THE
EVERYTHING®
GUIDE TO
EVIDENCE OF THE AFTERLIFE

Dear Reader,

For over a decade, we have been investigating the possibility of an after-life. We went into it with open minds, but wanted some concrete answers to how it could be true. Both of us are analytical thinkers, and used this ability to question and discuss the possibilities of connecting to the other side—if it was truly possible at all.

Through many hard hours of examination and development of our mediumship we realized that something extraordinary was happening. Time after time, information was being received that we would have had no access to; even some of the people receiving the readings had no idea of the information coming through, only to verify it later through a rela-tive or friend. The fact that both of us have witnessed paranormal phe-nomena in the past and wanted an answer to its cause made us natural collaborators for this book.

This book will open your mind to the very possibility of scientific evi-dence of an afterlife. It will make you think, make you wonder, and hope-fully make you understand that such a realm is not only possible—but in fact exists.

Joseph M. Higgins and Chuck Bergman

Welcome to the EVERYTHING® Series!

These handy, accessible books give you all you need to tackle a difficult project, gain a new hobby, comprehend a fascinating topic, prepare for an exam, or even brush up on something you learned back in school but have since forgotten.

You can choose to read an *Everything*® book from cover to cover or just pick out the information you want from our four useful boxes: e-questions, e-facts, e-alerts, and e-ssentials.

We give you everything you need to know on the subject, but throw in a lot of fun stuff along the way, too.

We now have more than 400 *Everything*® books in print, spanning such wide-ranging categories as weddings, pregnancy, cooking, music instruction, foreign language, crafts, pets, New Age, and so much more. When you're done reading them all, you can finally say you know *Everything*®!

QUESTION

Answers to common questions

FACT

Important snippets of information

ALERT

Urgent warnings

ESSENTIAL

Quick handy tips

PUBLISHER Karen Cooper

DIRECTOR OF ACQUISITIONS AND INNOVATION Paula Munier

MANAGING EDITOR, EVERYTHING® SERIES Lisa Laing

COPY CHIEF Casey Ebert

ASSISTANT PRODUCTION EDITOR Jacob Erickson

ACQUISITIONS EDITOR Lisa Laing

ASSOCIATE DEVELOPMENT EDITOR Hillary Thompson

EDITORIAL ASSISTANT Ross Weisman

EVERYTHING® SERIES COVER DESIGNER Erin Alexander

LAYOUT DESIGNERS Colleen Cunningham, Elisabeth Lariviere, Ashley Vierra, Denise Wallace

Visit the entire Everything® series at *www.everything.com*

THE EVERYTHING®

GUIDE TO EVIDENCE OF THE AFTERLIFE

A scientific approach to
proving the existence of life after death

Joseph M. Higgins and Chuck Bergman

adamsmedia
Avon, Massachusetts

This book is dedicated to the researchers, the
mediums, and free thinkers who did not care about
what society might say but persevered to search for
the truth no matter the consequences.

An Everything® Series Book.
Everything® and everything.com® are registered trademarks of F+W Media, Inc.

Published by Adams Media, a division of F+W Media, Inc.
57 Littlefield Street, Avon, MA 02322 U.S.A.
www.adamsmedia.com

ISBN 10: 1-4405-1008-3
ISBN 13: 978-1-4405-1008-3
eISBN 10: 1-4405-1143-8
eISBN 13: 978-1-4405-1143-1

Printed in the United States of America.

10 9 8 7 6 5 4 3 2 1

Library of Congress Cataloging-in-Publication Data
is available from the publisher.

This publication is designed to provide accurate and authoritative information with regard to the subject matter covered. It is sold with the understanding that the publisher is not engaged in rendering legal, accounting, or other professional advice. If legal advice or other expert assistance is required, the services of a competent professional person should be sought.

—From a *Declaration of Principles* jointly adopted by a Committee of the American Bar Association and a Committee of Publishers and Associations

Many of the designations used by manufacturers and sellers to distinguish their products are claimed as trademarks. Where those designations appear in this book and Adams Media was aware of a trademark claim, the designations have been printed with initial capital letters.

This book is available at quantity discounts for bulk purchases.
For information, please call 1-800-289-0963.

Contents

The Top 10 Tips to Finding Answers about the Afterlife **x**

Introduction **xi**

01 Afterlife Beliefs in Ancient and Modern Cultures / 1

Have We Always Believed in an Afterlife? **2**

Egyptian Mythology **3**

Ancient Chinese Afterlife Beliefs **6**

Death, Burial, and the Afterlife in Greece and Rome **8**

Early Celtic Beliefs **12**

Native American Rituals and Ceremonies **14**

Eastern and Western Cultural Beliefs **17**

02 Religious Beliefs and Theories of the Afterlife / 21

Christianity **22**

Judaism **24**

Islam **26**

Hinduism **28**

Buddhism **30**

Gnosticism, Esotericism, and Mysticism **32**

Universalism, Wicca, and Spiritualism **36**

03 Angels, Heaven, and Hell / 39

Angels: Messengers and Guides **40**

The Notion of Heaven **42**

Dante's Vision of Hell **44**

A Comparison of Various Heaven and Hell Realms **48**

Reincarnation and Past-Life Studies **50**

Case Studies: Angel Interventions **52**

04 Science Seeks an Explanation / 57

The Afterlife Experiments: Gary Schwartz, PhD **58**

Near-Death Experience Investigations: Raymond A. Moody, MD **61**

The Human Consciousness Project: What Happens When We Die **63**

The Scole Experiment **66**

Near-Death Experiences of the Blind: Dr. Kenneth Ring and Sharon Cooper, PhD **68**

Human Consciousness and Spirit Continuance after Death: The Rhine Research Center **70**

05 Consciousness / 73

The Brain and Consciousness **74**

Meditation: A Higher State of Consciousness **76**

Consciousness to Consciousness: Telepathy **80**

Communications with Coma and Nonresponsive Alzheimer Patients **82**

Transformation Consciousness, Wisdom, and Enlightenment **84**

Out-of-Body Experience (OBE) **86**

Case Studies **89**

06 Near-Death Experiences / 93

Near-Death Experiences Defined **94**

Clinical Death Versus Conscious Death **96**

Common Feeling, Sensations, and Sights **97**

Meeting Deceased Loved Ones **100**

The Life Review **101**

Scientific Studies **102**

Case Studies **104**

07 Can Quantum Physics Offer Proof of the Afterlife? / 107

Quantum Physics **108**

Substances That Make Up a Physical Being **109**

Quantum Physics and Biology **113**

Wave-Particle Duality **115**

The Heisenberg Uncertainty Principle **117**

The Search for the God Particle at the Large Hadron Collider **119**

08 Unraveling String Theory / 123

Uniting the Building Blocks of Nature **124**

M-Theory and the Existence of Multiple Dimensions **126**

Space and Time Here and in the Afterlife **129**

Dark Energy: The Unseen Force **132**

Parallel Universes and Multiple Existences **135**

09 Communication with the Afterlife / 139

Mediumship Through the Ages **140**

Types of Mediums **142**

Séance: A Group Event **144**

Scientific Studies of the Phenomena **147**

Individual Connections Through Thought and Prayer **150**

10 Afterlife Evidence from Mediums / 155

Personality and Trait Descriptions **156**

Relating Shared Experiences **158**

Objects of Significance **161**

Presence at Meaningful Events **162**

Secrets Exposed **164**

Cause of Death Revealed **165**

11 Solving Crimes with the Help of the Deceased / 167

Naming Suspects **168**

Providing Evidence **168**

Locating Bodies **169**

Locating Missing Persons **171**

Substantiating Current Undisclosed Evidence **173**

Pulling the Cases Together **174**

12 Signs from the Other Side / 177

Ways Contact Is Made **178**

The Dream State **180**

The Need for Contact **182**

Probability and Statistical Evidence **184**

Physical Methods Used to Gain Attention **187**

Case Studies **187**

13 Supporting Evidence / 191

Ghosts, Apparitions, and Hauntings **192**

Photographic Evidence **195**

Electronic Voice Phenomenon **197**

Apports: The Materialization of Matter **199**

Animal Reactions to Human Death **201**

Case Studies **202**

14 Deathbed Visitations / 207

A Long History **208**

What Is Seen and Heard **210**

Scientific Studies **212**

Case Studies **214**

15 Medical Personnel: Witnesses to the "Crossing Over" / 219

Afterlife Experiments in Medical Settings **220**

Hospice Workers' Stories **222**

Hospital and ER Personal Experiences **225**

Nursing-Home Events **227**

Transition Stories from Caregivers **230**

Unexplained Phenomena in Funeral Homes **233**

16 Miracles / 237

Visions by Multiple Witnesses **238**

Healings of Unknown Origin **240**

Physical Manifestations **242**

Unexplained Evidence **244**

Science and the Miracle Phenomena **247**

Case Studies **249**

17 **Skepticism about the Afterlife / 253**

When Skepticism Is Needed **254**

Weighing the Evidence with an Open Mind **256**

Paid Skeptics: The Industry **257**

When Skeptics Become Believers **260**

Case Studies: Fraudulent Afterlife Evidence **262**

18 **Do It Yourself: Conducting Afterlife Experiments / 265**

Using Physical Devices to Investigate **266**

Learning How to Meditate **268**

Opening Yourself to Communication **271**

Creating Studies to Present Evidence **273**

Recording Your Findings **276**

Participating in Established Current Research **278**

Appendix A: Glossary of Terms **281**

Appendix B: Additional Resources **284**

Index **286**

Acknowledgments

We would like to acknowledge some of the people who have been involved in this wonderful project for their time, support, and insights.

Chuck would like to thank:

His daughters, Charlene and Kimberly, and his son Jonathan.

Sharon, for her support and companionship. Your curiosity of the subject matter kept me motivated!

To Joe for putting so much time and effort into this book. What are we doing next?

Joe would like to thank:

Joe, Amanda, and Shannon, as well as Aaron, Shawn, and Kristen for their support and interest.

My sister Maureen and Chris Rossi for their continued support and ongoing questions about the other side.

To Tony, who came to me a week after he passed and told me we are living multiple existences on multiple planes at the same time.

A big thanks to Tom Frederick for his friendship, insight, and levity as well as his shamanistic abilities. Pierre Teilhard de Chardin was right: we are spiritual beings.

To Chuck for his friendship and insightful readings: I look forward to working with you again on a new project. Doesn't still amaze you how all this stuff works?

A special thanks to Nina, for her help with research, support, and understanding during the entire project: I love you with all my heart. Go Pats!

And to my guides, teachers, and supporters on the other side: I'll keep passing on the knowledge so we can help people enrich their lives while bringing peace to their hearts.

The Top 10 Tips to Finding Answers about the Afterlife

1. Keep an open mind; there are new discoveries every day.

2. Don't be afraid to know the truth, it could enhance your life.

3. Science and religion can work together.

4. The old skeptical excuses will not work with new evidence.

5. There is only true proof in the science of mathematics; the rest is subject to change.

6. Look at evidence from different sources in different fields of research.

7. Nothing is impossible when you look at the possibilities.

8. Record your dreams; you may have a look into another realm.

9. Trust your gut instincts; they are there for a reason.

10. Healings can take place on many different levels.

Introduction

THE QUESTION OF AN afterlife has been asked for thousands of years and might even be the most thought about concept known to man. Man has always been on the quest to understand what happens when humans die, and understand the causes of paranormal phenomena that have been witnessed for thousands of years.

Within the realms of religion and regional cultures, perceptions of an afterlife were developed and handed down through the ages. Some of these beliefs still exist today. But there have always been free thinkers wanting to know more—some were put to death for their theories, while others wrote in secret of their personal beliefs in the afterlife.

Mediums were at times held in high esteem; at other times in history they were put to death for their gifts. Today, once more, they are assisting with research and intermingling with scientists and theologians. Their gifts have helped solve crimes and have educated people on how to receive signs from their deceased loved ones. In this guide you'll learn how personalities and traits come with you when the time comes to cross over. Most importantly, you'll learn that you are never alone.

Clinical death—when the heart, brain, and lungs cease to function—was until now considered the point where the consciousness and mind cease to function, too. Doctors have staunchly held that the brain and the mind are one and the same. But recent studies have shown that this belief may be a fallacy.

With the development of modern scientific technology, researchers have opened the door to new possibilities of the existence of another realm beyond the physical plane that is seen by the world today. The study of consciousness has shown the possibility of the continuing of life after death. Have you ever had déjà vu, like having experienced a specific moment before in time? Do you feel at times like you have a sixth sense? Do you have vivid dreams with visiting deceased relatives? These are questions dealing with consciousness and how your mind might be able to separate from the physical body.

Quantum physics and string theory have revolutionized ideas about what everything is made of, including man himself. The possibility of multiple dimensions interacting with this one is no longer science fiction but on the verge of becoming reality.

From the everyday events surrounding the witnessing of paranormal phenomena such as ghosts, near-death experiences, and deathbed visits, you will learn how today, more than ever before, people are talking openly about these happenings in their daily lives.

This evidence does not have to eliminate your current belief system. It can coexist with the faith or cultural beliefs you have followed throughout your life. Judge the evidence with an open mind, accept what you can, and contemplate the rest.

The Everything® Guide to Evidence of the Afterlife will bring you up-to-date scientific studies, theories, and evidence of the afterlife. You will be asked to open your minds to the possibilities like you have never been asked before. As the evidence is presented, ask yourself the question that French philosopher and Jesuit priest Pierre Teilhard de Chardin asked almost a century ago: Are you a human being having a spiritual experience, or a spiritual being having a human experience?

CHAPTER 1

Afterlife Beliefs in Ancient and Modern Cultures

Cultural beliefs in the afterlife have had a great influence on organized religions. Many afterlife theories and concepts have transcended regional cultures and became the foundations of modern religious belief systems. From the earliest days of the ancient Greek and Chinese cultures, you will find many similarities to modern-day thought concerning the afterlife.

Have We Always Believed in an Afterlife?

From thousand-year-old cave paintings to modern-day texts, man has always found the idea of an afterlife not only interesting but also something that is a part of him. The biological makeup of the human species has not changed from the beginning of time. Therefore, the process of conscientiousness is the same as it was for our earliest ancestors. The human species has a self-realization, meaning there is awareness in the eventual death of the physical body.

Some of the modern-day phenomena, such as near-death experiences and deathbed visitations, also took place thousands of years ago. This led individuals to question if there is more to their existence than what they can observe. Out-of-body experiences, ghosts, and voices of dead relatives could have influenced early communities to believe in an afterlife.

In ancient cultures, myths based on folklore may have been used to explain the afterlife. These myths morphed into more organized structures as populations increased and moved throughout the world. All the great civilizations of the past have had some belief in an afterlife. They have varied in their specifics, but all have some type of explanation as to what happens after the physical body dies.

FACT

Afterlife-based belief systems have been the root of invasions, creations of great works of art, and the persecution of individuals and societies who wish to practice their own ideas concerning life and their eventual death.

Many of the belief systems seem to come from one another, with similar descriptions of heaven and hell in the West and reincarnation in the East. Some groups do not associate with an organized religion but consider themselves to be spiritual, to be connected to an outside source, and therefore connected to their own god.

Modern-day humans might try to relate their own mortality to their religious or cultural upbringing, but their awareness of their ultimate fate could cause them to question the true meaning of life.

Are We Hard-Wired?

Some believe we are hard-wired to believe in an afterlife—that it is built into our brain from the time of our birth. Neuroscientist Rhawn Joseph of Santa Clara, California, believes there is a neurological explanation for spiritual experiences and God. Humans experience God primarily through the amygdala, a part of the brain responsible for processing and memory of emotional reactions. He states, "These tissues, which become highly activated when we dream, when we pray . . . enable us to experience those realms of reality normally filtered from consciousness, including the reality of God, the spirit, the soul, and life after death." Others believe that if this is true, humans could use this part of the brain as a doorway to connect to the otherworld.

Often, modern-day reason is used to discredit the possibility of an afterlife. However, science has begun to open the doors to the possibilities of evidential proof of the existence of an afterlife through quantum physics and string theory, which will be discussed later in this book.

Egyptian Mythology

Ancient Egyptian culture has captivated our imaginations for centuries. This fascinating civilization left behind a legacy of mythological beliefs and fantastic, mysterious monuments, of which the pyramids are perhaps the most famous. The pyramids were built to house the bodies of deceased pharaohs, along with their families, servants, animals, and their worldly possessions. The Egyptians believed in an eternal afterlife, complete with possession of their earthly riches.

ESSENTIAL

Egyptologists agree that the ancient Egyptians were preoccupied with death and lived their lives in preparation for the afterlife. It is not surprising then that most of what we know about them comes from archaeological evidence uncovered in tombs.

In their overwhelming desire to secure a perpetual place in the afterlife, much time, effort, and thought was put toward preparing for death. The ancient Egyptians endured life as a means to secure a place in their ultimate destination, which they would enjoy side by side with the gods. They believed in a hierarchy of gods and goddesses, each of whom had a specific job and purpose. Egyptian priests told of the bliss and rewards in the Egyptian afterlife, and every Egyptian aspired to this perfect existence.

Preservation of the Body and Soul

One of the most important aspects of their belief system was the idea that if the soul were to live on in the afterlife, a person's body and identity must be preserved in this one. The body had to remain relatively intact, and offerings of food and drink were required to be made regularly.

The ancient Egyptians assured their place in the afterlife by:

- **Mummification:** Preserving and embalming the body and the internal organs separately
- **Protecting the body:** The body would be entombed and therefore safe from harm
- **Nourishment:** The deceased would receive regular offerings of food and drink, or illustrations of them in the tomb if no one was available to provide it

Inscriptions and illustrations describing the occupant's life were made on the tomb, along with adaptations of the myth of the soul's journey through the underworld. As well, figures known as *shabtis* were drawn to function as servants to the deceased. Inside the tomb there were various inscriptions, usually spells from the Egyptian *Book of the Dead*, various amulets of a protective nature, a decorated coffin, and sometimes a stone or wooden sarcophagus, inside which the mummy was placed for added safety.

FACT

Many underground tombs were well stocked with everyday items as well. A ruler like King Tut might need a dazzling golden mask in the next world, but according to Salima Ikram, professor of Egyptology at the American University in Cairo, Egypt, "Many tombs have included furniture, clothes, even underwear, jewelry and other smaller household items."

The ancient Egyptians believed that the soul was perishable and at great risk. The tomb, the process of mummification, rituals, and magic spells ensured the preservation of the soul.

The Steps to Eternal Life

Ancient Egyptian culture tells us the final journey to the underworld was a perilous one. Many tests and judgments had to be passed before eternal life was reached. There was no second chance at eternal life—if one failed the tests, he was consumed and ceased to exist. The ultimate goal was to reach the perfect blissful place that was an exact replica of Egypt in life. This place was called the Field of Rushes. An ancient Egyptian's status in the afterlife was dictated by his earthly means.

After death the soul would pass through four milestones:

1. The journey through the underworld
2. Reaching the Final Hall of Judgment and being held accountable by forty-two divine judges
3. The weighing of the heart
4. Either being allowed entrance to the afterlife in the Field of Rushes or devoured and cast into darkness

After undertaking the perilous journey through the underworld, contending with strange creatures, gods, and gatekeepers, the deceased would face his day of judgment at the Hall of Two Truths. Anubis, the god of the dead, would lead the soul through the underworld to the Hall of Two Truths, where the deceased would stand in front of the forty-two judges and gods.

The soul had to answer many questions, and if one stumbled, he could recite a spell from the *Book of the Dead* from an amulet that had been placed around his neck upon his earthly death. Once the soul passed this test, part of which was merely knowing what to say, he was then led to a set of scales where the heart, containing the deeds of his lifetime, was weighed against the feather of truth, a divine feather belonging to the goddess Ma'at. During burial, Egyptians removed the internal organs of the deceased and placed them in Canopic jars, so the separation of the heart to be weighed was already performed.

If the heart was found to be heavier than the feather, the soul was fed to the god Ammut, the "Devourer," and the *atman* (the soul) was cast forever into oblivion. However, if the scales were balanced, the deceased had passed the final test and was given over to the god Osiris, the god of the underworld and chief judge, who welcomed them into the afterlife, to the Field of Rushes.

The Field of Rushes

In this beautiful world the real life of the deceased was mirrored, but with none of his earthly problems—there was only happiness. The afterlife was seen as a perfect existence in an ideal version of Egypt. There were fields, crops, and an abundance of food, and a celestial version of the Nile River.

In this untainted land, the deceased met with his ancestors and loved ones who had gone before him. He continued working in the role he had undertaken in life. There was no hardship, only perpetual joy. There were no natural disasters and the crops grew bigger and higher than those found on the mortal plane. His leisure activities were replicated, as were all the pursuits of his mortal existence.

It is hard for us to comprehend today, but the highlight of an ancient Egyptian's life was ultimately his death and burial, which was a status symbol, followed by his longed-for journey into the afterlife.

Ancient Chinese Afterlife Beliefs

"What happens after a person dies?" is a common question that has been answered by different religions in different ways. The ancient Chinese had a unique perspective on the afterlife, which underwent a great change with the rise of Buddhism in China. The Chinese Taoists were greatly concerned with life after death and survival of an individual's soul even after his physical demise.

The Concept of the Soul

Chinese metaphysics is based on the polarity of negative and positive, the yin and yang, the two basic principles of the universe. Their philosophy teaches that each human being is an amalgamation of two souls, the yin and yang. These are together during the lifetime of an individual, but at the time of death, the two souls separate and go in different directions. This is exactly in harmony with the cosmos, which was also created after the integration of light and dark, the yin and yang elements.

Cary Baynes, a Jungian writer, summarized this concept in the following way: "In the bodily existence of an individual are two polarities, a *p'o* soul and a *hun* soul. During the life of the individual these two souls are in conflict with one another, each striving to gain supremacy over the other. Upon death, they separate and go different ways, while the *p'o* sinks to earth as *kuei* or ghost, the *hun* rises and becomes *shen*, a spirit or god."

Kuei and *shen* represent the two extremes, the lower, dark, and evil element, and the higher, spiritual element. The ancient Chinese idea of the soul was dualistic. The *p'o* was an earth soul that came into existence at the time of conception, while *hun* was made of chi, the life force, and came into existence at the time of birth. Each soul had its own afterlife; while *hun* went to heaven or a special underworld, the *p'o* went to the darker realms of the cosmos.

FACT

At the main entrance of many Taoist temples is an elaborately colored container. It is for joss sticks (incense sticks), which are placed there to be lit. The rising incense symbolizes prayers offered to heaven. On either side of the container will be carved dragons; similarly, there will be dragons on the roof of the temple. These symbolize strength, energy, and life force.

The ancient Chinese beliefs of the afterlife are largely a combination of Taoism and Buddhism. They believed that when a person died, messengers carried his soul to Cheng Huang, the God of Walls and Moats. Here the deeds and actions of the individual were judged, and those who were found virtuous were sent directly to paradise, a place inhabited by Taoist immortals. But those who led evil lives descended to hell to serve a fixed period of punishment. After the duration of punishment was over, the soul was given the Elixir of Oblivion and was prepared for rebirth.

Ancestor Worship

The ancient Chinese believed everything that exists flows out of Tao, and humans are a small component of Tao. The concept of dual souls is unique—the lower and dark soul perishes away with death but the good and pious soul is immortal and an object of ancestor worship.

Most Chinese believe that the soul of the deceased must be kept happy by offerings and worship. It is also believed that unhappy souls, those who weren't buried in the right way, or for whom no rituals have been performed, turn into ghosts and can attack human beings to receive their due. This is one reason why elaborate ancestor worship rituals are carried out, as a significant way to please the soul of the deceased.

The ancestor worship cult is an important part of the Chinese afterlife beliefs and is based on the premise that the living need to sustain the spirits of their ancestors and protect their graves.

Chinese Notions about Heaven and Hell

The concept of heaven as the dwelling place of gods is a very old Chinese notion. According to the Shang Chinese dynasty beliefs, heaven was also the place where the *hun* (the good soul) would go. However, only the powerful *hun*, those of earthy kings, could enter heaven; the rest would be given a place lower to heaven, or would be reincarnated with a longer life span.

The Chinese notion of the underworld of the Yellow Springs could be conceived of as hell. It was the destination of the evil souls, or *p'o*. Yellow Springs was a miserable place where the souls were punished for their bad deeds and were kept under the bondage of the Queen of Earth.

Confucius, the great Chinese thinker and philosopher, summarized these beliefs of life, death, and the afterlife. He stated: "Death and Life have their determined appointments; riches and honors depend upon Heaven."

Death, Burial, and the Afterlife in Greece and Rome

Death in many cultures is not seen as an end, but a beginning of a new life in the otherworld. Elaborate rituals and special burial ceremonies are conducted to bid goodbye to the deceased. As Socrates remarked, "Look death in the face with joyful hope, and consider this a lasting truth: the righteous man has nothing to fear, neither in life, nor in death, and the gods will not forsake him." The ancient cultures of Greece and Rome are the most popular for their elaborate death and burial rituals, and their fascination with life after death.

Death and Burial in Greek Culture

The Greeks believed that when a person dies, his spirit or psyche leaves the physical body in the form of a little breath or puff of air. The deceased was then prepared for burial according to Greek customs. The dead body was washed, anointed with oil, and dressed for the rituals. Relatives, primarily women, conducted the burial ceremonies, which can be divided into three main parts:

1. **The prosthesis:** This refers to the laying out and display of the body, so relatives, friends, and acquaintances could come and pay their respects to the deceased.
2. **The ekphora:** Ekphora is the funeral procession, where the deceased was brought to the cemetery for burial. Ekphora usually took place just before dawn, and it involved building the funeral pyre (if the dead body was to be burned) or filling up the grave with objects of daily use. More elaborate objects such as monumental earth mounds, specially built tombs, and marble statues were erected around the grave, to ensure that the deceased would not be forgotten.
3. **The interment:** The remains of the body, or ashes, if cremated, were placed inside the tomb specially built for the deceased. The tomb could be a family plot (*peribolos*), a communal grave (*polyandreion*), or a monumental tomb for the elite. Immortality lay in the continued remembrance of the deceased person by his family members.

ESSENTIAL

The burial ceremonies in the ancient Greek culture were a representation of the social and financial status of the deceased, as the tombs of wealthy men were built in an extravagant manner. Jewels and extravagant objects were considered essential grave offerings.

The Greeks believed those who were not buried or cremated in the appropriate manner would be destined to suffer between the two worlds and would not be given an entry into the underworld, the land of the dead, until these rites were completed.

Death and Burial in the Roman Culture

Romans could either bury or burn their dead, and depending upon the personal customs, people would choose one ritual over the other. Roman treatment of the deceased in terms of the cremation rituals perpetuated their life status.

Burial

The Romans believed the soul of a deceased person could only find peace when the physical body was buried in a proper manner and all ceremonies were conducted appropriately. If this was not done, the soul would haunt its home and other family members. It was the solemn religious duty of the living to perform solemn religious rituals for the dead.

Cremation

For those who preferred cremation over burial, there were strict religious rites to be performed. Also, the interment of the body, either the bones or ashes, had to be duly buried in the earth in order to bring happiness and peace to the soul of the deceased person. However, children less than forty days old and slaves were to be buried.

Ancient Greek and Roman Beliefs of the Afterlife

One way that human beings have come to terms with the tragedy of death is by their belief in the afterlife. In Greece, it was believed that all souls, whether good or bad, go to the underworld realm of Hades, the land of the dead. Tartaros was an area below Hades, where disobedient and evil spirits were punished. Elysium was a beautiful and tranquil place, inhabited by good spirits. When the concept of reward and punishment was introduced in the postclassical period, Tartaros became hell and Elysium became heaven.

When the hour of death arrives, red-robed deities come to take the spirit of the deceased to the land of the dead. To reach the land of the dead they must cross Acheron, one of the five underground rivers. Charon, the ferryman, takes the spirits of the dead to the other end of the river. Charon demands a small coin (*obol*) for this service; this is the reason why the dead are buried with a coin in their mouth.

After crossing Acheron, the soul of the deceased would be judged by Hades and all the sons of Zeus. The deceased would be assigned an eternal home depending on the deeds and the kind of life lived by the person:

- **For ordinary souls:** Neutral regions of Hades, a dull and drab place
- **For evil souls (those who committed many crimes):** Tartaros or hell
- **For pure and blessed souls:** Elysian Fields or heaven

All the burial rituals and beliefs of the Greeks point to the fact that they were fascinated by the concept of the afterlife. Through the brutal beliefs related to hell and the beautiful comforting thoughts of heaven, the Greeks wanted to lead their people on a path of righteousness.

The Roman Perspective

For Romans, much of their beliefs in the afterlife and burial ceremonies had an influence from Greek culture and viewpoints. Ancient Romans viewed life and death in a completely unique and different way. Life was viewed as a prison for the soul who had to serve the world, cultivate physical and spiritual qualities, and perform good deeds in order to be freed from the clutches of a physical body and find its eternal place in the heavens.

ALERT

Depending on the deeds performed in the mortal world, the soul would be assigned an afterlife in hell or heaven. The ancient Romans believed hell was a location where those who commit serious sins would be punished. The punishment was in the form of fire, and endless pain and suffering.

The mortal world was perceived as the center of the universe, and the physical body as the outer representation of the spirit. Romans believed all men to be gods, immortal beings who control their own bodies while being completely aware of the afterlife that awaited them beyond this world.

Just like the Greeks, the Romans believed that the soul of the deceased person was carried to the other end of the world by crossing the river Styx.

They believed that three judges—Minos, Rhadamanthus, and Aeacus—took an account of the deceased's life and activities and assigned an afterlife for the soul:

- Warriors and heroes were sent to the Elysian Fields or paradise.
- Good and honest citizens were sent to the Plain of Asphodel.
- Evil spirits, those that have offended the gods, were sent to Tartaros, or the Hall of Fury (hell).

The ancient cultures of Greece and Rome showed a strong faith in the afterlife, which is reflected in their elaborate ceremonies and burial rituals. While specific names and rituals might vary, the basic concept of heaven and hell is the same in both cultures.

Early Celtic Beliefs

The early Celts were a diverse group of tribes that were spread across Gaul, Britain, Ireland, Asia Minor, Central Europe, and the Balkans. Not much is known about their culture and beliefs, since they did not have written scriptures or codes of conduct. All information was passed on verbally, and most information on their beliefs and rituals was lost with the last Celts. However, from their burial sites, archaeological remains, and other sources, historians and philosophers have attempted to look into Celtic lives and beliefs.

A Brief Overview

Celts belonged to one of the world's earliest civilizations. The Celtic people practiced Druidism, a religion overseen by priests and priestesses called Druids. For Celts, the afterlife was as real as the mortal world. It was believed that after a person's death, her soul needed a clear path so it could travel to the otherworld, which is why all windows and doors were kept wide open when a person died.

In the Druidism culture, a priest would come and explain to the dying person how her soul would travel to its final destination and find eternal peace in the otherworld. In the case of sudden death of an individual, the priest would come and whisper this information to the deceased. Souls that did not get proper religious direction became targets for evil spirits, or may have roamed around restlessly, causing trouble for the living.

The Wake

The wake refers to the period the body of the deceased was laid out after the soul reached its afterlife. The body was washed with the waters from a sacred well to keep it protected and was wrapped in the *Eslene* (death cloth). It was then placed on a *bier*, or coffin, in the center of the house for mourners to come and pay their respects.

During the wake, mourners would come and sit by the corpse and share memories of the deceased. All mourners would "have a last drink" with the departed person. The body was laid out for up to a week, especially if it was that of a warrior or a king, before the funeral preparations began. Rush torches were kept burning throughout the days and nights until the body was taken for cremation or burial.

Funeral Feast

After the mourning period, there was a funeral feast. Usually a roasted boar or bull was served, and all the relatives and friends of the deceased were invited. A part of the food was given to the deceased person as "grave food," and then the body was finally buried or cremated.

The Celts considered funerals to be a celebration of the deceased's life. They believed that all men would one day die and be born again in a new life. During the time of funeral feast, the mourner praised all the accomplishments and contributions of the deceased person.

Celtic Burial Practices

The Celts preferred burial to cremation, especially for the great warriors, noblemen, and leaders. Mounts and tombs were built for such people; for everyday people, normal graves were dug. Stillborn babies were taken away by the priest and buried without any ceremony in a burial ground away from the settlements.

Were any objects buried with the ancient Celts?
With each body, goods such as objects of daily use, personal belongings, and food were also placed inside the grave. Weapons were placed with bodies of warriors, or any goods that were a mark of the profession of the deceased. Married women were buried with a comb and mirror, priests with a torch, and so on.

Finally, on the seventh day, the body would be buried or burned as per the tribal customs. The remains of the body, in case of cremation, were to be buried underground or dispersed in water. During funeral preparation, the body was to be kept as natural as possible without any chemical embalming or artificial adornments.

Celtics Afterlife Beliefs

Druids taught the concept of immortality of the soul—that even when a person dies physically, her soul continues to live. They believed that the soul was reincarnated as another entity in the living world, either as a plant or animal, or again as a human.

When one gained complete understanding of the immortality of the soul and the process of rebirth, she would be moved to a higher realm of existence, a different, outer world. This would continue until the soul reached the highest state, "the source," after which the process of reincarnation ended and the soul would be eternally rested.

Native American Rituals and Ceremonies

A common theme found in Native Americans' spirituality is the idea of finding god in nature. Understanding the world around them lead them to an interior understanding and connection with the divine. This Native American belief dates back as far as 60,000 years. Archeologists suggest that thousands of years ago people lived on a great continent, Pangea, which was responsible for a global uniformity of nomadic spiritual culture. These commonalities were responsible for the earliest forms of spiritual customs that developed into many of today's spiritual beliefs. From hunting they developed a belief in Animism, the idea that spirits exist in animals, and that the spirits and traits of each animal are a true expression of God. Farming brought forth food and medicine, and taught a respect for Gaia, the Earth Mother, who provided for her children. Shamanism (and shamans, the medicine men of the societies) helped induce healing and meaning to the spiritual forces seen and unseen in existence around everyone. These were the earliest forms of cultural connections.

The formation of the Bering Strait created a connection for movement across continents. With this movement, the early cultures of Africa, Asia, and Siberia entered into the Americas. Thousands of years of migration and settlement developed the native peoples of the present-day continents.

Modern Times

The root of these nomadic cultures is based upon the threefold concept of heaven, earth, and the underworlds. Everything is considered to be alive with a masculine or feminine expression of God—the trees, rocks, stars, animals, and all other entities are considered interconnected. All matter is considered an equal sentient being.

The earth is seen as a living, breathing conscious being. The earth is the "Mother" and the tribes are her children, nurtured and sustained by her love and grace. The need to live in harmony with the Mother rather than live off of the Mother is a fundamental to the future, spiritual advance, and survival of the Native American peoples. This is the primary and ultimate spiritual goal.

Afterlife

The understanding of the afterlife is as follows. The spirit is divided into two parts: the organic that returns to the Mother and the spirit that returns to the Father. This idea mirrors the Chinese concept of soul duality.

Indigenous belief systems vary from tribe to tribe. Even within one particular clan there can be multiple interpretations and beliefs, dependent upon the vision of the particular medicine man.

The following highlights common themes in Native American spirituality, as illustrated through the Oglala Lakota perspective:

- *Wakan tanka*—Literally translated this means "great mystery." It's considered the source, the creator of all, "the Great and Incomprehensible One." This meaning of the name expresses the idea that humans are incapable of ever truly and fully comprehending the ways of the Great Spirit.
- *Topa olowan*—The four directions is a complex ideology that recognizes the sacred four directions of north, south, east, and west as sentient beings that guard the four quarters of the world.
- *Ina maka*—This term translates as "mother earth."

All of these concepts are expressions of the *wakan tanka*, "one source," from which all things come.

These various beliefs are never questioned or debated, for it is at the very core of native spirituality that the direction (or one's spiritual destiny) is individualized, by an intimate connection with the Great Spirit. The process to achieve this intimate connection is called a *Hanblecheyapi*. This translates to "I cry for a vision."

FACT

The Lakota were nomadic, equestrian plains Indians who hunted buffalo and lived in tepees. They became famous for defeating Custer's forces at the Battle of the Little Bighorn in 1876. They followed the Seven Sacred Rites: the sweat lodge, crying for a vision, keeping of the soul, the sun dance, the making of relatives, preparing for womanhood, and throwing the ball. A modern additional practice known as *yuwibi* has been added and is used in worship.

Considered one of the seven sacred rites of Lakota beliefs, an individual seeks the assistance of a medicine man, and after a lengthy preparation process, goes to the mountain for one to four days to pray. If granted, a vision is given to the seeker and a process of understanding that vision ensues. This becomes the vocation or spiritual path. Here begins the glimpse into the true dynamic of this spiritual structure that sees everything as interrelated and connected. At the conclusion of all ceremonies, the words "All my relations" are stated.

As Godfrey Chips, Oglala Lakota Medicine Man, states:

When you gaze up at the evening sky, a thousand stars grace the dark night appearing as 1 million–plus points of light. These are our ancestors lighting the way that leads the Spirit on a journey home. As you look at the sky, the Milky Way is quite evident with its tightly compacted cluster of stars; this in Lakota Theology is the Spirit Road. Upon passing, the Spirit leaves the body and the Soul is guided by a Medicine person in prayer to reconnect the soul with the ancestors and urged to follow the Milky Way. Thus allowing the dualistic nature of the Soul to return to Wakan Tanka (Great Mystery).

Eastern and Western Cultural Beliefs

The idea of the existence of a soul or continuation of existence in the otherworld is one that has been adopted by Eastern and Western cultures, but their interpretations are different from each other. A handful of organized religions make up the majority of beliefs throughout the population of the world, and so their influences on cultural beliefs have had enormous ramifications for the Western and Eastern parts of the planet.

Western Religious Influences on Cultures' Beliefs

With the spread of Christianity toward Europe and the Americas, Western cultural beliefs began to accept the idea that your conduct on earth and your deeds are the main factor that will determine the kind of afterlife you will experience. They believe in heaven, which is an eternal place inhabited by the purer and virtuous spirits, and hell, where all evil spirits are sent. In hell, the evil spirits will be punished for their deeds and will be burnt in the eternal hellfire. The Catholic Church emphasizes a period of purgatory, a state between heaven and hell, which allows purification of the spirit so it can reach heaven.

Judaism is one of the earliest and most popular religions of the Western world. However, not all Jews believe in the afterlife and are more concerned about life in the mortal world. But they do believe that after a person dies, his soul goes to a place similar to heaven or enters the wheel of reincarnation. They also believe that souls of bad and wicked people are made to suffer in the afterlife, and are then finally destroyed.

According to the tenets of Islam, death marks the end of physical life and the beginning of a period of rest. This will continue until the Day of Resurrection, when everyone will have to appear in front of Allah, who will judge their earthly deeds and decide their eternal fate. In most Muslim teachings, heaven is described as an exquisite place where all men will be decked with jewels and drink holy waters and enjoy all earthly pleasures, while in hell evil spirits will be devoid of food and water and lead a miserable and painful afterlife.

Eastern Religious Influences on Cultures' Beliefs

Unlike the Western cultural beliefs, Eastern cultures were influenced by religions that were more inclined toward a psychological view of the afterlife. They place immense importance on the attainment of the highest level of consciousness.

ESSENTIAL

The cycle of life, that is, the process of birth, death, and rebirth, is something that every living being has to undergo, until it attains *moksha*, or liberation. The law of karma (cause and effect) is the real reason why a soul is born again and again in different forms—the necessity of "reaping one's karma" compels human beings to be reborn in successive lifetimes.

Belief in the afterlife is more with a view that a person would be reborn again as a different entity. Heaven and hell are not viewed as the final dwelling places, but more like a place of judgment where, based on your earthly deeds, you can be punished or rewarded, which is reflected in the next life you will have when you are reincarnated or reborn. The final destination of all souls is to become one with the Almighty, with the creator of the universe.

Hindus believe that the soul, or the *atman*, is immortal and is trapped in a physical body to undergo the process of birth and death. The main aim of a soul is to seek salvation, or *moksha*, and free itself from the cyclic pattern of the world (*samsara*). Reincarnation is an accepted fact, but one that is seen as a phase of suffering and pain.

Buddhist beliefs, to a large extent, are rooted in the Hindu ideologies of reincarnation and karma, and share the ideology that the final aim of a mortal being is to escape the cycle of birth and death. Gautama Buddha explained that desires keep a being attached to the mortal world and are the real reason why people are bound to the process of death and rebirth.

To escape the wheel of reincarnation, one needs to let go of all desires. Only then will a person attain nirvana, or liberation.

For Tibetan Buddhists, the spirit of the deceased person goes through a three-stage process called the *bardos*. Stage one begins at the death of an individual and is regarded as the time when the soul of the deceased person realizes that its mortal existence is over. In stage two of the *bardos*, or the luminous mind, the soul experiences hallucinations related to the karma/deeds of its life. The last stage is one in which the soul is prepared for its next life, the rebirth.

FACT

According to Tibetan Buddhists, those who have highly evolved intellects and have raised their consciousness to the highest levels are able to completely forego the process of *bardos* and directly attain nirvana, the ultimate destination for all mortals.

Basic Differences Between Eastern and Western Beliefs

In Eastern cultures, reincarnation is a core belief, and the fact that you will be reincarnated does away with the need for a permanent heaven or hell. Also, the law of karma is put into action and you will be rewarded or punished for your deeds in your next incarnation.

In Western cultures, however, there is only one life, which is why your sins or good deeds will be the ultimate determinant for your afterlife. Heaven and hell are properly described planes of existence that are also referred to as the otherworld, and your final existence will be decided based on your physical life.

ESSENTIAL

In Eastern beliefs, the aim of mortal existence should be to gain a permanent release from the cycle of life, and become one with the divine. Western cultures focus on living a life in a virtuous and right manner, so the soul of the deceased can go to heaven in its afterlife.

Eastern cultures consider release from ignorance, ego, and suffering as the key to finding the ultimate bliss, in the form of nirvana, or liberation; however, Western cultures considered release from the mortal body as the main purpose of afterlife. Eastern cultures view reincarnation as a means to reward and punish individuals for the acts and deeds done in this lifetime. In Western traditions, a person will be rewarded or punished for his life's deeds, and the kind of afterlife a person experiences after he dies is dependent upon these deeds.

As Dr. Charles E. Osgood, a well-known American psychologist and cross-cultural researcher aptly summarized, "Western culture constantly strives to seek and establish 'the truth,' while Eastern religions focus more on accepting the truth as given and in finding the right balance."

CHAPTER 2

Religious Beliefs and Theories of the Afterlife

The origins of organized religions have dated back a few thousands years, while man's individual connection to God or a higher realm can be traced back to the beginning of recorded time. The possibility of life after death has always been a subject of interest for many, spurring long, heated debates among philosophers and theologians. This possibility also exposed various differences as to the existence or nature of an afterlife among the world's religions, as well as each individual's inner quest to acquire the answers.

Christianity

Christianity, a monotheistic religion, can be broken up into many different denominations. Catholicism, Protestantism, and Eastern Orthodoxy are the largest, which have similarities and differences in their theories of the afterlife. Most Christians believe in an afterlife, described as heaven and hell. Heaven is a beautiful paradise where souls reside with God and enjoy all his love and support. The opposite is hell, a place lacking any presence of God and his love.

Catholicism

The afterlife belief of this denomination starts with the concept of baptism. The sacrament of baptism represents the acceptance of Jesus as your savior, and allows you the opportunity to enter into heaven when it is time for you to cross to the other side. There are also other obligations one must adhere to in order to be accepted into heaven, including confessing and repenting ones sins.

Once considered a physical place, it is now accepted as an eternal relationship with God. Pope John Paul II stated to the General Audience on July 21, 1999: "Heaven is neither an abstraction nor a physical place in the clouds, but a living, personal relationship with the Holy Trinity. It is our meeting with the Father which takes place in the risen Christ through the communion of the Holy Spirit."

If one commits a mortal sin and has not confessed and repented that sin, he will go to hell. Once believed to be a place of eternal fire and torment, the Catholic Church now states that hell is "the pain, frustration, and emptiness of life without God."

According to Pope John Paul II, "hell is the ultimate consequence of sin itself. . . . Rather than a place, hell indicates the state of those who freely and definitively separate themselves from God, the source of all life and joy."

The Catholic Church also believes in a realm called purgatory. According to the doctrine of purgatory, stated in the *Catechism of the Catholic Church*, "All who die in God's grace and friendship, but still imperfectly purified, are indeed assured of their eternal salvation; but after death they undergo purification, so as to achieve the holiness necessary to enter the joy of Heaven." Pope John Paul II explained that physical integrity is necessary to enter into perfect communion with God; therefore, "the term purgatory does not indicate a place, but a condition of existence," where Christ "removes . . . the remnants of imperfection."

FACT

A Gallup telephone poll conducted in 2010 indicated that 16 percent of Americans do not have a religious affiliation, while nearly three out of ten say religion is out of date. Gallup has been tracking religious identity since 1948.

Protestantism

Protestantism is a group of Christian denominations that separated from the Catholic Church during the sixteenth-century Reformation. Their concerns about how one gets into heaven forged their move to independence; for example, they believed that one could enter heaven through faith alone, and only Christ could forgive sins. The Bible is the most important basis for the Protestant Church, and it is the final word for all practices and beliefs.

The ceremony of baptism is an important and distinguishing aspect among Protestants, as it varies among the different branches of the Protestant denominations. For example, Quakers and the Shakers do not perform the ritual, while Lutherans and Episcopalians still practice infant baptism. Baptists and Methodists have adopted the practice of adult baptism.

There is no purgatory, as in the Catholic Church, where souls need to be purified before entering heaven. Faith, a gift from God, is their salvation.

A difference of opinion has emerged between the conservative and liberal wings of many Protestant denominations. The conservatives believe in a literal place of hell, while the more liberal tend to believe that a loving God could not put people into such a place of torment. They feel it is more likely an eternity separated from God himself.

Some Christian Fundamentalists disagree with Catholics about the physical location of hell. R. A. Mohler, Jr., president of the Southern Baptist's Theological Seminary in Louisville, Kentucky, commented, "My concern here is the temptation to make hell a state of mind, to psychologize hell. As attractive as that may be to the modern mind, that is not the hell of the Bible."

Eastern Orthodox

The Eastern and Western Churches split in the eleventh century over the disagreement of the authority of the pope. The Eastern Churches denied the authority of the pope and believed the Holy Spirit to be only of the Father, while the Western Church stated that the Holy Spirit came from the Father and the Son.

Eastern Orthodox beliefs teach that after the soul leaves the body there is an anticipation of judgment. This occurs in either heaven, where there is a sense of light, or hell, where there is a sense of darkness. On Judgment Day, their bodies are reunited with their souls to fully experience heaven or hell.

Judaism

Judaism is one of the oldest world religions. It is believed to have originated around 2000 B.C.E. It is an Abrahamic religion, that is, Abraham is its patriarch. The Book of Genesis describes the account of how Judaism came into being under the leadership of Abraham, Moses, and Jacob.

Basic Religious Beliefs

Judaism teaches that death is not the end of one's being, and primarily focuses on life now rather than the life to come. A person's current actions are more important than the beliefs in *olam ha-ba*, the afterlife. The Torah, the most important Jewish text that establishes the laws Jews live by, emphasizes implementing your responsibilities to others and to God now.

According to the main tenets of Judaism, all men are entitled to respect and dignity. These tenets are implemented in daily life by following the Holy Scriptures. An effective study of the Torah includes reading the text itself along with an understanding of the interpretations. When carried out in this way, the Torah is said to show the believer the path to salvation.

Concept of Reward and Punishment

The Torah speaks of the equal and just consequences for all actions within the life span of earthly beings. This focus on the balancing of bad deeds with punishment and good deeds with rewards within a lifetime precludes any specific detailed mention of death and events of the afterlife, according to some scholars. However, others believe that these messages are simply concealed and become apparent when interpreted correctly. The widely accepted belief is that the good will be happy in company of loved ones until the arrival of the Messiah when the soul is resurrected, while the bad will not receive this grace.

The Concept of an Afterlife

The concept of afterlife is contained in the Talmud, which comprises of the Mishnah (written text of the Oral Commandments) and Gemera (interpretation of the Commandments). The journey of the deceased is described in this Scripture in detail.

When a person dies, his soul is brought for judgment. Those who have never swerved from the teachings of the Scriptures and have led a pure life are ushered into the *olam ha-ba*, or world to come.

The unrighteous go to a place referred to as *sheol* after death. The earth splits apart to swallow these souls and send them to *sheol*. Here the soul may be given a chance to review past actions and gain an understanding of how much wrong it has committed. Through this process, the soul gains wisdom. Some believers view this period as that set aside for punishment for bad deeds during life. At the end of a one-year period, the soul is elevated to a higher plane and can now move on to the world to come.

ESSENTIAL

Judaism does not preach the concept that all bad souls are sent to hell for eternity. However, some evil souls that have carried out deeds of great wickedness are punished for eternity. Another school of thought holds that such souls are simply destroyed, never to be resurrected again.

In the Book of Enoch, *sheol* is described as being divided into four planes. The first plane is occupied by the pristine souls, who are merely waiting for resurrection. The second is occupied by the lesser mortals, who have many virtues and good deeds to their credit. The third contains the bad souls awaiting punishment, while the fourth contains the truly evil souls who will never be resurrected.

Resurrection

Rambam's Thirteen Principles of Faith speaks about resurrection. According to this concept, when the Messiah arrives, he will create the perfect world, or the world to come. The good souls awaiting resurrection in paradise will be given a new life in this world of peace and happiness so that they can enjoy the fruits of their good deeds.

Some followers of Judaism hold that the process of rebirth is a continuous one, and the righteous souls are sent back to earth to help make it a better place. Still others believe that only souls that are yet to complete earthly duties are reincarnated so that they may have a second chance to finish their work.

The different movements of Judaism have varying thoughts concerning the afterlife, but these are all speculative. They consider it a distraction to focus on the afterlife, instead placing their attention on their actions during their daily lives. It is believed God rewards the good and that it is right to leave it in his hands.

Islam

The concept of an afterlife plays an extremely important role in Islam and it governs, to a large extent, the Islamic way of life. According to the Koran, the very purpose of life is to live in a way that is pleasing to God (Allah) so that one may achieve paradise in the afterlife. Followers of Islam believe that an account of each person's good and bad deeds is opened at the time of puberty, and this record is used to determine the person's fate in the afterlife.

The Koran, God's words to Muhammad, is the holy book of Islam and is meant as guidance to Muslims and others who wish to learn the meanings of Islam. It clearly states the idea that people should live their lives in a certain way if they want to live a good afterlife. Although this concept of actions (in current life) and reward (heaven or hell in afterlife) is present in many religions, the impact that it has on Muslims is much more than in any other religion.

Islam incorporates the concept of a soul. Each person is considered to be the combination of a body and soul. Similar to the Judeo-Christian tradition, the idea that a physical body is needed for life after death is also present in Islam. The Koran speaks of the Day of Reckoning or the Day of Resurrection (*Yawm al-Qiyamah*), when the dead will be resurrected and given an afterlife according to their deeds.

Afterlife Before Resurrection

Muslims believe that for a spirit, the period after the death of a person and before the Day of Resurrection is like the period spent by an unborn child in the womb. The Resurrection is thus the second birth of a spirit, but it takes place after an extremely long period.

During this period, the level of consciousness of the spirit increases. As the Day of Resurrection comes closer, this embryo (spirit) becomes more and more peaceful and blissful if it is supposed to go to heaven, and it becomes more and more impatient if it is supposed to go to hell. During this period, it is said that a window is opened into the grave: a window from heaven for a pious person, and a window from hell for an evil one. It should be clarified that this refers to a symbolic grave (more like a womb) and not a physical one. It is also believed that just as the beginnings of an embryo are drastically different from the final form of the baby at birth, similarly, the final form of the spirit at the time of resurrection is far removed from its original state.

FACT

It is also believed that when a spirit is resting in the grave, the grave is transformed into a luxurious place if the person has done good deeds, or an oppressive, constricting space if the person's faith is imperfect or if he has sinned. The sinner faces horrible pain as the rib cage of the corpse collapses and worms begin eating the flesh. This is referred to as the torture of the grave.

Communicating with Spirits

On the possibility of making contact with the spirits of the deceased, the views of Mirza Tahir Ahmad, a famous Muslim scholar and a caliph of the Ahmadiyya Muslim Community, are noteworthy. According to Ahmad, the belief that spirits can return and can communicate with the living is incorrect.

He pointed out that according to the Koran, it is completely forbidden for a spirit that had left this world to return to it, and that there is no way you can summon a spirit to visit you. However, he emphasized that communication with spirits is possible through mediums like prayer, dreams, etc., and that it has been observed many times in the past, as well as mentioned in the Koran.

Afterlife after Resurrection

The Koran also speaks about the specific nature of heaven and hell. According to the Koran, paradise (*firdaws*), also called "the Garden" (*Janna*), is a place of physical and spiritual pleasure, with lofty mansions (39:20), delicious food and drink (52:22), and virgin companions called *houris* (56:17–19). There are seven heavens (17:46).

Hell is mentioned as having seven doors (39:71, 15:43), and the Koran states, "The unbelievers among the People of the Book and the pagans shall burn for ever in the fire of Hell. They are the vilest of all creatures" (98:1–8).

Hinduism

Hinduism adheres to the principle of an afterlife. It is seen as a very real and powerful concept within the perspective of religion and metaphysics. Death is a natural aspect of life. Like many other religions, Hinduism firmly believes in this as well. But death is not seen as the end, but rather the beginning of a new life. The idea of transmigration is broadly classified into two major categories: *linear*, the belief that a human is born only once and after death is judged on the basis of his deeds, and *cyclic*, wherein an individual's soul is reborn as a new human being and the deeds of the past life are carried on to the next.

The *atman*, or *atma*, is the soul of a human being, or the "true self," and it exists without any form. When you are born, a soul is transferred into your body in the form of life, and when you have completed your life in the physical world, your *atman* leaves your body.

Atman is pure and is the essence of divinity. Each human being is connected to the supreme being through his soul. Just like energy, the *atman* can neither be created nor destroyed and is immortal. It keeps moving from one body to another until it finally comes together with God.

Karma

Karma is the act or deed that runs the circle of cause and effect called *samsara*. Also referred to as the "wheel of karma," it is the fundamental law, governed by three major concepts:

- The Act
- Principle of the Act
- The Consequence

Karma is the infrastructure put in place by God to keep a check on the deeds of human beings, whether good or evil. Your fortune and misfortune are a result of your karma, and it takes into account not only your present life but your past life karmas as well.

Karma can be good or bad based on the actions of a human being. Good deeds are rewarded and bring you closer to God, but bad karma takes you away from God and puts you back into the routine pattern of birth, death, and rebirth.

ALERT

The Bhagavad-Gita, a sacred Hindu scripture, highlights the impact actions have on a person's life: "The senses have been conditioned by attraction to the pleasant and aversion to the unpleasant: A man should not be ruled by them; they are obstacles in his path."

Moksha means "liberation" in Sanskrit, and is described as the state when the *atman* gains salvation. When God liberates a soul from the wheel of karma and merges it into himself, the *atman* achieves *moksha*. The Vedas, sacred Hindu scriptures, describe some methods to help a human attain *moksha*:

- **Karma yoga:** This is a way to reach God through your actions and deeds. As described by Lord Krishna in the Bhagavad-Gita, karma yoga is doing the right thing without any regard of the consequence or personal interest.

- **Bhakti yoga:** *Bhakti*, or worship, is a method of reaching God.
- **Jnana yoga:** This refers to achieving complete understanding of the *atman*, passing on this knowledge to other human beings, and showing them the path to attain *moksha*.
- **Raja yoga:** This refers to gaining complete control over your mind, so your thoughts and your soul are completely purified. It is a realization of your "true self" achieved through meditation and through purification of the mind and the soul.

Punarjanma, or rebirth, refers to your next life (in Sanskrit, *punar* means "next" and *janma* means "life"). As mentioned above, your karma (your deeds) will decide how and where you will be reborn and what kind of life you will have. Lord Krishna succinctly described the concept of rebirth in the Bhagavad-Gita:

"As a man casts off his worn-out clothes and takes on other new ones, so does the soul cast off its worn out bodies and enters new ones."

Ultimately, good or bad karma will determine how and if you will get out of the "wheel of life" and finally merge with God for eternity in the afterlife.

Buddhism

The Buddhist perspective concerning the afterlife is somewhat of an eccentric concept for the typical Westerner. Whereas Abrahamic religions embrace the notion of the afterlife as being a wonderful existence, which is the opposite of the suffering on earth, the Buddhists adopt a somewhat different perspective.

Specifically, Buddhism holds the view that life on earth is the embodiment of suffering, and that people will undergo multiple reincarnations based on how morally and justly they lived their previous lives. However, whereas other world religions have a very clearly defined and ordered body of moral law designed to regulate human conduct, Buddhism departs from this way of thinking to cut straight to what it identifies as being the root of all problems. Specifically, Buddhism identifies that the notion of desire, the coveting of anything in the world—whether it be material or sexual—brings pain and suffering.

Buddhism and Its Views on the Afterlife

Buddhists do not believe in the concept of a soul as such, and so they use the word *anatta* to embody their firm view that all things in existence are transitory, fleeting, and temporary. Because all things are in a state of constant flux, this means that there is no concept of immortality within Buddhism.

QUESTION

What is the difference between *anatta* and *annica*?
While *anatta* is used to refer to the fact that nothing is eternal in the world, *annica* is the Buddhist word used to refer to the continual process of change. It basically refers to impermanence, which according to Gautama Buddha is the key to understanding *dukkha*, suffering, and *anatta*.

The countless negative emotions, such as disappointment, frustration, and anger, that we face in our daily lives are a result of our ignorance of the law of nature, which is "impermanence." Nothing in this world remains constant or forever, and to get rid of our sorrows we need to understand this fully.

Buddhist leader of the Soka Gakkai International organization, Daisaku Ikeda, sums up this process eloquently: "Buddhism holds that everything is in constant flux. Thus the question is whether we are to accept change passively and be swept away by it or whether we are to take the lead and create positive changes on our own initiative."

Nirvana/Nibbana

Another fundamental precept of Buddhism related to the afterlife is that the attainment of perfection, the liberation from pain and suffering of our stressful existences, is achieved through nirvana.

The ultimate state of perfection within Buddhism philosophy is called *nirvana*, and in keeping with the philosophy identified thus far, nirvana is the achievement of total oblivion, the extinction of a person both as an entity as well as a concept. Nirvana refers to the state of purity, a mental state where all desires, selfishness, greed, and anger have been extinguished and eliminated. To achieve nirvana means to enter a state of absolute bliss and enlightenment.

There is a clearly defined process within Buddhism of the various channels of the afterlife. Whenever a person's physical being comes to an end through death, this means that their spirit will then endure a process that lasts for a total of forty-nine days. This forty-nine-day process is identified within Buddhism as the *bardos*, and during this time there will be one of two possible outcomes:

1. The spirit of the deceased person will be promptly returned to earth in order to recommence the cycle of birth, suffering, and death.
2. The spirit of the deceased person will reach a level of enlightenment so as to entitle him to reach the ultimate goal of nirvana.

At the initial stage of the *bardos* process, commonly referred to as the *chikai bardo*, the deceased person will come to the realization that he has indeed died, and that his soul has been duly separated from his physical body.

During the second stage of the *bardos* process, commonly referred to as the *chonyid bardo*, the spirit of the deceased person will then have to face the trials and tribulations of a number of distressing visualizations that will appear before him, which are the physical embodiment of the actions of the deceased during his time on earth. Gautama Buddha summarized the way to achieve nirvana: "The whole secret of existence is to have no fear. Never fear what will become of you, depend on no one. Only the moment you reject all help are you freed."

Gnosticism, Esotericism, and Mysticism

Gnostics have a unique religious belief that maintains that knowledge is salvation. This does not denote knowledge of the material world but that of spiritual reality and an understanding of the cosmos. It is now believed after the discovery of the Nag Hammadi scrolls that Gnostics learned the principles of their religion directly from Christ's disciples.

According to Gnosticism, all humankind was created by Demiurge, a deity that has a dualist nature—a physical form and a divine spark, which lies within. Those who have not gleaned the supreme knowledge continue to move toward Demiurge's Garden of Delights—condemning their divine spark to lie concealed, even after death. *Beyond Death: The Gnostic Book of the Dead* by Samael Aun Weor explains how unenlightened souls live in a world of illusion, both during life and in the afterlife, unless they learn spiritual knowledge of where they originated and where they must go.

Salvation signifies the release of the divine spark from its physical bondage to merge with the supreme God at death instead of being reincarnated. This salvation can be attained through gnosis, or knowledge. According to the Gnostic Gospel of Thomas, Jesus explains that humans must comprehend the supreme God while on earth in order to gain salvation at death. The physical body of a being that has failed to complete the work of gnosis is destroyed at death, and the divine spark is transferred to another body to remain on earth in search for the true knowledge. This cycle continues until the being achieves gnosis.

Earthly beings are assisted in their search for supreme knowledge by the Messengers of Light, such as Jesus, Seth, and the Prophet Mani, sent by God. Jesus and Sophia, the embodiment of wisdom, wait, in a place called Pleroma, for those who have followed the divine guidance to gain gnosis. Here, these divine entities aid the being to merge with the supreme God. Those who have almost gained the supreme knowledge are allowed to exist in a heaven-like place at the entrance of Pleroma. Here, they increase their awareness and ultimately rise to the level of the enlightened being that merges with God.

Esotericism

Esotericism holds that a deep insight into the hidden meanings of spiritual texts is necessary in order to gain an understanding of the ultimate truth. These hidden meanings have been concealed herein by the divine to be unveiled through introspection by earthly beings, which have attained higher spiritual levels. By understanding these hidden realities the earthly being can align actions, the way of life, and thoughts, so that after death it can merge with the supreme God. The concept of esotericism can be found in many religions, including Buddhism.

Buddhism and Esotericism

Vajrayana Buddhism, a key esoteric belief system, speaks of the path that leads to knowledge and thus to nirvana, or the escape from the cycle of life and death. Religious teachers ask disciples to carry out good deeds, think good thoughts, and follow the sutras (Buddhist teachings or scripture) so that they can gain a higher birth after death. In this manner, the being is expected to move constantly higher toward nirvana. Mahayana Buddhists believe that good souls are reborn in the Pure Land where they may continue their good deeds without interruption for all eternity. Evil souls are meted out punishment by Yama, in proportion with the magnitude of the bad deeds they have accumulated in life. Tibetan Buddhists believe that the soul exists in *Bardo*, or in a kind of limbo, until rebirth.

Hermeticism

In Hermeticism, a leading esoteric religion in the West, followers believe that godlessness is the worst kind of evil perpetrated by man. This evil is punished in the afterlife by demonic spirits who torture those beings after death when they are in purgatory. The good souls avoid this by turning to God in life (*De Castigatione Animae*, chapter 10.7).

Rosicrucianism

Rosicrucians also follow esoteric beliefs. According to them, when a person dies, his ego, or the manifestation of his earthly self, leaves the physical body but continues to hover around it until they both degenerate over time. The transition from life to death takes a while and at the end of this time, the ego breaks free from the connection to the physical form. It takes on the same physical appearance and enters the "desire world." Here the ego has to rid itself of the coarse desires that were built up during life. It also has to understand the consequences of the sins committed in life. Only after this stage can the ego move up to heaven.

Mysticism

Mysticism finds place in many religions across the world. From the ancient Egyptians to Judaism, Sufism, and Christianity, numerous religions reveal elements of mysticism in various forms. The mysticism school of thought holds that it is every living being's eternal quest to find the pathways and processes to attain the ultimate goal of reunion with a supreme power. This quest takes the form of a communion with oneself by keeping all external influences at bay. However, different mystic forms of religions describe this ultimate salvation in different ways.

Mystic Christians

Mystic Christians believe that enlightened souls attain the final goal of oneness with Christ wherein they become Christ. The New Testament has several references that mystics refer to, like Galatians 2:20: "I have been crucified with Christ and I no longer live, but Christ lives in me." The underlying belief is that by experiencing Christ as the believer would experience himself, through prayer and devotion it is possible in time to elevate the soul to a higher place. In this plane, the soul achieves union with the essence of God. Traditional Christianity, as opposed to mystic Christianity, speaks of reaching God's heaven through unswerving faith and devotion but does not dwell on elevating the soul to the level of Christ through spiritual knowledge.

Kabbalistic Judaism

Flavius Josephus, a first-century Jewish historian, wrote about the beliefs prevalent in rabbinic Judaism at that time. He stated that the souls of the evil are punished in the afterlife while good souls are given a new life in a physical form on earth. Although esoteric elements exist in rabbinic Judaism, such leanings become evident in the kabbalistic Judaism teachings, which clearly define the mystic aspects of rabbinic Judaism. According to the Zohar, a religious text of kabbalistic Jews, it is the evildoers who are consigned to resurrections on earth after memories of previous births and actions are erased. These souls must rectify past wrongs in the reincarnated life to attain salvation.

Sufism

In Sufism, God assesses all souls on the Day of Judgment, or *Yawm ad-Din*. Those who have surrendered themselves to the belief and practice of worshipping God will be granted a place in paradise (*jannat*) while nonbelievers will be sent to hell (*jahannum*). As opposed to traditional Islam, Sufis believe that paradise brings them closest to the Supreme and allows the veil between the souls and Allah to be lifted. In this way, they are reunited with the Supreme Being to become one with him.

Universalism, Wicca, and Spiritualism

In his position paper entitled "Universalism and the Bible," Yale philosopher and researcher Keith DeRose defines Universalism as "the position that eventually all human beings will be saved and will enjoy everlasting life with Christ." DeRose cites various biblical verses found in the New Testament which use the word "all" in reference to who will be saved in the afterlife. He maintains that you don't have to be a Christian or to believe in Christ to be saved, because the Scriptures make no distinction as to who Christ will save. For some, "all" may even include the devil.

FACT

While some Universalists believe in punishment or retribution in the afterlife, they maintain that any punishment will not last forever or will not be "unending," although the Bible speaks of "eternal" punishment. They explain that the Bible's original Greek text used the word *aion*, which means "age enduring" or "pertaining to an age," and took a different interpretation when it was translated in English as "eternal."

Wicca

Wicca is an eclectic religion that is associated with witchcraft traditions, although its followers are quick to point out that Wiccans are not necessarily witches. Well-known Wiccan author Gary Cantrell explains that Wicca is based on "harmony with nature and all aspects of the god and goddesses divinity."

Wiccans believe in the Threefold Law that says that all the good you do will return to you threefold in this life. Conversely, all the harm that you do will return to you threefold as well. This law of cause and effect is not viewed as punishment but as a natural result of your action. It may come before death or even soon after the action is done.

They also believe that all souls go to a place called Summerland after death, where you can meet those who have gone before. Summerland is pictured as a place of beauty and peace, where you can see and experience all that you hold close to your heart in full beauty for eternity.

It is not a place of judgment but rather a place of self-evaluation where your soul can review its past life and gain an understanding of its total impact on the world. Only after learning your lesson in Summerland will your soul be reincarnated so you can try anew, although you won't be able to remember Summerland when you reach the physical plane again.

Spiritualism

"Thinking about death and dying can be morbid, unless you believe in an afterlife that has meaning," says ordained Spiritualist minister Joanna Bartlett-Gustina in her article "What Spiritualism Teaches About Death."

ESSENTIAL

Universalism, Wicca, and Spiritualism may maintain different views of life after death, but they all share the common idea of continuity of life. This continuity of life can be a source of comfort to both the dying and the grieving.

Unlike materialism, which holds that all life ceases in the death of the physical matter, Spiritualism maintains that your spirit survives death and can communicate with the living through a third party, usually a medium or spiritualist minister. This interaction of the dead with the living is based on the idea that the dead are able to observe the living from a distance and often want to give knowledge and advice to living friends and relatives through a medium.

Death is not viewed as the end but a transition from one state of awareness to another. While they believe in life after death, they do not propose a place of punishment or reward such as a heaven and hell.

CHAPTER 3

Angels, Heaven, and Hell

The concepts of otherworldly entities and places of the afterlife have been with mankind since the beginning of time. Almost all religions and cultures have a belief in angelic beings that act as messengers and help protect those in need. While various versions of heaven and hell have taken shape throughout history, their interpretations are still being debated and continue to shape the world today.

Angels: Messengers and Guides

The word "angel" has been derived from the Greek word *angelos* which means "messenger." Angels have played a pivotal role in many world religions, perhaps most acutely in the context of Christianity. Angels were primarily the emissaries of God, providing people mentioned in the Bible with due and proper instruction as to what God intended for them. Sometimes their role extended beyond mere mouthpieces for the heavenly master; they were avenging creatures sent to punish and destroy the wicked.

ESSENTIAL

Saint Augustine, the popular theologian and philosopher, aptly described angels: "Angels are spirits, but it is not because they are spirits that they are angels. They become angels when they are sent. For the name angel refers to their office, not their nature. You ask the name of this nature, it is spirit; you ask its office, it is that of an Angel, which is a messenger."

Angels, as Interpreted by Major Religions

Angels have something of an irrational portrayal, with some cultures and belief systems hailing them as the absolute embodiment of purity and mercy, and others as terrifying creatures of righteous wrath.

Two angels were sent to redeem and spy on the cities of Sodom and Gomorrah, cities of ill repute, according to the Bible. When the angels were sexually assaulted, God decided that the cities were to be destroyed, despite the pleas for clemency urged by the angels.

Michael the Archangel is given an especially important and pivotal role in the Bible, and his cameo appearance is specifically mentioned in the Book of Revelation, which heralds and discusses the "end of days" in great detail. Michael, it is claimed, will defeat the "great dragon" (Satan) and then seal him in hell for all of eternity in order to usher in an eternal calm.

Angels in Buddhism

Despite its general rejection of an afterlife as such, Buddhism does make provision for the existence of angels. Unlike Christian angels, angels in Buddhism (commonly referred to as *devas*) came into being when a pure-hearted person reached a sufficiently high level of enlightenment, which allowed her to reach a higher spiritual plane. However, just like their Christian counterparts, they are not supposed to directly meddle in the affairs of men, and to do so is a divine offense. They do act as custodians of moral conduct, rewarding those who are virtuous and kind, and harassing those who are wicked and selfish.

Angels in Islam

Unlike other religions, where the belief of angels is a voluntary elective, it is a mandatory perquisite for a true Muslim. Indeed, a rejection of the existence of these celestial beings will render that person the status of non-*mu'min*, or nonbeliever.

A common theme noted within all religions is that angels are directly prohibited from acting directly in human affairs, whether by active choice or merely a design quirk. By this, it is meant that they cannot make decisions for you or take control of your life.

Angel Interventions

According to angeologists, the intervention of angels in human lives is not just limited to our physical death. Angels guide souls to the divine light and love of God and help them reach their ultimate destination. And while people are in this world, angels provide healing, love, guidance, and protection whenever a person calls upon them and seeks their help. Guardian angels are spiritual beings, and each person has at least one angel watching. They are present during an individual's graduation ceremony, a birthday party, or other happy occasions that mark a turning point in life, to guide that person on the right path. And when people face emergencies, such as a life-threatening situation, angels can help them avoid all dangers and keep them safe if it is meant to be.

People have reported hearing voices in their heads that have guided them toward incredible achievements that normally would not have been possible; some people talk about how a stranger or loved one suddenly arrived and saved them in a life-threatening situation. There are numerous instances where everyday people have reported encounters with angels.

Encounters can happen through a light or a distinct voice, or angels might assume human form—appear in front of a person—as a friend, relative, or stranger, to assist him or help him in his times of need.

FACT

According to a March 2004 Gallup poll, belief in angels and demons is on the rise, at least in the United States. In 1994, 72 percent of Americans said they believed in angels; in 2004, 78 percent indicated belief in angels. Belief in the devil has risen even more dramatically, increasing from 55 percent in 1990 to 70 percent in 2004.

As Doreen Virtue writes in her article "Calling All Angels," you can connect with your angel and ask for help by writing a letter spelling out your need, visualizing them, or just calling out aloud and asking for their guidance and assistance.

Angels can act as messengers and guides, but only when a person is prepared to listen to them. Intuition can help people hear the signs and messages given by angels, since they are always working to protect humans against unpleasant events and to help them achieve life's real purpose.

The Notion of Heaven

"Heaven" basically refers to the physical place beyond the earth's atmosphere. It is imagined as a seemingly endless stretch of the universe, a plane of existence different from our universe. Most religious philosophies and spiritual books talk about heaven as a place that is accessible only by good, pious, and kind spirits. Those that helped people and performed good deeds would earn a place in heaven after they left the mortal world.

The Traditional Doctrines

Heaven can be defined based on one of the following three philosophies:

1. **The reward theory:** The main purpose of heaven is to reward people for leading honorable earthly lives and depicting the highest standard of behavior.

2. **The individual existence:** In this concept, heaven is a plane of existence for the higher consciousness of an individual.
3. **The permanence theory:** Heaven is the place of eternal existence for a soul, which is freed from the cycle of life.

Heaven as Seen by Different Religions

In some early religions, especially the Egyptian and Greek faiths, heaven was considered as a far-off plane of existence beyond the earth. It was a place beyond the universe, a dark space where no stars were present. The soul of the deceased person would have to travel literally from this end of the world to the other to reach heaven. Another popular notion was that heaven was a place beyond the clouds from where angels and gods watched over man.

As each era passed, religions developed strong beliefs and notions about heaven. The word *paradise* was coined by the ancient Persians (followers of Zoroastrianism), who believed heaven to be a beautiful garden. The concept of heaven as suggested by Zoroastrianism was later adopted by the Jews, Christians, and Muslims. However, one unique aspect about Zoroastrianism is it claims that eventually all people (good or bad) will get a place in heaven, though the evil souls would go through a period of purification first.

Just like in Zoroastrianism, the Islamic view of heaven is also of "paradise," a garden inhabited by immortal souls. Those who fulfill their purpose on earth and lead their lives abiding by the path laid out in the Koran will be given an eternal place in heaven, where they will be surrounded by "bashful, dark-eyed virgins, chaste as the sheltered eggs of ostriches," and will be dressed in silks and jewels. Inhabitants of heaven will be rewarded in every way for leading virtuous lives, and for being Allah's true sons.

The Afterlife, Justice, and Judgment

Religion and faith are powerful pillars of strength and guidance. The concept of heaven, hell, and the afterlife have been perpetuated to show humans the right path to achieving enlightenment and to provide answers that science has not been able to establish so far.

Bishop John Shelby Spong, a former Anglican bishop popular for his unique and provocative position regarding religious faith, described the concept of religious beliefs as follows: "We humans are self-aware enough to realize that our lives are counting down toward some unknown end. And it scares us, so we invented religion to give us solace. Religion tells us that good deeds in this life will be rewarded with a place in heaven in the next, while bad people will be sentenced to hell."

The strong beliefs in an afterlife can also be attributed to the desire for justice. The mortal world can be an unjust and cruel place for many people, and most ancient cultures and religions promise a final justice in the afterlife. While struggling with the cruelties and hardships of the physical world, it can be very comforting to know that when you die you will be relieved of all sufferings, pain, and adversities; you will reach a place where there will be peace, happiness, and God's love. Many are comforted by the thought that good people will eventually be rewarded, even if the evil seems to win in the physical world.

Dante's Vision of Hell

Dante Alighieri (1265–1321) was a preeminent Italian poet of the medieval times. His greatest work, the epic poem the *Divine Comedy*, is highly regarded in world literature. The poem describes Dante's journey through hell, purgatory, and heaven to reach God's home. The poem is allegorical and represents the soul's journey toward God.

Dante's journey in the *Divine Comedy* begins in a dark forest, which leads into the *Inferno* (hell). *Inferno* is followed by *Purgatorio* (purgatory) and *Paradiso* (heaven), which finally leads to the Empyrean, or the abode of God. The journey through hell is an allegory for recognition of the various sins and rejection of them to cleanse the soul of these vices.

Dante begins his journey in the *Divine Comedy* in 1300 on the day before Good Friday. At the beginning, he is lost in a dark forest with a view of the distant and silent sun. Three creatures assail him, each of which are representative of three kinds of vices: the she wolf (avarice, or greed), the lion (ambition, pride, violence), and the leopard (fraudulence, incontinence). These creatures are shown preventing Dante from climbing the mountain of joy and keeping him away from the sun (an allegory for God) in the darkness of the woods. Virgil (70 B.C.E.–19 B.C.E.), a famous classical Roman poet, appears before Dante in this situation and offers to guide him through his journey. It is then that they start their journey toward and then through hell.

Hell is divided into nine concentric circles, each circle representing a specific sin (or sins). The souls that reside in each circle have been damned for their sins, and are doomed to reside there for eternity.

ESSENTIAL

In Dante's journey through hell and beyond, he often came across instances of nonbelievers of different categories condemned for not having faith in the Christian God or not following religious teachings. Dante was a strong believer, and his poem exhibits this belief throughout.

The souls that are thrown into hell after death are of people who have committed sins in complete awareness. The nine circles of hell described by Dante have been highly influential in shaping the Christian vision of hell.

Inferno's Nine Circles

First circle—Limbo:
This circle is for those who were either unbaptized or did not believe in the Christian faith. This realm of hell has green fields, villas, clear skies, and clean air, unlike the other circles of hell.

Second circle—Lust:
This circle is the first realm of punishment in the true sense. It is reserved for souls who were swayed by excessive lust, which led them to commit sexual sins such as adultery. These souls are punished by being blown around by strong winds that lash and spin them with great force.

Third circle—Gluttony:
This circle of hell punishes those who indulged in excessive and addictive abuse of food and other substances. As a punishment, they are thrown into foul-smelling slush and are beaten down by icy rain and storms. The three-headed, ravenous dog Cerberus guards this circle. In Dante's poem, Dante and Virgil escape the dog by throwing mud in his mouth.

Fourth circle—Avarice and Prodigality:

In this circle, the hoarders and the wasters are punished. Plutus, the Greek god of wealth, guards this realm. Misers and excessive spenders have been condemned to push large bags of wealth eternally.

Fifth circle—Wrath and Sullenness:

This circle is filled with the stinking swamp of the river Styx, which has a thick fog hanging over it. The wrathful float in the swamp and fight each other, while the sullen lay gurgling beneath the surface. The sullen are referred to as those who find no joy in anything, be it man, God, or material.

Sixth circle—Heresy:

This is the beginning of the "lower hell," where the most malicious of sins are punished. In the sixth circle, heretics are punished eternally by being stuck in hot iron tombs or in the walls of a large white marble mausoleum. This place is the city of Dis, and the air here is hot and dry.

Seventh circle—Violence:

This circle of hell has three rings associated with three kinds of violence. The outer ring holds the souls who have committed violence against people and property, and are hence immersed in the river of blood. The middle ring punishes the souls for violence against self or suicide by entangling them in thorny bushes, which is being eaten up by the Harpies. The last and the innermost ring is for souls who have committed violence against God or nature, that is, blasphemers, sodomites, and usurers—these are eternally confined in a hot desert, where fiery rains pour from the sky.

Eighth circle—Fraud:

Greyon, a creature that personifies fraud, guards this circle; it has an honest man's face but the body of a serpent with a poisonous sting in the tail. This circle is comprised of ten different, abhorrent ditches, each representing a kind of fraud or treachery. These include panderers, flatterers, simonists (the crime of paying for sacraments), false prophets, corrupt politicians, hypocrites, falsifiers, evil counselors, thieves, and cultivators of schism and discord.

Ninth circle—Treachery:

This circle is reserved for those who Dante considers as the biggest sinners of all, the traitors. This circle of hell is unbearably cold and consists of four concentric zones. Each zone is for a different kind of traitor, which includes traitors to kindred, guests or hosts, country, and benefactors. (Interestingly, it was only after Dante's description of hell that Satan started getting depicted in a blue color, as opposed to red, as the deepest level of the *Inferno* was an eternally cold place with a blue frozen lake.)

Cultural, Social, and Religious Influences of Dante's Vision of Hell

Dante is often considered one of the early torchbearers of the Renaissance. Though a firm believer and devout Christian, his epic poem the *Divine Comedy* has multilayered, thought-provoking allegories, excellent character sketches, great symbolic descriptions of the three realms (hell, purgatory, and heaven), and includes several scientific concepts of his time.

It has been suggested and argued that Dante's vision of the *Inferno* was inspired by the Islamic hell. No conclusive evidence of this has been found, but it is a distinct possibility. Similarly, some pagan influences are also evident throughout the work, possibly because Virgil (who was a pagan) was highly regarded by Dante.

Dante's vision of hell and his detailed imagery gave Christians the abhorrent image of the "burning" hell, where souls were damned for eternity for their sins. The Christian image of hell as an "ever-burning, endless pit" was greatly influenced by this work, which was adapted by several painters, sculptors, architects, and other visual artists such as Auguste Rodin, Stradanus, Eugène Delacroix, Gustave Doré, and William Blake. Several musicians and writers have also drawn inspiration from Dante's *Inferno* to create works of great importance. Some notable figures are Geoffrey Chaucer, T. S. Eliot, Franz Liszt, and Peter Ilich Tchaikovsky.

Dante's *Inferno* is much more than a gory picture of hell; it is a detailed investigation into the nature of man, sins, and a map of medieval Christian spirituality. The *Inferno*'s detailed description of hell made it an even more feared place to end up after death—a thought that Christians have absorbed through the ages. The influence of Dante's *Inferno* on Christianity was immense.

A Comparison of Various Heaven and Hell Realms

Heaven and hell have a big significance in most religions of the world. Both concepts are a means of explaining what happens to you after you die. They are also a way of instilling responsibility in humans for their actions and beliefs during their lifetime.

Heaven is the place of supreme happiness (or in some religions "eternal happiness") that you reach after death (if you have been good during your life). The criteria for earning a place in heaven differs slightly among religions. Some, like Hinduism, believe that it is a result of good actions during your lifetime, while in others, like Christianity, it is also dependent on how devoted you have been to God or the religion's beliefs.

Hell, on the other hand, is where people who have done wrong or sinful things in life are sent as punishment. It is a place of great unhappiness and agony. Some religions portray hell as a fiery place of suffering, torture, and agony, and some have portrayed it as cold, depressing, and gloomy.

ESSENTIAL

For some, heaven and hell are the ultimate destinations after death. However, in other religions that believe in the recurring nature of life or the belief in reincarnation, they are seen as a transitional environment. Some religions also suggest that heaven or hell are not a single destination, but have multiple realms, where a person can end up depending on his sins or actions.

Christianity

According to the *Catechism of the Catholic Church*, "Those who die in God's grace and friendship and are perfectly purified live forever...This perfect life with God . . . is called heaven. It is the ultimate end and fulfillment of the deepest human longings, the state of supreme, definitive happiness."

Protestants believe salvation is a gift of God, a proper relationship with God, granted by faith. For Protestants this life is a journey toward either heaven or hell. All people will be resurrected on the Day of Judgment; those who have had faith will join God in joy and happiness. Those who have rejected their faith will go to a place of agony.

Buddhism

The core of Buddhist belief is *samsara*, which is the endless cycle of life, death, and rebirth. Heaven and hell are destinations between death and rebirth—they are not the final or the ultimate destination, but temporary phases or terms that a soul has to go through depending on its karma. There is even heaven and hell in this physical world itself.

Most prominent and often discussed are the six realms of existence. These include *deva-gati*, the realm of heavenly beings (the equivalent of heaven); *asura-gati*, the realm of Titans, characterized by desire and envy; *preta-gati*, the realm of hungry ghosts; *narka-gati*, the realm of hell; *tiryagyoni-gati*, the animal realm; and *manusya-gati*, the realm of humans. The souls continue to move in and out of these temporary realms, and the only escape from this cycle is attainment of enlightenment. This can be achieved only in the human realm or form, and hence is the most important of all phases of the cycle.

Hinduism

Hinduism also has various realms or planes to which the soul can ascend or descend depending on one's karma on the earthly plane. Above the earth are the six heavenly realms or planes, and below are the seven nether planes, followed by twenty-eight hellish planes, and finally the waters of destruction, the Garbhodaka Ocean. The final goal of the soul is attainment of *moksha*—the eternal liberation from the cycle of birth and death.

Islam

In Islam, heaven and hell are split into various levels, attainment of which depends on the human's actions during his lifetime. Maalik guards the gate of hell, and there are both hot and freezing realms of hell in Islam. The heaven described in the Koran, the holy text of Islam, has many levels, and one of the highest is the seventh level.

Other World Religions

Other religious groups do not focus on the realms of heaven and hell—they believe that what is important is what is experienced right now, in people's daily lives. Why look toward one of these realms when your focus should be on what you are doing today?

Reincarnation and Past-Life Studies

Reincarnation is the phenomenon whereby the soul leaves the body at death and enters a new body at the beginning of a new life. The word *reincarnation* derives from the Latin term meaning "the re-entering of the flesh." Millions of people believe in reincarnation, and some religions, such as Buddhism and Hinduism, are in part focused on the premise of reincarnation and rebirth. For people who belong to these religions, reincarnation is regarded as a natural phenomenon. Reincarnation belief structures center on notions like karma and moral consequences—what one does in any given life has consequences and an aftermath that carries on to the next one, be it good or bad. According to many cultures, faiths, and belief systems, one experiences many lifetimes, working through karmic-type issues, until the soul attains a level of spiritual evolution that will allow it to be freed from the earthly plane and the cycle of incarnation. Many people have come forward claiming to have memories of past lives. However, many people who have memories of previous lives have no background in such beliefs, revealing it to be a universal phenomenon.

Remembering Past Lives

Therapies, such as past-life regression, help people to relive moments and experience memories of past lives. Some allow participants to work through traumas from past lives that are affecting them in the present, in order to heal psychologically. Extremely traumatic past experiences are believed to be more likely to leave an imprint on the current life.

Children and Reincarnation

Often it is young children under the age of five who show evidence of past-life memories. They often recount tales of experiences they can't possibly have had and share information that children of this age wouldn't know. Likewise, these memories most often fade as children get older. For example, a case study report by Erlendur Haraldsson from the Department of Psychology at the University of Iceland, published in the *Journal of Scientific Exploration*, investigated four children in Sri Lanka who claimed to remember a previous life at the early age of two to three years:

> *Detailed written records were made of the statements of three of the children before any attempt was made to examine their claims. In two cases, these statements made it possible to trace a deceased person whose life history fit to a considerable extent the statements made by the child. In these cases, no prior connection of any kind was found to have existed between the child's family and that of the alleged previous personality. The pattern of these cases resembles those earlier reported. . . . The children are at a preschool age when they start to make claims about a previous life; they usually start to "forget" at about the time they go to school; some of them claim to have died violently earlier; they express the wish to meet their earlier families or visit their homes; and some of them show behavioral idiosyncrasies that seem to differ from what they observe and would be expected to learn from their environment.*

While critics hold that children this age are subject to a belief in fantasy, many consider these types of reports compelling proof of reincarnation.

Remembering Past Lives

Scientists are working on assembling evidence of the past lives of those who claim to remember them, and are determining what causes people to have these memories. Some people have highly compelling graphic memories of past lives that are often seen as genuine proof of reincarnation. According to the article "The Mystery of Reincarnation" by theological scholar Patrick Zukeran, proponents and scientists studying the reincarnation phenomenon suggest that "hypnotic regression, déjà vu, xenoglossy, birthmarks" are proof that past lives exist.

With hypnotic regression, the subject often recounts people, places, and events with stunning and descriptive accuracy that they seemingly would have no way of knowing. Psychologists that specialize in past-life therapy conduct the sessions of hypnosis. However, it has been found that hypnosis is not 100 percent reliable, as it can make the mind susceptible to manipulation (intentional or otherwise), distortion, and conflation of fantasy with reality.

ALERT

Critics believe that individuals are manipulated by therapies such as hypnosis that are used to recapture past-life memories and that these "memories" have no validity. However, some people have experienced the often near-miraculous healing of physical illness upon the recollection of past-life experiences where the ailment or illness in the present mirrors an ailment or experience from a past life.

Although there are multiple explanations for déjà vu—including the assimilation of present experience with a past one from memory, forms of dream recall, and neurological distortion—proponents of reincarnation attribute déjà vu to memory elicited from past lives. Xenoglossy involves an inexplicable and abrupt ability to speak a language that a person has never learned before. This also is thought to indicate a past-life experience. Those who believe in reincarnation often suggest that a person's birthmarks can resemble those of a deceased individual—although this is difficult to substantiate.

So, is there "proof" of reincarnation, a phenomenon believed by millions the world over, from a vast plethora of cultural and religious backgrounds? While it is always difficult to prove anything with scientific certainty, reincarnation and past lives are fascinating subjects that continue to compel further research

Case Studies: Angel Interventions

Millions around the world believe in angels. From every culture and geographic location and period in history, we have heard about angels. Angels are known as spiritual beings, messengers of God, or spirits of the dead transformed after passing that are historically described as God's task force, protectors, and guides for people in the earthly realm. They are often portrayed in art, literature, and other media as winged beings, filled and shrouded with light, often androgynous looking, sometimes with halos, and dressed in white, resplendent in the qualities of love, kindness, protection, joy, glory, destiny, healing, justice, protection, and celestial power.

FACT

In the Judeo-Christian traditions, there are also archangels, who appear to have special significance and proximity to God. In fact, many religions hold strong to the notion of angels, their mission-related purposes, and their roles in human life.

Tales of angel interventions have appeared throughout recorded history in religious texts, such as the Koran and the Bible (where there are hundreds of references), as well as religious and mystical texts in many of the world's religions, such as Judaism, the Bahá'í faith, Christianity, Zoroastrianism, Sikhism, and others. For example, in the Bible, angels intervene to share messages or bring news, provide comfort or enlightenment, and sometimes to perform tangible tasks, such as the rolling back of the stone before Jesus' tomb after he was crucified.

Angels are depicted as being the messengers of God, acting as the go-between for humans and God. Angel interventions are known to occur in order for the recipient to transcribe their messages, producing scriptures as is seen in the Koran, the works of Rumi, and various Christian mystical texts. There have been many famous stories of angel interventions for artists and historical figures alike, guiding their acts and works, from Joan of Arc, to Handel, to William Blake. Contemporary research and literature have also documented accounts of angel interventions.

These visitations can involve visions, audible information, smells, and tactile sensations. Angels are also often reported to appear as similar to regular human beings, as stated by Daniel Benor in *Personal Spirituality: Science, Spirit, and the Eternal Soul*. Benor claims that angels are "described as looking like normal people who appear out of nowhere, give their assistance, and then disappear again into nowhere. They may communicate in gestures, words or telepathically."

Life-Saving Interventions

Angels often intervene to prevent accidents and death. In an account from firefighter Mark Kuck, retold in *The Big Book of Angels*, an angelic voice gave warning and instruction to the firefighter, allowing him to save his life and the life of his partner. While fighting a fire in a mobile home, Kuck was caught in a fatal flashover:

He heard a clear male voice: "Mark," it said "you need to go." Mark was astonished. The voice was audible, yet it couldn't be his partner—he was too far away to be heard. And an air pack distorts a voice. . . . Not like this voice, so distinct and close it was almost at his ear. Nor were there any openings in the trailer where someone outside could yell through. What was happening?

After Kuck and his partner retreated, the flames advanced into the room they had been in, and if they had not left at the moment they heard the voice, they would have perished. Later, as the fire waned, Mark thought more seriously about the voice. It had been a young voice, something like his own, firm but not intimidating, a voice that he instinctively knew he could trust and obey. And, yes, he had heard it once before, when he was seventeen and involved in a serious automobile accident. Wasn't it this same voice that had calmed him as he crashed, reassured him that all would be well? But how could this be?

In another account from bush pilot Terry Baldwin, retold by Daniel Benor in *Personal Spirituality: Science, Spirit, and the Eternal Soul*, we again find a human-sounding voice said to be an angel intervening. Baldwin was flying passengers through the bush when they were caught in a dangerous storm, and his instruments began to fail. An apparent air traffic controller led them to safety through the storm, evidently using only radar instructions, as the passengers prayed openly. However, Baldwin lost touch with the voice when the radio broke off, and another voice appeared suddenly, just as the plane touched down to safety. At this point, Baldwin said:

"Thanks tower. There's little doubt that you saved our lives today." The controller's reply cast a stunned silence over the men in the plane.

"What are you talking about? We lost contact with you about forty miles out."

In this case, as in many other accounts, prayers often come directly before an angel intervention.

According to Carmel Reilly in *True Tales of Angel Encounters*, aside from miraculous life-saving encounters, we often hear of angel interventions where angels appear as guardian angels in everyday experiences, angels appearing in dreams, angels seen during meditation or prayer, angels sharing messages or news, angels performing real physical acts, and angels as spirit guides and ghosts.

Angels and Near-Death Experiences

There are also many recounted instances of angels present in near-death experiences as well as out-of-body experiences. As professor Craig R. Lundahl stipulates in an article entitled "Angels in Near-Death Experiences," "Angels are personages with whom the near-death experiencer does not usually recall having previous acquaintance. Angels serve as guides, messengers, or escorts in the NDE." Lundahl says that in one account of a near-death experience, "a man . . . came close to dying as a result of being ill during a tooth extraction, and took a trip to Heaven where he saw angels." In another account, there was a woman "who described angels holding hands to form a stairway to Heaven" before she was revived.

Children and Angels

Children often tell compelling stories in which they encounter angels. According to Carmel Reilly in *True Tales of Angel Encounters*, there are "a large number of reports of guardian angels helping children who were ill or lost," as well as many other situations in which a child was in distress. In one account, Lundahl explains, during a near-death experience "a 9-year-old boy was met on the other side by a group of angels whom he described as having no wings, glowing, and seeming to love him very much."

In Brad Steiger's *The Big Book of Angels*, a woman narrates a story where she was given a message by an angel: "When I was five years old an angel came to me at my preschool to let me know that my grandmother had passed away. When my mother and uncle came to pick me up from school, I walked up to my mother and told her that grandma had died. She looked at me with a perplexed expression and wanted to know who told me as she had not called the school to let them know. My reply was that God had sent one of his angels to me." Reilly explains that many researchers theorize that children are often the recipients of angel interventions for reasons such as that they are more "vulnerable" and "less rigid" than adults, being more open to contact with the unknown and the divine.

From the mouths of babes, to the elderly and dying, and from all corners of the globe in all periods of time and in all cultures, human history is inundated with tales of angel interventions. Perhaps, given that, and the fact that most of the earthly population to this day believes in angelic spirits, we would do well to listen to these stories and to the research into these phenomena, for validation or divine inspiration.

CHAPTER 4

Science Seeks an Explanation

Throughout the ages, cultures and religions have tried to explain the concept of an afterlife to the masses. Each group cultivated its own beliefs and ideas, which then spread throughout the world. Many of these concepts are very similar to each other, though at other times they can be significantly different. In the last few centuries science has taken a major role in organizing research into the possibilities of life continuing after the death of the body. Outside of religious and cultural barriers, more in-depth scientific research continues into the possibility of continued consciousness beyond the grave.

The Afterlife Experiments: Gary Schwartz, PhD

Well-known paranormal investigator Gary E. Schwartz's *The Afterlife Experiments: Breakthrough Scientific Evidence of Life After Death* continues to create curiosity and controversy regarding mediums and the possibility of contacting the dead. The investigation is a collection of case studies and experiments in which Schwartz, a former Harvard University professor, and his associates monitored mediums interacting with sitters (nonmediums present at séances and readings).

Dr. Gary Schwartz

Dr. Gary Schwartz is director of the Laboratory for Advances in Consciousness and Health (formerly known as Human Energy Systems Laboratory) at the University of Arizona. He is currently a professor of psychology, medicine, neurology, psychiatry, and surgery at the University of Arizona. He is a graduate of Harvard University, and has taught at both Harvard and Yale, holding the positions of professor of psychiatry and psychology for nearly three decades. He has published more than 400 academic papers.

Schwartz's interest in the paranormal developed after he began teaching at the University of Arizona and after the death of his father-in-law. His wife's grief and her desire to make contact with her father spurred him to begin studying the survival of consciousness after death. Since the late 1990s, Schwartz has studied mediums and the afterlife, having the opportunity to observe famous mediums such as John Edward and George Anderson under laboratory conditions.

He has done considerable work with other top mediums, who have consistently received messages from the dead, to investigate whether there is life after death. Comprehensive reviews of mediumship research indicate that certain people—mediums—can report specific and accurate information about the deceased relatives, friends, and coworkers of people (the "sitters") without having any prior knowledge about the sitters or the deceased people.

Receiving Information from Mediums Using Triple-Blind Protocol

The primary purpose of this study was to gather accurate information of deceased individuals through research mediums under highly controlled experimental environments. More innovations than single-blind and double-blind experiments were employed to remove any traces of fraud.

The triple-blind design had blinding at three levels:

1. The research mediums were blind to the identities of the sitters and the deceased.
2. The experimenter was blind to the identities of the sitters and the deceased.
3. The sitters evaluating the transcripts were blind to the origin of the readings.

Participants

Eight adult mediums, one male and seven females, who had earlier demonstrated abilities to report accurate information, were chosen for the study. Undergraduate students from the University of Arizona (approximately 1,600) were asked to answer "Yes" or "No" to a survey questionnaire about their belief in the afterlife, mediums, and their willingness to be sitters. Finally, eight sitters were chosen (three males and five females). A research assistant who did not interact with the mediums collected information about the discarnate and his or her associated sitter. Each medium performed two readings and they had no prior knowledge about the sitter.

QUESTION

What is a double-blind study?
A double-blind study is a type of clinical trial or experimental procedure in which neither the subjects nor the people overseeing it know the aspects of the experiment, thus helping to prevent bias. A triple-blind study would also have a statistician, who conducts the analysis of the data, unaware of the enrollees and the nature of the experiment.

The key studies described were:

- Potential Medium to Departed to Medium Communication of Pictorial Information: Exploratory Evidence Consistent with Psi and Survival of Consciousness
- Accuracy and Replicability of Anomalous After-Death Communication Across Highly Skilled Mediums
- Accuracy and Replicability of Anomalous Information
- Evidence of Information Retrieval Between Two Research Mediums: Telepathy and Continuance of Consciousness

Findings

Schwartz's findings showed that the mediums he studied had an 85 percent accuracy rate, well above the 36 percent rate logged by a control group of university students—a difference of almost 50 percentage points.

Schwartz's study of the mediums and their interaction with sitters led him to what he describes as a "scientific" conclusion that the mediums he observed were actually communicating with the dead, and that life after death was therefore proven.

The conditions in which Schwartz conducted his experiments were stringent—in one experiment, mediums Laurie Campbell, Suzanne Northrop, and John Edward had to interact with sitters who were not allowed to talk to them—and their results supported the conclusion that the mediums involved were more than just hucksters or skilled cold readers.

"I can no longer ignore the data and dismiss the words," Schwartz wrote in *The Afterlife Experiments*. "They are as real as the sun, the trees and our television sets, which seem to pull pictures out of the air."

Schwartz's experiments, and their conclusions, have stirred up considerable debate. While the academic world was able to dismiss similar conclusions by less well-pedigreed academics, Schwartz's credentials have compelled the academic world to take his findings seriously.

Near-Death Experience Investigations: Raymond A. Moody, MD

Arguably, the most credible evidence on the existence of an afterlife is the series of near-death experience investigations conducted by Raymond A. Moody, a medical doctor who holds postgraduate degrees in philosophy. During the 1960s, Dr. Moody began studying the experiences of people who died, or almost died, and then recovered. He referred to this phenomenon as "near-death experience," or NDE. After investigating the NDEs of approximately 150 people, he published his findings in a book that became a bestseller in 1975, entitled *Life After Life*.

In his book, Dr. Moody identified some elements or experiences that occurred during most NDEs:

- **Strange sounds:** Many recall hearing a buzzing or ringing noise while having a sense of being dead.
- **Peace and painlessness:** Those who felt intense pain while dying relate how pain disappears and is replaced by a sense of peace and calm at the moment of physical death.
- **Out-of-body experience:** Dying moments were accompanied by the sensation of rising up and floating as they watch their bodies from above. They describe the feeling as comfortable and say that their spiritual bodies felt like an energy field.
- **Tunnel experience:** Some recall feeling being drawn into a dark tunnel at an extremely high speed until they reached a realm of radiant golden-white light. While some felt scared during the tunnel experience, they did not sense that they were going to hell or falling into it.
- **Rising rapidly into the heavens:** Some didn't have the tunnel experience but relate how they rose rapidly into the heavens and saw the earth and the celestial sphere at a distance.
- **People of light:** Upon reaching the end of the tunnel or after rising into the heavens, the dying report meeting people who glowed with an inner light. Some also mentioned seeing departed friends and relatives who greeted them.

- **The being of light:** A powerful spiritual being appeared as well, whom some identified as God, Jesus, or some religious figure. Dr. Moody notes that the accounts of the bright-light experience vary and "seem to be largely a function of the religious background, training, or beliefs of the person involved."
- **Life review:** The being of light presents the dying with a panoramic review of everything they have ever done. As they relive every act they did in their lives, the prevailing feeling is that love is the most important thing in life.
- **Reluctance to return:** After the life review, the being of light sometimes tells the dying that they must return to life. Others recall being given a choice of staying or returning. Often they are reluctant to return but some maintain that they only chose to return because they have loved ones who they did not want to leave behind.

Bright-Light Experience

Of particular interest is the experience with the bright light, which many are unable to describe in adequate terms. They recall that this bright-light experience starts out as a dim light that rapidly grows into an unearthly brilliance. It does not hurt or dazzle the eyes, as the dying are still able to see their bodies and the people that surrounded them at the time.

Being of Light

Central to the bright-light experience is the encounter with a being that does not take a human form and who communicates without speaking. Without producing a physical voice or sounds, communication is described as "direct, unimpeded transfer of thoughts," similar to telepathy. And communication is "in such a clear way that there is no possibility of misunderstanding or lying to the being of light."

Because communication with the being of light is not in human language or words, participants of the NDE studies expressed the messages they received from the being of light in the form of questions such as: "What have you done with your life?" "Are you ready to leave?" "Was it worth it?"

Some members of the medical and scientific community remain skeptical about accounts of near-death experience and propose that drugs, lack of oxygen, severe psychological stress, or some other explainable disorder can cause hallucinations and lead people to believe that they are experiencing an NDE. However, when each cause is looked at, they do not account for the majority of the true near-death experiences. For example, common drugs used in the medical facilities (most not having any side affects) could mimic some of the vivid experiences that have been associated with a NDE. Some, like ketamine, an IV-injected anesthetic, were not administered; many of these events happened before medical treatment began. If lack of oxygen, severe psychological stress, or other disorders were the cause, then everyone who flat lines would have an NDE, and this is not the case.

QUESTION

Does it make a difference what your religion or your faith is in order to have a near-death experience?
NDEs have been experienced throughout the world among all the major religions and cultures. There can be slight variations in the descriptions of the events depending on your beliefs.

Nevertheless, some elements of near-death experiences, particularly details witnessed during out-of-body experiences, have been corroborated by testimonies of medical personnel present at the time of physical death. People recount very detailed observations of medical personnel working on them. These include hearing conversations, seeing medical procedures, and even witnessing events in other rooms nearby.

Current studies will continue to examine the nature of the near-death experience phenomena and could some day enlighten the scientific community to the point of acceptance of an afterlife.

The Human Consciousness Project: What Happens When We Die

Research by independent sources has brought some startling facts to light. A significant percentage of those who have suffered cardiac arrest and have been successfully resuscitated have claimed clear recollection of what happened around them when they were "clinically dead." Their recollections include the phase when doctors working on them detected no brain activity, that is, their brain was not functioning. How then can they have comprehended, assimilated, and retained these memories? The answer lies in exploring consciousness or the mind as distinct from the brain.

Human Consciousness Project

The Human Consciousness Project aims to unravel the truth behind what happens in a situation when a person is clinically dead, and to comprehend the difference between the brain and the consciousness. Dr. Sam Parnia, Dr. Peter Fenwick, Professor Robert Peveler, and Professor Stephen Holgate will lead the project. Twenty-five medical centers across the United States, Europe, and Canada will participate in the study. The Horizon Research Foundation, the UK Resuscitation Council, and the Nour Foundation in the United States are funding the research.

The project will begin with the AWARE study, where the consciousness and the brain of a patient undergoing cardiac arrest will be studied by attending physicians. Dr. Parnia, acknowledged expert in the study of the brain and consciousness during death, believes that the human consciousness is still a mystery. He says, "We have no evidence that tells us at what point the human consciousness and mind cease functioning during clinical death." Dr. Parnia believes that this study will help unravel the mystery.

The Basis of the Study

The study is based on the belief that death is not an event that occurs at a single point in time but a process that gradually unfolds. During this process, the physical organs may fail but the mind and consciousness may continue to be in a state of awareness. The study is aimed at evaluating this awareness during the "clinical death" phase. In his lecture at Goldsmiths, University of London, Dr. Parnia described how he has found evidence that suggests a continuation of mental and cognitive functions for an unknown period of time after the process of death has begun.

Methods

About 1,500 cases are to be evaluated under this study, and the participating physicians will undertake special analysis of the patient during the cardiac arrest phase. This analysis will include testing the recollection of these patients during the time they were dead.

ESSENTIAL

The INVOS Cerebral Oximeter is a noninvasive monitoring system for brain blood oxygen saturation in cardiac surgery patients. Its use has showed significant reductions in stroke and other cerebral conditions. It will continuously monitor changes by transmitting infrared light through sensors placed on a patient's head.

Testing Cognizance During "Death"

In most of the reports of near-death experiences, the person describes a feeling of floating above his own body and over the doctors trying to resuscitate him. They describe the scene unfolding under them in the room as if they were watching from a height. The study will test this experience by placing some images on shelves high up in the room where they will be invisible to anyone at floor level. After resuscitation, the person will be asked if he can describe any of these images.

Testing the Physical Manifestations of Death

In addition, the physicians will also monitor the blood and oxygen flow to the brain during the time when the heart has stopped. Special equipment like the INVOS Cerebral Oximeter, a noninvasive monitor, will be used to conduct this evaluation.

Conclusion

The Human Consciousness Project will hopefully bring us closer to understanding the complexity and the mystery of the human mind and consciousness. The research in evaluating the level of awareness during clinical death will play a crucial part in improving the general care and medical treatment provided to a patient under such circumstances.

It is too early to tell whether the findings substantiate the theory of Nobel laureate neuroscientist Sir John Eccles that the human mind and consciousness are a distinct entity separate from the brain. But lead research scientist Dr. Parnia has no doubt that the study will open up new lines of thought in this subject—though it may well just scratch the surface of this mystery. In spite of the great technological advancements and scientific discoveries achieved by us until today, the human mind still retains its deep secrets.

The Scole Experiment

The Scole experiment is one of the recent demonstrations of the existence of an afterlife. The experiment took place in the presence of eminent scientists and investigators. The first sitting of the experiment was conducted in the English village of Scole in 1993, and subsequent sittings took place across the United States, Germany, Spain, Switzerland, and Ireland over a period of six years. With no signs of fraud or trickery identified by those in attendance, including representatives from the Society for Psychical Research (SPR), the Scole experiment is considered by some as irrefutable evidence of the existence of an afterlife.

An Account of the Experiment

Mediums Robin Foy, Sandra Foy, Alan Bennett, and Diana Bennett were prompted by spirit entities to prove that there is life beyond death and that discarnate beings from another dimension exist. This demonstration was performed in full view of an audience consisting of intellectuals, scientists (including those from the NASA), paranormal investigators, and established names from the scientific community. Those in attendance included SPR researchers David Fontana, Arthur Ellison, and Montague Keen, who would later publish "The Scole Report," a critical account of the phenomena they had witnessed.

The sittings were in dark rooms with the mediums wearing luminous wristbands to ensure that they did not use their hands in any way. Those present recounted hearing voices of spirit entities, and some experienced physical touches, such as light kisses and handshakes. Levitations of objects, apports (transference of an article from one place to another), trumpet sounds, and drum beatings were just some of the many live demonstrations. Says medium Robin Foy: "We suddenly discovered what could actually be achieved with the right combination of people at the right time, all of whom had the right attitude of co-operation with our spirit friends."

ESSENTIAL

The Scole Group had shown no financial or publicity motives for the experiments and had refused financial assistance from the Society for Psychical Research (SPR). Two of the mediums had wanted to remain unknown to the public, but eventually their names came out in a national newspaper article.

An interesting phenomenon involving photographic films was also recorded. Unopened film rolls kept at the scene of the experiment were imprinted with images of people, places, drawings, and verses. The rolls were kept in a locked box that was not accessible to any of the mediums or people present. Another fascinating phenomenon was the materialization of complex patterns of "dancing" psychic lights that passed through solid objects and even entered the bodies of those present, with healing results in some cases.

SPR researcher Montague Keen was startled when the discarnate entities played a classical music piece (Rachmaninoff's Second Piano Concerto) that he had loved as a boy and had a strong association with. "They must somehow have divined my buried memories," said Keen.

Support and Criticism

The Scole experiment is well documented, having been discussed in detail by skeptics and believers alike. Australian lawyer and paranormal researcher Victor Zammit, who has closely followed the Scole sittings across different locations, calls the Scole experiment "the greatest recent afterlife experiment conducted in the Western world." Fontana, Ellison, and Keen, in "The Scole Report," have endorsed the authenticity of the experiments, supporting the concept of an afterlife. The fact that no medium or magician has accepted their invitation to replicate the phenomena under the same conditions proves that the Scole experiment cannot be dismissed as trickery.

In fact, well-known magician James Webster, who has more than forty years of experience in stage magic (and is a psychical researcher himself), has admitted that a professional magician could not replicate the phenomena observed at Scole. The phenomena have never been replicated following a discontinuation of the experiments, and those who have dismissed it as fraud have failed to explain the "tricks" employed by the mediums.

If you are unable to make up your mind about these experiments, remember that though it is good to be a skeptic and question things, it is also important to have an open mind about phenomena that cannot be explained by mainstream science.

Near-Death Experiences of the Blind: Dr. Kenneth Ring and Sharon Cooper, PhD

When people are declared clinically dead and then resuscitated, they sometimes undergo an experience during the time they are proclaimed dead. These experiences are termed near-death experiences, or NDEs. During the NDE, they travel away from their bodies and are able to view themselves from far away and see people doing things to their body. Some of them review the entirety or parts of their lives again as an onlooker. Some have reported that they have a feeling of traveling in a tunnel and seeing a being of light at the end of the tunnel. Most of them say that they have experienced a feeling of great love and peace in their experiences. During these experiences, people often find themselves feeling a oneness with everything and everyone. This often impacts their outlook on life in incredibly profound ways, as they've come to understand that how they impact others is in fact how they impact themselves as they feel the pain or joy they have inflicted on others.

Most do not want to return to earth. However, when they do so, they feel transformed and are more caring and giving toward others.

Near-death experiences are often described in visual detail. It is interesting, though, that near-death experiences of the blind are also recounted in visual terms, often with the same descriptions as those of sighted people.

The Researchers

Dr. Kenneth Ring, PhD, is cofounder of the International Association for Near-Death Studies and professor emeritus of psychology at the University of Connecticut. He has authored several books on NDEs, including *Life at Death*, *The Omega Project*, and *Mindsight: Near-Death and Out-of-Body Experiences in the Blind*. Sharon Cooper, PhD, has been researching near-death studies since the early 1980s and has studied yoga and Eastern spirituality. She has published studies on religion, spirituality, and near-death experiences.

When the Blind Have an NDE: The Study

Over a two-year span during the 1990s, Ring and Cooper interviewed and studied thirty-one legally blind people, fourteen having been blind since birth, who had near-death and/or out-of-body experiences. Out of these, twenty-one people had a complete near-death experience (NDE), while the remaining ten had an out-of-body experience (OBE). Fifteen claimed to have had vision, while nine out of the ten OBE cases claimed sight.

QUESTION

Do congenital blind people, blind since birth, "see" in their dreams? It has been shown in studies that people who have been blind since birth do dream but rely on more emotional and tactile senses in the dream state. This would not be unusual, as they rely on these senses more than people who have the gift of sight.

Vicky Umipeg

One such account provides a good example of this phenomenon. It was described to Dr. Ring in his detailed interview with Vicky Umipeg, a forty-five-year-old woman who was blind from birth. She described herself as having discovered herself floating above her physical body in the hospital's emergency room after an automobile accident. She knew she was close to the ceiling as she watched the doctor and nurse try to repair her body.

Umipeg had a distinct recollection of coming to the realization that the body they were working on was indeed her own. She later expressed what a remarkable experience it was for her, saying "This was, the only time I could ever relate to seeing and to what light was, because I experienced it." She also found herself being taken up a tunnel-like structure toward light and coming into a new world where she "saw" trees, birds, and flowers, and encountered deceased friends and relatives who were "made of light."

It is noteworthy, though, that regardless of their age, cause of the NDE, race, religion, beliefs, or sight ability, the experiences of all those studied were remarkably similar. The subsequent experiences of the congenitally blind interviewees were largely parallel to the accounts of sighted near-death experiences.

Near-death experiences in the blind are significant because if people who have been born blind or become blind very early in their infancy can in fact "see" in a near-death state, then it could very well imply that there is some kind of transcendental state of spirit in death. It would go a long way to proving that there is a "soul" as well as adding weight to the belief of the existence of an after life.

Human Consciousness and Spirit Continuance after Death: The Rhine Research Center

The primary focus of the Rhine Research Center is the study of the parapsychological aspects of the human consciousness, its nature and potential. The center explores answers to the basic questions about consciousness through a combination of informal research and empirical study of the available data and information. The Rhine Center aims to prove paranormal experiences and beliefs that have so far been set aside for lack of hard evidence.

Rhine Research Center—the Past and the Present

Dr. J. B. Rhine, a prominent American parapsychology scientist, was one of the first to experiment and research with parapsychological phenomena (psi). In fact, he is credited for coining the term *parapsychology*. His monumental work in Duke University's Parapsychology Lab led to recognition of parapsychology as a distinct field of study. In 1965, he set up the Foundation for Research on the Nature of Man (FRNM) as an independent research unit in the field. In 1995, the FRNM was renamed the Rhine Research Center in acknowledgment of the immense contribution to the field by Dr. J. B. Rhine and his wife Louisa.

Even as early as 1940, thirty-three experiments, involving about a million trials, had been carried out in this field, according to the book authored by the Rhines, *Extra-Sensory Perception After Sixty Years.* Twenty-seven yielded significant results supporting their views on parapsychology.

Today, the Rhine Center continues the legacy of parapsychology research, led by prominent researchers, such as Bonnie Albright, Carl Blackman, William Higgins, John Palmer, and Sally Rhine Feather, daughter of J. B. and Louisa Rhine. These acknowledged experts in the field continue to explore the mysteries of human consciousness and its connection with parapsychological phenomena. The studies conducted by the Rhine Research Center have yielded scientific evidence pertaining to ESP, paranormal activity, psychokinesis (PK), precognition, and other related phenomenon.

The scope of research has significantly expanded since the center's inception. The methods used by the Rhines have been replaced with modern techniques such as measurement of physiological or bio energy in persons with proven psychic talents. By using such verifiable evaluation methods with an open-minded approach toward the paranormal, the Rhine Center today offers undeniable proof of many phenomena that have been cast aside as impossibilities in the past.

Current Focus of Research and Activities

The center is engaged in research on various subjects like human biofields, mind over matter, and telepathy. Researchers are also exploring the depths of human consciousness through studies on health, consciousness enhancement through prayer and intent, heightened perception, harnessing of ESP, and consciousness survival after death.

The Rhine Center conducts seminars and workshops on these subjects from time to time, where renowned experts share their views and the outcome of their research. The center also conducts monthly meets of various work, volunteers, and research groups. The research undertaken in the center is presented in the form of educational offerings through conferences, classes, webinars, study groups, and lectures.

The Rhine Center also publishes the *Journal of Parapsychology*, which is considered an authoritative resource in this field. The *Journal* is peer reviewed, and this ensures that the content is of the highest quality and substance. The *Journal* has been presenting the best of the empirical and theoretical research conducted in this area since its first publication in 1937. The center also publishes a newsletter containing the latest studies, discussions, and thoughts by in-house researchers and other experts in the field.

FACT

Psychokinesis is a form of psi, which includes ESP and psychic healing, and is a technique of mind over matter through invisible means. Psychokinesis includes telekinesis, the paranormal movement of objects, bending of metals, and determining the outcome of events. It can be both an unconscious and conscious process. Levitation and materialization are also associated with psychokinesis.

Rhine Center Director James C. Carpenter, who is also a former editor of the *American Academy of Clinical Psychology Bulletin*, has said, "In the minds of a lot of people, the Rhine Center still is the gold standard for scientific credibility in this field." This holds true to date.

The Rhine Center today continues to seek statistical and quantifiable evidence to prove various parapsychological occurrences. The pathbreaking psi research conducted by the Rhine Research Center has been used as the foundation of many further studies in the field. Although J. B. Rhine and Louisa used older methods, such as Zener cards, the outcome was no less convincing than achieved from the more credible methods of current times. Today, the Rhine Research Center uses modern scientific techniques and state-of-the-art equipment to carry out experiments and analysis in various fields, including telepathy, ESP, remote viewing, precognition, and other paranormal phenomena. The basis of all Rhine Center research lies in the carefully collated empirical data and verifiable tests. This is what makes the center an authoritative source for parapsychological studies, even seventy-five years after Joseph B. Rhine began his journey into the world of the unknown at Duke University's Parapsychology Lab.

CHAPTER 5

Consciousness

The debate on understanding the connection between thoughts and the physical workings of the brain has fascinated science and mankind for ages. What was once believed to be one in the same originator of ideas, the brain and consciousness are now believed to have separate origins that rely on each other in order to manifest reality. As more data and studies come into existence, the understanding of how consciousness can exist on its own becomes more of a reality.

The Brain and Consciousness

Despite sophisticated scientific knowledge and the ability to map genes through thousands of years, there remains a mystery that will almost certainly never be solved: the brain and its relationship to consciousness. The mechanical and biological workings of the brain have been mostly defined and mapped, but how those workings relate to consciousness remains unknown. How does "awareness" really form, and what inputs are involved? You might want to believe that the five senses are the sum of the inputs. If that were so, how would you describe intuition when events are at a geographical and metaphysical distance that prohibits the use of senses?

Our Brain Makeup

Before exploring the brain and consciousness, a quick review of the brain itself is needed. The brain has approximately 100 billion cells and the vast majority are neurons. The neurons are often compared to an electrical system with impulses firing and creating a chemical that enables the impulse to travel from neuron to neuron. Triggering these neurons requires inputs of some kind, like those processed through the senses, but there is certainly more at work.

According to D. H. Pink in *A Whole New Mind*,

The brain is divided into a left and right hemisphere. The right side can interpret inputs simultaneously, can deal with context, and can combine separate inputs into a whole. The left side interprets serial inputs, can deal with text, and is proficient at analyzing details. The brain does not fire up and shut down when needed. Both sides are continually working and trying to make sense of the world.

The entire set of brain cells is overlaid by the cerebral cortex, which R. Thompson, in *The Brain, an Introduction to Neuroscience*, says:

. . . makes humans what they are. Within the vast human cortex lies a critical part of the secret of human consciousness, our superb sensory capacities and sensitivities to the external world, our motor skills, our aptitudes for reasoning and imagining and above all our unique language abilities.

The previous description makes it sound like brain functioning is mostly understood, but that is not true. Researchers only understand approximately 25 percent of the brain's workings, and their approach to consciousness is primarily mechanical. That's why so much research continues to be conducted on topics like brain injuries, autism, epilepsy, posttraumatic stress disorder, and many other problems known to be connected to the brain.

Relating the Brain with Consciousness

So what is the relationship of consciousness to the brain? That's a good question, and one medical researchers have been unable to answer. J. Cornwell states in the article "A Question of Mind Over Matter":

Most researchers agree that research progress is hampered by what they call "the hard problem." Consciousness involves the impression of a subject gazing from a private inner world to an objective outer world: how can I encapsulate the authenticity of that outward-gazing subject by treating consciousness as an object? This "hard problem" has encouraged skeptics to declare that consciousness is an insoluble enigma. Meanwhile, the optimists press doggedly on. Some believe the search requires the discovery of a new kind of physics; some hope to make complex machines in which consciousness will simply emerge; others, such as Nobel prize-winner Francis Crick, think it will be explained, or explained away, by studying the electronic oscillation of brain cells.

This new physics could be quantum biology, which will look at the brain consciousness connection from a subatomic perspective.

B. K. Min stated in an article in the journal *Theoretical Biology and Medical Modelling*, "The subjective experience of consciousness is central to our everyday life. However, whether such subjective experiences have neural correlates remains unsolved and open to hypothesis and investigation."

J. Cornwell further states:

There are two schools of thought concerning consciousness. One school believes that consciousness is merely a mechanical process that relies on objective structures and processes that one day can be replicated. Another school believes that consciousness is an indefinable process that relies on far more than obvious objects and sensory stimuli and is based in moral and imaginative agency leading to breakthroughs of the irrational in the form of dreams and other unrestricted emanations.

D. H. Pink, in *A Whole New Mind*, offers further explanation:

Carl Jung, the Swiss psychiatrist who was the founder of analytical psychology, proposed the idea of a collective unconscious. Jung explored much more than biological processes of the brain and studied both Eastern and Western philosophies and sociology. The collective unconscious mind represents humanity itself and is not personal in nature. Collective consciousness, according to Jung, is not developed . . . it is just within us as humans.

F. David Peat is a well-known physicist and writer. He explores the question of what operates independently of the brain. He points out that the brain does not explain the whole mind, though researchers studying the issue begin with the "hard problem" mentioned earlier. He writes that consciousness is not fully explained by the brain and suggests that it is possible "that the mind was present in the universe at the beginning . . . or that the mind is of a totally different order and makes it liaison with matter via the medium of the brain." (F. David Peat, Talk given in Padova, October 1995, to Club of Budapest)

There is no defined connection between the brain and consciousness. That is probably why, despite years of study, researchers have been unable to agree as to where the mind begins. Does it begin in the brain? Is it just part of us as members of the universe? And how do you define what is objective versus irrational?

The brain is a highly complex biological organ. Consciousness, on the other hand, seems to transcend biology, and therefore could transcend death as we know it.

Meditation: A Higher State of Consciousness

Most of the population are constantly in pursuit of worldly pleasures they believe can bring them happiness and fulfillment. But it is well recognized that the happiness derived from these material pleasures is temporary and brings with it stress and anxiety. To drive away stress, calm the mind, and experience inner joy, a technique known as "meditation" is practiced in the East as well as the West. The purpose of meditation is to focus on the inner self, away from the outside world.

FACT

Meditation is said to have a profound impact on the mind and the consciousness of the individual. It awakens the inner consciousness and makes the person practicing it realize different aspects of life that he would never have pondered before.

The word *meditation* is a word taken from the Latin word *meditatum*, formed from the root *med*, which means "to measure, or to ponder." Meditation has been practiced for centuries by isolated individuals to achieve a higher spiritual consciousness and by modern societies for relaxation, stress reduction, and inner peace. Meditation can be studied in a spiritual as well as a scientific context. On a spiritual level, meditation helps in attainment of peace, serenity, and bliss. Scientific observations of the brains of Buddhist monks have shown that meditation has a positive affect on the brain's gamma wave activity, which is responsible for neurological functions such as attention, perception, and memory.

Connecting with the Universe

The state of meditation does not take you away from worldly realities; it is a medium that allows you to dissociate yourself from the regular mind-body processes and worldly matters, and observe them from a higher plane of being or state of consciousness. This state of consciousness or awareness that can be achieved through the disciplined practice of meditation encompasses both the spiritual and earthly planes.

The goal of a person practicing meditation should be to experience his thoughts and body objectively, without being limited by his existence or feeling trapped inside them. Liberating the mind from the limitations of existence in the earthly plane is one of the key objectives of meditation.

Meditation also gives you the ability to connect with the universe and feel your soul as a part of the larger and all-encompassing universal consciousness. Experiencing this may not be the easiest of things, but regular and disciplined meditation practice can get you closer to the pure consciousness, which is much more blissful than the surface level reality of the physical world.

ESSENTIAL

"There is no need to go to India or anywhere else to find peace. You will find that deep place of silence right in your room, your garden or even your bathtub."—Elisabeth Kübler-Ross, MD

Types of Meditation

There are different forms of meditation, some of which include keeping the body immobile and focusing attention on the inner self, an expressive form where the body is let free. Broadly, meditation can be classified under two main categories: concentrative meditation or mindfulness meditation.

Concentrative Meditation

In concentrative meditation, concentration is focused on a particular object. The mental image you choose to focus on can be something that is of spiritual significance to you, or if you concentrate on a phrase or word, it can be one that has a deep spiritual meaning. It could be your breathing, a word/phrase, an object, or a mental image. When the mind is at ease, each breath is regular, deep, and slow. In this form of meditation, you have to focus on every inhalation and exhalation of breath.

Mindfulness Meditation

Mindfulness meditation helps achieve a nonreactive and calm state of mind. In this form of meditation, the mind is focused on the present. According to Dr. Joan Borysenko, an expert on mind-body connection and integrative medicine, mindfulness meditation is an awareness of the present sensations, feelings, images, and thoughts without getting involved in actually thinking about them. The United States Army has now employed this meditative technique to help their soldiers in Iraq cope with mental stress.

Tai chi is a popular Chinese meditative form, which combines slow movements, postures, and deep, controlled breathing. There are also yogic breathing techniques that relax the body and calm the mind.

Buddhist meditative practices are diverse and vary according to the schools of Buddhism. "Right Concentration," "Right Mindfulness," and "Right View" are three of the several techniques taught. A popular technique is "Vipassana," which involves focusing attention on the coolness in the nostrils during breathing, the breathing process felt around the stomach, and the breath itself. This can be practiced at any place and time.

How Does Meditation Work?

All meditative practices focus on getting rid of cluttered thoughts and calming the mind. Research on the subject shows that meditation brings a decrease in heart rate, pulse rate, and the stress hormone cortisol. Studies conducted on transcendental meditation by Dr. Robert Keith Wallace, pioneering researcher in the neurophysiology of higher states of consciousness, indicate that during meditation, not only does the body achieve a state of profound rest, but the mind and brain also become more alert. The nervous system activity is also reduced, making the mind quiet and relaxed. There is also a drop in blood pressure levels of those practicing meditation on a regular basis.

How Can Meditation Help You

Studies show that meditation has a positive impact on a person's physiological and psychological health. Apart from lowering blood pressure, stress hormones, and cholesterol levels, meditation has been found to help asthma patients by improving airflow to the lungs.

QUESTION

What are some of the health benefits associated with meditation?
Research by Harvard Medical School professors has found that there is an increase in the body's blood flow and a faster delivery of oxygen to muscles during meditation. Practitioners of transcendental meditation have been estimated to be up to twelve years younger than their actual chronological age. Regular meditative practices have been found to retain youthfulness and prevent diseases associated with aging.

Meditation has been found to cure disorders related to stress, anxiety, and depression. Practitioners have reported feeling less irritable, happier, and having improved emotional stability. As mentioned earlier, meditation has a positive effect on brain wave activity, which results in better reasoning skills and improved creativity. All this evidence points to how consciousness can control and help the body, including the physical brain, and how the human being is not just a physical being but made up of thoughts and energy.

Consciousness to Consciousness: Telepathy

Telepathy is the parapsychological phenomenon of transference of thoughts, information, and ideas from one individual to another without the use of the five senses. The word *telepathy* comes from the Greek *tele* and *patheia*, meaning "distant" and "feeling," respectively. F. W. H. Myers, a classical scholar, coined the term in 1882. He was also the founder of the Society for Psychical Research in the United Kingdom, which is a nonprofit organization dedicated to the study and research of paranormal or psychic phenomena in an unbiased way.

The transference or communication of thoughts in telepathy is said to happen through psi, or the "mind soul," which facilitates paranormal cognition. Deductions from bodily gestures, body language, or physical observation do not count as telepathy. Telepathy is pure mind communication, unaided by our senses.

Types of Telepathy

Telepathy can be broadly classified under two categories: intentional and spontaneous communication. Intentional communication involves transference of thoughts by the sender through mind concentration in an effort to pass on the thoughts to the receiver, who may or may not be aware of this intent of the sender. Such communication can be more successfully carried out on hypnotized subjects. Spontaneous communication, on the other hand, refers to unintentional transfer of thoughts or ideas from one person's mind to another's. This includes intimation of illness, danger, or distress, despite physical distance and no sensory communication between the subjects.

Another common classification is precognitive, intuitive, and retrocognitive telepathy. Precognitive telepathy refers to instances where you, as a receiver, get information about the future of the subject. Similarly, intuitive and retrocognitive telepathy is the transfer of information to the receiver from the present and past of the subject.

Telepathy Versus Clairvoyance

There have been several debates surrounding how the parapsychological phenomena of telepathy and clairvoyance are different. Clairvoyance refers to the ability to see into the future or past and know what will happen to an object, individual, or at a particular place.

Though there is no consensus on how the two are different, the key distinction often cited is based on the source of the information. In the case of telepathy, the source of information is the mind of another person, while in clairvoyance it is a direct external intangible source. It is believed that a clairvoyant taps information from a spiritual realm or a larger consciousness.

Scientific Studies, Discussions, and Evidence

Like other forms of parapsychological phenomena, telepathy too has been the topic of many studies. Several experiments and research studies have been conducted to prove or disprove the existence of telepathy. Interestingly, supporters of telepathy not only come from believers in the paranormal, but also from the scientific community, which has researched the subject extensively.

One of the earliest studies conducted in the area was by John E. Coover, a psychologist from Stanford University, in 1912. He did a number of telepathic tests involving guessing playing cards, with results pointing toward the existence of telepathy. Starting in 1927, J. B. Rhine from Duke University conducted several ESP (extrasensory perception) tests, which included telepathic experiments following stricter protocols. Results of these experiments were published in his book, *Extra-Sensory Perception*.

Since then many other experiments and studies have been conducted in this field. The Ganzfeld experiment, devised by Wolfgang Metzger in the 1930s, is one of the most notable experiments that have established the existence of the phenomenon. This experiment has offered some of the strongest quantifiable results to date about telepathy.

ALERT

As telepathy is an extrasensory phenomenon that transcends time and space, its explanation within our current understanding of physics and science may not be possible. However, researchers and physicists are trying to understand telepathy within the realm of science. Some recent efforts have also tried to link telepathy to quantum physics.

The proponents claim that our mind provides a platform for electrical and quantum impulses, which can be received by other minds. Recently, a group of Chinese researchers developed a primary model of how quantum telepathy would work. Their argument is based on the fact that if you bring consciousness into the picture, the premise of nonlocality in quantum theory can be challenged, and quantum superluminal communication will be possible.

Telepathy, Technology, and the Future

In the future, the concept of telepathy may see a convergence with technology. Scientists claim that cybernetics will enable a connection of two human minds using computers, and the future may see increased use of such technology for communication. This may not be telepathy in the purely psychic sense of the concept, but it would certainly see more and more application in the future.

Communications with Coma and Nonresponsive Alzheimer Patients

Coma is defined as a state of almost total unresponsiveness to external stimulation in which the patient lies with his eyes closed. It is a condition in which the normal cognitive and communicative functioning of the patient is hampered.

However, ongoing research in the field has found out that there may be small "islands" of consciousness, even in persistent vegetative states. This could be another example of how the conscious is separate from the physical body.

Success in communicating with a comatose patient lies in identifying these islands wherein there may be some form of eye movement, vocalization, or change in facial expression of the patient.

It is believed that in a comatose patient, the attention is fixed in the past, that is, before the incident that led to the coma. So the aim of communication with such a patient is to make him aware of the present. One method of doing this is to place an object in his hand and tell him what it is. (The faculty of hearing remains intact until the very last breath.) This method of interacting with a coma patient is called "unconscious patient assist."

Newer methods, which utilize measurement of brain activity in response to certain stimuli and convert them into bio-signals that can be read by EEG or computers, are also under research.

FACT

Nonverbal communication plays an important role in interaction with a comatose patient or one in an advanced stage of Alzheimer's. While communicating with such patients, touch therapy is said to work wonders. Merely touching the patient tenderly can establish a physical connection with them and the care providers.

Music Therapy

This type of therapy also allows these patients to communicate with us on social, emotional, and cognitive levels. Music is said to be a preverbal function of our brain, that is, it developed before the function of deciphering language evolved. The different elements of music, like rhythm, pitch, and melody, are processed by different parts of the brain. The emotions attached with the music are processed in the limbic system. Comprehending music thus provides a form of mental exercise to all parts of the brain.

There is ongoing research to develop more effective means of communicating with comatose and nonresponsive Alzheimer's patients. There are reported cases where psychic mediums have made contact with coma and nonresponsive Alzheimer patients, who communicate that they are aware of their current surroundings, people in their lives, as well as past memories. They relate that they are not in any pain and even have had contact with deceased loved ones, which bring them great peace. This information from the medium is related to a loved one who authenticates the facts that the patient has communicated. This reinforces the belief that consciousness is separate from the actual physical brain, and when the body can no longer function and dies, an afterlife is possible.

Transformation Consciousness, Wisdom, and Enlightenment

Do you have a sense of separateness in relation to your body and your mind? Do you have moments when you experience a sudden vision of a deeper emotion, a greater understanding of the world around you, or an awareness of the universe?

This self awareness is intended to make you realize that there is more to your existence than that bound by cultural biases and your environment. If you are like most people, your ego rules your life. The ego referred to is not a sense of inflated self-worth but rather the organized, rational part of your mind that has been structurally defined by life events, trauma, images, other people's influences, and the senses.

Psychotherapists have done many studies trying to define the impact of perception on thoughts and the role of consciousness. And of course there are many theories that have been developed in an attempt to define consciousness. The explanations focus on introspective psychology, networks of cultural meanings, neural systems, and even bio-energies that exert force on the conscious. Yet these explanations focus on the individual's reaction to the world rather than considering what arises from within the individual as a state of awareness representing the union of the internal and external domains.

Simply stated, if you limit your state of awareness with perceptions, then you suppress the state of awareness that enables you to fully experience the inner and outer world as a unit. The net effect is that you limit your ability to become enlightened.

Dr. Tom Lombardo, director of the Center for Future Consciousness, described Walter Truett Anderson's prediction of an emergence of New Enlightenment published in *The Next Enlightenment: Integrating East and West in a New Vision of Human Evolution*. Anderson is a political scientist, professor, futurist, and author. Dr. Lombardo wrote:

He [Anderson] describes enlightenment as an expansion of consciousness—a liberation from mental constraints. He sees it as involving the experience of "oneness" and connectedness, where the conceptualized boundary between the self and the world is transcended. As he notes, the boundary of self and other is frequently a protective and defensive posture, as a way to preserve stasis and prevent change within; enlightenment is the overcoming of this ego-defensive state. Enlightenment is a form of transcendence—of the capacity to stand back from everyday experience and gain a broader view of things.

Another way to state it is if you allow perceptions to limit your consicousness, then you also limit your wisdom, enlightenment, and spiritual awakening. Ken Wilber, prolific writer and lecturer recognized for developing the theory of the holon or unity, explains that transcending the ordinary means understanding that consciousness:

does not, and cannot, arise on its own. . . . There is no private language, there is no radically autonomous consciousness. The very words we are both now sharing were not invented by you or me, were not created by you or me, do not come solely from my consciousness or from yours. Rather, you and I simply find ourselves in a vast intersubjective worldspace in which we live and move and have our being. ("An Integral Theory of Consciousness." Journal of Consciousness Studies)

This theory says that understanding the cosmos requires considering the interior and exterior individual, and the interior and exterior collective. These make up the four quadrants of intentional, behavioral, cultural, and social actions.

Ordinary perception is not enough to comprehend consciousness. The roots of understanding consciousness lie in mysticism, because mysticism involves eliminating the arbitrary restraints and reaching enlightenment where the collective universe is allowed to present itself. You overcome the "I," or the self-centered egoism.

ALERT

In *The-Crest Jewel of Wisdom*, Sankaracharya writes that man must "discriminate between things permanent and transitory" to achieve wisdom. To reach wisdom you must accomplish tranquillity, self-control, cessation, forbearance, faith, and deep concentration. Sankara (known as Sankaracharya) was an Indian sage who lived from 788 to 820 C.E. and is considered by many to be the greatest among historical Hindu sages.

This philosophy is also found in the Chinese Consciousness-Only School of Buddhism, but here there are eight levels of consciousness. The first five levels are the senses including the body; the sixth level is the cognitive process; the seventh level is the ego; and the eighth level is the storehouse consciousness.

Out-of-Body Experience (OBE)

The term *out-of-body experience* was coined by parapsychologist G. N. M. Tyrrell. A person having an out-of-body experience (OBE) will have a sensation of leaving his physical body and observing the world as well as his own physical self from a different location. Out-of-body experiences are often observed in people close to death; however, others have also reported having this experience.

One out of every ten people has an OBE in her lifetime. Researchers have tried to induce the experience in laboratories using various techniques. Out-of-body experiences have been practiced across ancient Indian, Chinese, and Egyptian cultures. There are also many known modern-day practitioners of OBE.

Types of Out-of-Body Experiences

An out-of-body experience can occur spontaneously or be induced through various techniques. A spontaneous OBE is often experienced by persons who are in a state of lucid dreaming or a sort of sleep paralysis, a condition where the subject is unable to move her body despite the willingness to do so.

Extreme and strenuous physical activity has also been observed to cause an OBE. Mountain climbing can trigger a sensation of bilocation, or appearing to be present at two different locations at the same, causing an experience similar to an OBE. Another type of spontaneous out-of-body experience is associated with near-death experience (NDE). Persons undergoing a major operation or a life-threatening accident have accurately described what went on during the course of the operation or at the scene of accident, as if they were observing it from a place outside the scene of the event.

Dutch cardiologist Pim van Lommel, after observing instances of OBEs in patients in near-death situations during cardiac arrests, says that consciousness in a person can exist independent of the brain. His patients correctly described what happened at the scene of their cardiac arrest despite the absence of neuronal activity in their brain.

Ways OBEs Can Be Induced

There are also several ways of inducing an OBE. Deep meditation and a subsequent trancelike state can cause a sensation of drifting out of one's physical body. Hallucinogenic drugs, such as *Salvia divinorum*, ketamine, and phencyclidine have also been known to cause out-of-body experiences.

Mechanically induced OBEs include employing brain wave synchronization methods as well as electrical or magnetic brain stimulations to create a "body asleep/mind awake" state.

OBE researcher Robert Monroe (1915–1995) classified OBEs into Locale 1 and Locale 2 experiences. In the Locale 1 experience, the person feels that she is experiencing the phenomenon in an existing realistic environment. The person may perceive very strong psychological sensations like vibrations, fast heartbeats, and tingling. On the other hand, in a Locale 2 experience, the person may find herself in an unrealistic world. Vibrant colors are commonly seen in this experience.

Many ways of inducing an OBE have been suggested. Psychical researcher Hereward Carrington (1880–1958) suggested that an OBE could be induced when a strong desire by the subconscious provokes the body to experience such a phenomenon. Robert Monroe, in his book *Journeys Out of the Body*, describes a method of inducing an OBE in which the person has to first go into a state of near-sleep and subsequently enter a "vibrational state," which will prepare her for a complete separation.

FACT

Neurology experts have also found that certain portions of the brain, when stimulated, can induce an OBE. Swiss neurophysiology professor Dr. Olaf Blanke found that stimulations of the right parietal-temporal region of the brain could cause an OBE.

Explanations for Out-of-Body Experiences

Doctors and researchers have been able to successfully simulate out-of-body experiences in laboratory conditions. The explanations for OBEs mostly fall in the neurological domain. According to British psychologist Dr. Charles McCreery, a relaxed (sleeping or lying down) or hyper-aroused (such as during childbirth or mountain climbing) state of mind takes the form of a lucid dream, which turns into an OBE, indicating that the phenomenon occurs at very low or very high states of arousal. According to another British psychologist, Dr. Susan Blackmore, an out-of-body experience occurs when all sensory contacts from the physical body are lost, even as the person remains conscious. Perceptions are not drawn from the physical senses, and the person has the illusion of having a physical form/body.

Out-of-body experiences have been also associated with astral projections, where the astral body (vehicle of consciousness) travels anywhere it chooses in the astral world (world of thought). But some researchers, including Blackmore and British psychologist Dr. Celia Green, believe that the phenomena of astral projections is separate from OBEs, as most OBEs do not involve astral travel.

Case Studies

To most, consciousness is an easily defined concept that is taken for granted in everyday life. However, the mind's intricate design makes awareness and even bodily functions far more complex than one would imagine. In *The Blackwell Companion to Consciousness*, professors Max Velmans and Susan Schneider, leading authors in the field of consciousness, explain: "anything that we are aware of at a given moment forms part of our consciousness, making conscious experience at once the most familiar and most mysterious aspect of our lives." Clearly, there is a bountiful amount of information beyond the scope of science and human perception.

The definition of consciousness is commonly thought to require an awake, aware, and breathing person. Solid medical documentation and research have proven that the scope of consciousness delves much deeper. Tibetan monks' astounding mastery of their bodily functions, medical studies conducted on near-death experiences, and the eerie correlation between Buddhism's beliefs regarding the passage between life and death alongside medical science's discoveries essentially blur the line between hard science and spirituality.

Fascinated by Tibetan monks' bewildering mastery over their physical bodies, Herbert Benson, MD, an associate professor at Harvard Medical School, traveled to remote monasteries in India in order to research what could only be considered a medical phenomena.

Benson stated: "I wanted to investigate what advanced forms of meditation can do to help the mind control physical processes once thought to be uncontrollable." According to an article written in the *Harvard Gazette* by William Cromie, through "g *Tum-mo* meditation," also known as heat meditation, these dexterous monks are capable of consciously increasing the temperature in their hands and feet by seventeen degrees Fahrenheit. As astonishing as these results may be, Professors J. D. E. Young, adjunct professor at the Laboratory of Cellular Physiology and Immunology, Rockefeller University, and E. Taylor, lecturer on psychiatry, Harvard Medical School, used the following study in their article analyzing meditation as a wakeful process:

> *Individual practitioners . . . have gained phenomenal control over normally involuntary bodily processes. Tibetan monks studied in their natural environment in a Himalayan monastery practicing* g Tum-mo *yoga*

have been shown to first enter any one of several states of quiet medita-
tion, after which they are able to generate such body heat that they can
dry wet sheets on their back in freezing weather.

Clearly, Tibetan monks have accessed and learned how to control a portion of the brain that the majority of the population can merely connect to
through the body's natural response to extreme temperatures—by slipping
into a sweater and coat to combat chilly weather.

In addition to their phenomenal heat meditation, Tibetan Buddhists have
"made a true science out of the process of dying." Instead of seeing death as
an ultimate end, they view it as an unfolding passage, a metamorphosis, as
stated by Tsering Palmo in the article "Tibetan Buddhist Practices for Dying"
(*Afternoon Session*, Jodo Shu Research Institute):

From a Buddhist perspective, death is a stage of transition. It is merely
an exchange of a rugged and old body of this life with a new and young
body of the next, like changing of your clothes when they are old and
worn out. Buddhists see death as a process and not as an end.

Astonishingly, this perspective can be paralleled to reports of cardiac
arrest patients who were resuscitated and able to recount the event. There
are many different types of experiences a patient may encounter when clinically dead. According to a renowned cardiologist, Dr. Pim van Lommel:

A near-death experience can be defined as the reported memory of the
whole of impressions during a special state of consciousness, including
a number of special elements such as out-of-body experience, pleasant
feelings, seeing a tunnel, a light, deceased relatives, or a life review.

A near-death experience where the patient perceives "a position outside and above their lifeless body" is called an out-of-body experience,
which correlates closely to the viewpoint of Tibetan monks. While enduring an out-of-body experience, patients "have the feeling that they have
apparently taken off their body like an old coat and to their surprise they
appear to have retained their own identity with the possibility of perception, emotions, and a very clear consciousness." Surrounded by reports of

near-death-experience patients accurately recounting specific events during their trauma, Dr. van Lommel became intrigued. He stated, "scientific curiosity started to grow, because according to our current medical concepts it is not possible to experience consciousness during a cardiac arrest, when circulation and breathing have ceased." Evidently, spirituality and hard science have intertwined.

The blurred line between spirituality and science reveals the degree to which human consciousness remains unknown. Both perspectives have proven documentation, leaving even scientists to question which fragments of the brain remain beyond their grasp, and how Tibetan monks have accessed portions of the mind that the remainder of the population cannot. The true depth of human consciousness remains unknown to all and a great mystery for scientists, religious figures, and the human population as a whole to examine until its secrets are unraveled and exposed.

CHAPTER 6

Near-Death Experiences

Have you ever thought of your own death—what actually happens when your body shuts down? Some people have actually experienced an event that is so close to death that it could be that glimpse into the afterlife that people have searched for since the beginning of time. Research and studies have shown that these experiences, called near-death experiences, can be so overwhelming that they leave an everlasting impression on the subject that changes their outlook on life forever.

Near-Death Experiences Defined

Throughout the ages there have been numerous reports of phenomena surrounding people who have briefly died and come back to report experiences of an afterlife. From the ancient Greeks to modern-day Native Americans, history is filled with stories of encounters with the other side. Many experiences were thought to be specific to various religions or cultures, but with time and the advancement of technology, these experiences have begun to be investigated and discussed openly throughout the world.

The expression near-death experience (NDE) has become the generally accepted term for this experience since the publication of Dr. Raymond Moody's 1975 bestselling book, *Life After Life*. Dr. Moody investigated hundreds of cases of people who were clinically dead and brought back to life to report similar extraordinary experiences from the other side.

There are many similarities in NDEs among people who have experienced them. Common phenomena include the feeling of being outside of the body, the sensation of entering a tunnel, and the presence of a strong, white light. Many people report encountering deceased loved ones, and some experience a series of powerful memories from throughout their lives.

Many people who have a near-death experience return with a new outlook on life that is based on universal values and a deeper sense of spirituality. Whatever their prior beliefs, they often feel a greater appreciation of life itself and a renewed sense of purpose. Their priorities may shift toward more compassionate interactions with others and increased focus on current relationships.

FACT

According to a Gallup poll, approximately 8 million Americans claim to have had a near-death experience. Many have reprioritized their lives after the experience.

NDEs in Different Cultures

Near-death experiences have been reported in all religions and cultures. NDEs have been related among atheists, Christians, Muslims, and

Jews. They have been experienced and described by Hindus, Native Americans, and by people of other cultures throughout the world.

These events have not been selectively associated with adults only, as many children have also experienced these episodes. The fact that some children have recounted similar experiences without having a lifetime of religious and cultural attachments is very intriguing and has been the focus of some investigations.

Science and NDEs

Not very long ago, when people encountered sudden medical emergencies that brought them to the precipice of death, there was often nothing that could be done for them and they naturally died. With the advent of modern medical devices, many individuals who have been face to face with their own demise have experienced a reversal of the dying process at the very time of their transition. Medical personnel who have witnessed the NDE phenomena and researchers have begun a vast amount of studies in search for the explanation of these events.

Some scientists have theorized that the NDE phenomena are caused by biological conditions occurring during the time of death. For example, the optic nerve could be affected, thus causing the tunnel-like experiences. The lack of oxygen to the brain has also been thought to cause some of the phenomena.

However, some of these theories have opened up more questions than answers with their conclusions. If an NDE were a totally natural biological event, then why wouldn't every patient who experienced cardiac arrest have one? If patients were clinically dead, how would they remember the event in vivid detail? How can children describe meeting deceased relatives that they have never met or even known about before the NDE?

Dr. Pim van Lommel, when referencing a study conducted in the Netherlands, said: "In our study 282 patients (82 percent) did not have any memory of the period of unconsciousness, 62 patients (18 percent) however reported a NDE with all the 'classical' elements. Between the two groups there was no difference in the duration of cardiac arrest or unconsciousness, intubation, medication, fear of death before cardiac arrest, gender, religion, education or foreknowledge about NDE."

Clinical Death Versus Conscious Death

The idea of "death" has many forms, definitions, and philosophical implications. Death seems relatively easy to determine. If the body does not respond to stimuli, is immobile, and shows no sign of breathing or a heartbeat, the person is considered dead, right?

However, as medical education advanced, new possibilities began to form concerning when and how a person had achieved her biological end. With the use of ventilators and other medical apparatus, it was not always apparent when the real end of consciousness had occurred because machines could be used to continue the breathing process and assist the heart.

QUESTION

Are NDEs caused by the clinical death of the brain?
Some scientists have theorized this could be the case. However, evidence that people return to consciousness with previously unknown knowledge, and that some are given the choice to stay on the earth while others are not, brings into real question the fact that all brains die basically in the same biological way.

In 1968 a Harvard Medical School committee determined the benchmark for constituting the legal death of a human: "whole brain death." The Uniform Determination of Death Act, which the National Conference of Commissioners on Uniform State Laws in cooperation with the President's Commission on Medical Ethics passed, provides the legal definition of death as "irreversible cessation of all functions of the brain, including the brainstem." Brain death is considered legal death in the United States and throughout most of the world.

Conscious death, the ability to lose self-awareness of being and connection to the environment, is much more difficult to define. Some scientists associate conscious death with clinical death, while others separate it into its own category of study. Philosophers are probably better suited to answer this question, but modern technology does have some input into the possibilities.

The question of clinical death versus conscious death might be like comparing apples to oranges. Clinical death is based on a physical determination of events on a biological physical being, while conscious death might be an invalid term altogether. Scientific studies into near-death events, out-of-body experiences, and quantum physics open the door to the possibility of consciousness surviving after the declaration of clinical death.

FACT

The "dead-donor rule," observed as law in all states, requires patients to be declared clinically brain dead before organ transplantation can occur. Medical assisting devices are often still in use until proper transplant authorization is obtained.

Ongoing studies of consciousness suggest that it might be separate from the physical body but have an interaction with the living tissue of the brain. This brings up the dilemma of the real human essence. Is a human being just a chemical and biological interacting physical structure—the body—or a spirit conscience? Someday, it may be shown that perhaps the physical body houses the spirit conciseness.

Common Feeling, Sensations, and Sights

What makes a near-death experience so interesting to researchers is the fact that so many of the people who have experienced them report common elements. Religious or cultural backgrounds do not seem to alter the main characteristics of the experience. Ruling out these possibilities as the cause of the phenomena can help researchers focus on other areas of study, such as the mind-body connection.

The Out-of-Body Experience

A common sensation of an NDE is the feeling of leaving the physical body and floating free of the confines of the physical world. This is the point where the individual realizes that something extraordinary is happening to him and he begins to observe his altered surroundings. A person having an out-of-body experience sees himself along with the surroundings, often from "above." People have reported the exact movements and conversations of medical personnel in the emergency room after being declared clinically dead.

The Silver Cord

The silver cord has been described as a thin iridescent light membrane that connects an individual to the physical body during an out-of-body event. People who have experienced this phenomenon often report they realized that if the cord were severed, they would continue on to the afterlife and not have the ability to return to the physical world.

The Tunnel and Light

After an NDE, many people talk about seeing a tunnel, often with a light at the end of it. People report feeling drawn to the tunnel by an outside force and once entering it, feeling as if they are being propelled through it at a high rate of speed. NDE subjects commonly describe a slim glimmer of light at the end that brightens to an extreme degree and becomes what has been described as a living entity of light.

ALERT

Ketamine is a hallucinogenic anesthetic drug that has been shown to lead to symptoms that are similar to NDE characteristics, like out-of-body sensations. However, not every NDE involves the use of ketamine.

Concept of Time

NDE subjects report an altered perception of time during the experience. An event that actually lasts a few minutes can seem to go on for hours or days. People also remember feeling as if time does not exist. There seems to be no beginning or end to this new existence they are experiencing.

Knowledge

The knowledge that is transferred during the NDE does not seem to be a surprise to many, as they remember the essence of the discussions, the meaning, but not always the details. They remember that it all makes sense, but are not sure how or why it makes sense. It is like having a gut feeling about something; you're not sure why you feel a certain way, but you trust yourself that it's right. A common answer to "what is the most important thing in our lives?" is love, to give love, to accept love, and to learn from love.

FACT

According to Dr. Pim van Lommel, "When the heart stops beating, blood flow stops within a second. Then, 6.5 seconds later, EEG activity starts to change due to the shortage of oxygen. After 15 seconds there is a straight, flat line, and the electrical activity in the cerebral cortex has disappeared completely. The respiratory center shuts down as well as the pupil response and swallowing reflex."

The Life Review

Another common element of an NDE is called a life review. People report experiencing a review of their complete lives, often with lightning speed and clarity. Some people report a greater understanding of how their actions have affected others after undergoing a life review.

The Light Being

People report coming into contact with a being of light, who accompanies them during their life review. This being, which can be communicated with telepathically, is described as loving and compassionate.

Encountering Deceased Loved Ones

A comforting part of some near-death experiences involves encountering deceased relatives, friends, and loved ones. People say that these entities seem to appear to help with the transition from the physical plane to the other side. Some people report the presence of other beings who are not recognized but seem to have an emotional family connection.

Telepathic Communication

A person who has experienced an NDE often describes communication that takes place without words being spoken. Questions seem to be asked and answered through mental connections. Another commonly reported experience is a question that goes unanswered, as if it's too soon to know the answer.

A Choice

Some people realize that a choice is to be made concerning the future—either to join some kind of afterlife or to return to their physical body. This choice is sometimes made by the individual, and at other times, it seems as if it's made for them.

Meeting Deceased Loved Ones

One of the most common elements of a near-death experience is the presence of deceased relatives and friends. People have also reported seeing figures that they don't recognize but feel a connection to. These meetings are often described as being surrounded by love, compassion, and understanding, even if the entities are not recognized.

It's not uncommon for someone else to recognize the unidentified figures once the NDE is over and the person describes it to others. Often, friends and relations can identify a relative who died without ever meeting the NDE participant. This happens often with younger children.

ESSENTIAL

According to Michael Sabom, MD, in *Light and Death*, "It used to be thought that the point of death was a single moment in time. But it is now thought that death is a process, not a single moment."

The loved ones encountered seem to be there to help with the transition of the spirit from the physical to the nonphysical realm. Many report a sense of being home. The environment sometimes appears to be a past residence. The powerful awareness of these connections is a common trait of a near-death experience.

Nonfamily Encounters

Those who have had a near-death experience sometimes report encountering religious figures, angels, or guides. They may feel as if they have known this entity for a lifetime or even more than one lifetime.

Family pets have also been observed in these surroundings. The feeling of being reunited with a well-loved and missed pet brings great joy to the owners.

People say that contact with deceased friends, work associates, and distant relatives can have a tremendous positive effect on them, even if they were never previously close. These people often provide insight into ongoing events or reassurance that a reunion with loved ones will happen at some time in the future.

The Life Review

The life review is one of the most interesting parts of a near-death experience. Of course, it's different for each individual, but the experience shares common themes among many who have had an NDE.

A panoramic review of an entire life seems like an overwhelming concept, but people who have gone through an NDE say that it can be a learning experience, and many people describe feeling surrounded by support and unconditional love.

The experience of a life review has been described as watching an intricately detailed movie in an instant. People say that they seemed able to relive every thought and every encounter they ever had. They also felt as if they experienced the reactions and emotions they caused in every person they ever came into contact with. This complete empathy makes people realize how influential their interactions have been to others.

People also report a sense of judgment, not by others, but by themselves. Dannion Brinkley, a participant of multiple NDEs, says in his bestselling book, *Saved By the Light*, "you are the toughest judge you will ever have." The review seems to give individuals the opportunity to reprioritize their lives in the future. After such a profound experience, many people say they have lost their fear of death and have become more compassionate, caring individuals.

ALERT

Not all reported NDEs have the traits of peace, love, and understanding. Some people report coming into contact with a dark void, lacking any compassion or light. They feel as if they're surrounded with negative energies that are filled with anger and arrogance and lacking the concept of love.

Some people say that they were given the choice to stay and continue their existence or pass to the other side, while others report being told "it's not your time," followed by a reconciliation with their physical bodies. People who have reported having the choice often say that they were torn between choosing this peaceful loving state or returning to the physical realm in order to care for their children or other loved ones who may need them. For those whose time has not come, there seems to be unfinished business, things to be learned and experienced, for either themselves or others they might interact with at a future time.

Scientific Studies

There are hundreds of published research papers and scientific studies on the phenomena of near-death experiences, and many are being conducted today throughout the world. As more studies are done, the field of NDE investigations is growing and the mainstream scientific and medical communities are taking notice.

A Children's Study

P. M. H. Atwater is one of the original researchers in the field of near-death studies. In her research, she studied over 270 children who have had NDEs. Her findings revealed the following:

- 76 percent reported a comforting "initial" experience. Such experiences involved up to three elements: things like a "loving nothingness," a friendly voice, a visitation by a loving being, an out-of-body experience, and/or the peacefulness of either a safe light or safe dark place.
- 19 percent reported a pleasurable or heaven-like experience.
- 3 percent reported a distressing or hell-like experience.
- 2 percent had a "transcendent" experience in which they felt they acquired special knowledge.

The most commonly reported type of childhood NDE is the "initial" experience.

In an episode of meningitis, a six-year-old reported being out of her body with a sense of being completely free of pain and totally surrounded by love. She reported feeling like a soul—neither boy nor girl, neither grownup nor child. She felt a sense of absolute peace and completeness. When she looked down, she saw a girl lying in bed and empathized with her pain. On reflection, she realized she must be that girl, and with that thought, she was back in her body.

Children offer a unique look into NDEs as they offer a more "uncluttered" view of the event. They have not been exposed to various theories, beliefs, or life situations as an adult.

The Dutch NDE Study

Dr. Pim van Lommel, a cardiologist at Rijnstate Hospital in the Netherlands, studied near-death experiences of cardiac patients for almost two decades after noticing similar experiences of patients who survived cardiac arrest.

Dr. van Lommel and colleagues began a study in 1988, which consisted of 344 survivors of cardiac arrest. This study was created to observe and record the patient's experiences under controlled conditions at ten different hospitals. Similar studies were carried out in Britain and the United States with more than 500 total participants. In 2001 this major study was published in the medical periodical *The Lancet*.

The study found that some patients experienced a form of increased consciousness after cardiac arrest, which should not be possible as breathing and circulation of the blood to the brain had stopped. The patients recalled out-of-body experiences, meeting deceased relatives, and seeing their entire life played out in front of them.

According to Dr. van Lommel, "Several theories have been proposed to explain NDE. However, in our prospective study we did not show that psychological, physiological or pharmacological factors caused these experiences after cardiac arrest."

Seattle Children's Hospital Study

Dr. Melvin Morse, a pediatrician at Seattle Children's Hospital, has been researching near-death experiences in children for over twenty-five years. His work in critical-care medicine at the hospital was the driving force in his decision to study NDEs in the pediatric setting. In his work, he encountered children who told him stories about experiences they had while under his care, such as climbing a staircase to heaven, after being resuscitated. In one of the very first studies of NDEs in children, Dr. Morse states, "We studied 26 critically ill children compared to 131 who were seriously ill, and found that 23 of them reported being conscious while dying, and having some sort of conscious experience. Typically that involved the perception of a loving light, a 'light that had good things in it.'"

Case Studies

Tens of thousands of people have reported experiencing NDEs. Here are some of their stories.

>> CASE: A BOATING ACCIDENT

While out fishing one day my boat started to take on water so I called for help, but just before they arrived a wave capsized my craft and I went into the water. I tried to swim to the rescue boat but I started to swallow a lot of water. The next thing I knew I was in the ER looking at the doctors as they were working on me. All of a sudden I felt like I was going to faint, and then I was out cold. The next thing I knew I seemed to be up near the ceiling of an operating room looking down at myself. There was a lot of commotion going on and I heard a nurse say "we lost him." The doctor said, "we only have a short time." They all were trying to revive me. I was then in this dark tunnel. The tunnel seemed to be made of rings, and I felt like I was being pulled through it. I saw a bright light and I remember seeing my father and a few other people whom I knew. There were others there too. Some I did not recognize, but I felt like they were not strangers but people who I felt comfortable with.

I was told I had to return to finish my learning. I was surrounded by overwhelming joy and comfort until I felt snapped back into my physical body. The doctor said "welcome home." I was too weak to tell him that I had felt at home on the other side.

›› CASE: THE TRUCK ACCIDENT

I was on my way to work on a farm early one morning with a friend of mine. I was driving my truck about 75 mph because we were late. I started to turn the radio on and when I looked up I was leaving the road. I tried to quickly turn the steering wheel the other way but it just rolled the truck over and down an embankment.

I was thrown from the truck into a ditch. I broke a bunch of bones, cut myself up, and banged my head bad. I was out cold. My friend called for help and I was put into an ambulance.

I felt out of my body at this point. I could see the EMTs working on me, but I felt no pain. It was weird—it was like watching someone else being worked on. Then I saw a light and started to go toward it, I noticed all my relatives there, smiling at me. My uncle came up to me and said I had to go back. "It's not your time," he said.

Before I knew it, I was in the ambulance feeling like I had been hit by a house. I will always remember the loving feeling that was all around me when I was in that light. It's difficult to explain.

›› CASE: POSTOPERATIVE COMPLICATIONS

I was in a dark void with nothing around me, and then I noticed a small white light that began to grow as I moved quickly toward it. The light seemed to be alive. It had an unbelievable feeling of love to it and I just smiled as it surrounded me.

My whole life was then shown to me. I saw everything I had ever done, good and bad. I wish I hadn't done some things in my past but I had a feeling that it was all right.

Everything happened so fast. I asked questions and knew the answers at almost the same time I asked them. I was not talking like we do but was communicating through emotion and my mind. There was an all-knowing understanding. I realized that the only thing in life is love. I have changed my life to be more kind toward others. There is definitely a God. Maybe not with a robe and beard, but love is the way to recognize him.

›› CASE: MY DROWNING

I was at the beach one afternoon and got caught in an undertow. I tried very hard to swim, but I slipped under the surface. I started to inhale water and realized I was drowning. I blanked out and began to see shadows of people I didn't know. I did not recognize them but I seemed to know they were family. How I knew this I don't know. I just knew. I began to hear this beautiful music and was moving through a tunnel toward a being of light. I knew it was God because it was surrounded with pure love. Just as I was getting close to this being I shot back into my body and I awoke lying on my side on a rescue boat. I now have no fear of dying, I know what's on the other side and it's great!

CHAPTER 7

Can Quantum Physics Offer Proof of the Afterlife?

While classic physics has been the accepted science for the explanations of how large objects interact with one another, quantum physics looks at how things react from the smallest subatomic levels. The astounding discoveries of what makes up physical matter has revealed the possibility that the physical world is not what it seems to be. Quantum physics ponders the possibility of an afterlife from a purely scientific point of view, and this starts to bring spirituality and science closer together.

Quantum Physics

What most believe to be commonsense reality is based on an implied belief that the things that are experienced in the world are not only real, but that they exist objectively and independently of ourselves. You assume that what you're able to see, hear, taste, smell, or touch actually exists as an independent reality.

Now consider the subatomic world of quantum physics. This world of the tiny subatomic stuff, which makes up the big stuff like cars, buildings, and galaxies, has its own set of rules that are drastically different from the large-object world you experience in your daily life. Not only does this quantum world play by a different rulebook, but you, as an observer, have much to do with the manifestation of the reality you are observing.

The underlying subatomic fabric does not behave in a way that our minds can easily understand. For instance, a subatomic object appears to have properties of both a particle with mass and a wave (like sound waves) with energy. The way an individual will see a subatomic object, as particle or wave, depends on how the individual constructs the experiment. But when you're not observing it, any subatomic object exists in a stable and undefined state called "a stationary probability wave." Fixed points of reality do not really exist in the pre-observational subatomic world. When an observation is made, the object "actualizes" by collapsing into one of the many forms dictated by its probability wave, and the particle appears to come into being in that instant. So in reality nothing exists until you look at it.

ESSENTIAL

Don't forget that the human body is also made of this small stuff. However, an electron really has no path, no exact location, and no exact momentum. Our observation freezes one of those potentialities in time, causing it to become real. Where the object appears next can't be known with certainty; it can only be expressed as a probability.

If we could observe an electron's (a subatomic particle) movements through time, what we would see is a discrete energy bundle that appears to jump in an irregular series of seemingly random leaps, collapsing from wave to matter and just as quickly disappearing again into another wave-cloud of probability. These particles would seem to flash in and out of existence before our eyes with such rapidity that they might appear like a cloud.

"Spooky Action at a Distance"

Another aspect of quantum physics is the principle of entanglement. To understand entanglement, imagine a pair of parallel subatomic particles generated in a laboratory; one of the pair might have a subatomic property called "spin up," and the other a property called "spin down." These two particles can be described as entangled, since neither particle can be fully described without referring to the other. What's interesting about entangled particles is that even though they are separated and do not make physical contact with each other, they somehow seem to know enough to maintain the opposite spin from the other. If you intervene and cause the subatomic particle that had a spin-up property to reverse and spin down, what we find is that its entangled particle reverses itself simultaneously, switching from spin down to spin up. Albert Einstein called this phenomenon "spooky action at a distance." What makes it even more "spooky" is that this information exchange theoretically occurs more rapidly than the speed of light, and the implications of that are still being realized.

With the discovery that consciousness plays a fundamental part in shaping reality, we have moved away from the mechanical systems of classical physics and now have a physics that includes the human component as an integral part of the process. Currently, quantum biologists are trying to determine if the properties described by Einstein as "action at a distance" (as well as entanglement) play a role in the functioning of our human mind, and consciousness itself. These possibilities could open up the reality of who you really are and how you might create your own existence, now and in the afterlife.

Substances That Make Up a Physical Being

Even as the medical community tries to unravel the many mysteries of the human body (made up of atoms and subatomic particles), doctors and spiritualists have acknowledged the existence of an "energy field" around the human body. This energy field, or aura, extends externally and internally, interacting with everything around us. It is comprised of energy bodies that exist in succession and coexist in the same space.

It is also known through quantum physics that subatomic particles can "phase in and out" of existence, depending on the moment of observation. It also explains that we are both particles (matter) and energy waves. As stated in the first law of thermodynamics: energy cannot be created or destroyed, but only changed from one form to another. Therefore, a part of us must continue to exist after physical death, and perhaps this is a form we take in the afterlife.

FACT

In the late twentieth century, scientists made the discovery that organs and tissues produce particular magnetic pulsations or biomagnetic fields, which can be measured using a SQUID magnetometer (possibly the most sensitive measurement device known to humans), as proof of our existence beyond just the physical visible form.

It is believed that the human energy field is an instrument of wellness. Once disregarded by the medical community, alternate forms of healing such as Reiki and therapeutic touch, a technique to stimulate energy fields, has become a popular and accepted form of treatment, and has shown a reduction in postoperative recovery time.

Different Models of the Human Energy Field

One of the first references to the human energy field comes from the ancient Vedic traditions of India, which believe that human beings exist on five *koshas* (layers/levels). The physical body is the outermost layer, followed by the energy body, which is the life force supporting the five senses. The third *kosha* is the mental body, where emotions and thoughts are processed. The next, wisdom body, is a provider of intuition, helping humans reflect upon and evaluate the deeper meaning of life. Human consciousness is subtly manifested in the bliss body, which provides transcendental experiences.

Influential spiritual writer Alice Bailey (1880–1949) described human energy fields in relation to *chakras* and *nadis*. The literal translation of the

Sanskrit word *chakra* is "spinning wheel." *Chakras* refer to energy centers, in the shape of rotating vortices, which serve as focal points for transmission and reception of energies. The human body is said to be composed of seven major *chakras* and a number of minor *chakras*. Every *chakra* spins at different rates and absorbs those energies from the universal energy field that is harmonically related to its individual frequency. *Nadis* are channels or conduits that make up the subtle body. Vital force, or *prana*, flows through these *nadis*. According to Bailey, there are distinct human and spiritual energies that affect a person's life. The soul is said to express itself through four human mechanisms: the dense physical body, etheric energy body, emotional (astral) body, and mental body.

ESSENTIAL

"All matter originates and exists only by virtue of a force. . . . We must assume behind this force the existence of a conscious and intelligent Mind. This Mind is the matrix of all matter."—Max Planck, Nobel Prize–winning father of quantum theory

World-renowned healer and bestselling author of *Hands of Light: A Guide to Healing Through the Human Energy Field*, Barbara Brennan has described a seven-layer model of the human energy field, which is widely accepted by healers around the world.

Seven-Layer Model of the Human Energy Field

The seven-layer model is based on the three planes of existence: physical, astral, and spiritual. The physical plane consists of the physical body, thoughts, and emotions. On a higher plane of consciousness is the astral plane, which is composed of feelings and thoughts of humanity. Many human interactions take place on this plane, influencing thought processes. The spiritual plane deals with higher and more important visions, perceptions, and universal oneness. It is not as easily accessible as the other two planes. The seven layers of the human energy field are clearly defined and have specific functions.

Etheric/Vital Energy Body

Existing on the physical plane, this body is said to exist up to two inches from the human body. It is a provider of health, life, and vitality, maintaining the body's yin/yang balance. Its consciousness is expressed in terms of physical sensations such as pleasure or pain.

Emotional Energy Body

Extending 1–3 inches from the physical body, this body's consciousness is expressed in terms of personal emotions such as love, fear, and hatred. It is the field through which the emotional energy flows.

Mental Energy Body

This is a structured body extending 3–8 inches from the physical body. Its consciousness is expressed in terms of thinking that include words, thoughts, and images.

Astral Energy Body

This is an amorphous body, extending 6–12 inches from the physical body.

Existing on the astral/psychic etheric plane, it is a provider of imagination, desires, and psychic abilities. Dreams, hallucinations, fantasies, and visions are all astral experiences.

Etheric Template Body

Existing on the spiritual plane, it extends about 1½–2 feet from the physical body. It is expressed in terms of higher will—those who fail to get things done are believed to have a weak etheric template body.

Celestial Energy Body

Existing on the spiritual plane, it extends 2–2½ feet from the physical body. Associated with feelings of unconditional love and joy, spiritual ecstasy can be experienced through this layer.

Ketheric Template Body

Extending about 2½–3½ feet from the physical body, this body is associated with knowledge of higher concepts and enables creative thoughts. Its consciousness can also be expressed in terms of a higher spiritual inspiration.

Quantum Physics and Biology

Quantum physics and biology are two fields of scientific study that have often been viewed as unrelated branches of knowledge. Quantum physics describes the world of microscopic phenomena, a world of inanimate electrons, photons, and atoms. It assumes a worldview in which classical rules of physics do not apply, a world where quantum entanglements, coherences, tunnels, and quantum probabilities hold sway for subatomic particles and energy waves. Basically, it's the small stuff—the really small stuff—that makes up everything.

On the other hand, biology is a natural science that concerns itself with the study of life and living organisms. In the past century, biology and the life sciences have made remarkable strides in understanding the makeup of various cell processes, and this came about primarily through the study of molecular cellular structures. However, there are many biological processes that are not yet completely understood. Could quantum mechanisms be responsible for some of the most inexplicable processes of life?

Quantum Theory and Photosynthesis

In 1944, Austrian physicist Erwin Schrödinger suggested the need for the quantum theoretical study of genetics when he wrote his book *What Is Life?* Since then, interdisciplinary biologists and physicists have taken up that challenge, and the field of "quantum biology" has evolved. Today it has a role to play in understanding procedures as diverse as plant photosynthesis, the sense of smell, and even the consciousness of the human brain.

Consider the process of photosynthesis, the transfer of light energy to chemical energy, in which one molecule of the pigment chlorophyll absorbs one photon of light, and in the process releases one high-energy electron. This electron is then directed along a series of molecular transports until it reaches reaction-center proteins in the cell that store its energy in another chemically energetic molecule. The cell can then use this energy to power its internal processes. What is notable about this process is that the amount of energy lost during these transport mechanisms is amazingly small: the process of photosynthesis is 95 percent efficient.

One aspect of quantum mechanics is the idea of coherence: that every given particle has a probability of being in many different locations and in a sense occupies all those places at once. Physicists typically refer to this aspect of a particle as the particle's wave function. When an observer makes a measurement on the system, that wave function will "collapse" to a single point, making the particle observable at that moment.

Using high-speed lasers, a team of quantum biologists, led by Gregory S. Engel at UC Berkeley, devised a way to follow the movement of the light energy during photosynthesis so that they could detect quantum-level processes. What you might expect to find, based on the classical approach of physics, was that the energy of the electron would simply select one path for transport. Instead, what Engel's team discovered was that the electron first appeared to travel along every possible path simultaneously. You can think of these paths as a group of all the quantum possibilities that the transported electron might take. Once the shortest and most efficient path in the transport process is determined, the probability wave for that electron collapses and the most efficient transport path is selected. Engel explains in the journal *Nature*, "This wavelike characteristic of the energy transfer within the photosynthetic complex can explain its extreme efficiency." In other words, the quantum system "cheats" by looking at all the possibilities in advance before committing itself to one path.

Consciousness and "Quantum Tunneling"

Today, there seems to be no biological process to which quantum theory might not apply. Quantum biologists may even discover that our minds are quantum in nature, and consciousness itself may be a manifestation of a quantum leap. The phenomenon of "quantum tunneling," wherein an electron disappears in one location and suddenly reappears somewhere else without appearing to travel through any intermediate point, is another example of the use of quantum mechanics to explain a biological process. In this case, our sense of smell may ultimately be based on this tunneling aspect of quantum mechanics. The study of quantum biology is still in its infancy, but it holds promise for explaining much biological phenomena.

Wave-Particle Duality

The wave-particle duality, in modern science, refers to the concept that all matter, including light, exhibits both wave-like and particle-like properties. This apparent paradox owes its origin to the centuries-old debate among scientists over the nature of light.

Earlier, light was considered to be a wave, and not matter, for the very obvious reason that it could neither be touched nor felt like any other matter. It was believed to be much like a sound wave, which travels at different speeds in different settings. This theory successfully explained the phenomenon of refraction of light through a lens, prism, or a brilliant diamond. René Descartes supported this wave theory of light, as did Christiaan Huygens, who proposed light to be a wave spreading in a straight line. The wave theory of Huygens satisfactorily explained the known phenomenon of light, such as reflection, refraction, and diffraction.

Newton's Theory

However, Isaac Newton supported the corpuscular theory of light in his work "Hypothesis of Light" (1675), because waves were characterized by the tendency to bend around obstructions, but light, unlike waves, was observed to travel in a straight line. He proposed that the light consisted of small particles. Newton's theory remained unchallenged for over a century.

ALERT

"When science begins the study of non-physical phenomena, it will make more progress in one decade than in all the centuries of its experience."—British cosmologist, Dr. Fred Hoyle

Revisiting Huygens's Wave Theory

Experiments carried out by the scientists Thomas Young and Augustin-Jean Fresnel in 1803 showed that when light is sent through a grid, a characteristic interference pattern is observed, very similar to the pattern resulting from the interference of water waves. The double-slit experiment demonstrates the inseparability of the wave and particle natures of light and how just observing the experiment may alter the outcome.

Further, light was also observed to exhibit the phenomenon of polarization, which could not be possible if it consisted of particles. The discovery by James Clerk Maxwell in the late 1800s of the existence of self-producing electromagnetic waves traveling through space at a constant speed equal to the speed of light led him to conclude that light is a form of electromagnetic wave. He supported his discovery by a full mathematical description, known as "Maxwell's equations," which were experimentally verified by Heinrich Hertz in 1887. As a result, the wave theory of Huygens again became widely accepted.

By the late nineteenth century, however, certain phenomena were observed that could not be explained by the wave theory, as detailed in the following sections.

Black Body Radiation

It had been known for a long time that metal (a thermal object) when heated glows red and upon further heating glows white. The classical theory predicted the spectrum of such electromagnetic radiation to be a continuous one. However, the spectrum was actually found to be comprised of discrete lines.

To explain this phenomena, Max Planck hypothesized that the black bodies, theoretical objects that absorb 100 percent of light and emit no reflection (thus the "black" appearance), emit electromagnetic radiation only as discrete bundles or packets of energy. These packets were given the name *quanta*, the particle of light was called *photon*, and the theory came to be known as "quantum theory."

Photoelectric Effect

The incidence of high-frequency (ultraviolet) light rays on metals was found to cause an electric current in the circuit. As it had already been discovered that the electric current was comprised of moving electrons, it was readily concluded that such high-frequency light knocked the electrons out of the metal, causing current to flow. It was also observed that while a dim blue light was enough to cause a current in a certain metal, even the strongest, brightest red light caused no current at all.

Einstein explained this phenomena by adopting Planck's black body model and postulating that the electrons can receive energy from the electromagnetic radiations falling upon it only in discrete quantities (that were called *photons*) before it can be knocked off. Hence, only photons of a frequency higher than the threshold value could knock an electron free.

ESSENTIAL

The earlier mentioned developments led to the concept of wave-particle duality in which the light was characterized as having both properties—that is, the properties of wave as well as of particle (photon).

The de Broglie Hypothesis

Subsequently in 1924, Louis Victor de Broglie put forward the de Broglie hypothesis, extending the concept of wave-particle duality to all matter, not just to the light. De Broglie's hypothesis was later experimentally confirmed for electrons. Since then, the experiments conducted to verify the quantum mechanical wave-like properties of other known atomic particles such as neutrons and protons as well as certain atoms and molecules have successfully demonstrated the truth of the "wave-particle duality" hypothesis.

The Heisenberg Uncertainty Principle

In 1927, while working at the Niels Bohr Institute for Theoretical Physics at the University of Copenhagen, German physicist Werner Heisenberg published a groundbreaking theory of quantum mechanics that provided a new way of thinking about atomic interactions, and a new way of looking at the world.

His theories resulted in a major shift in how scientists think about the nature of reality itself. The Heisenberg uncertainty principle tells us that we cannot exactly determine both the position and momentum of a subatomic particle at the same time. The reason for this is simply watching requires an energy intermediary, such as a photon of light, to interact with what we are observing, and in the subatomic world that interaction can change the makeup of the observed particle. According to Heisenberg, "the path comes into existence only when we observe it." And this is not predictable using the classical mechanics of physics.

The Classical Understanding

In the common day-to-day world, all large objects appear to be fixed things that exist even if no one is there to observe them. It's commonly understood that you can measure objects, whether they are at rest or in motion, and you can make predictions as to exactly where they will be located based on that information. Radar and sonar work like this. That's how ships and airplanes can be tracked. In baseball you can measure a ball's mass, and if the ball is thrown through the air, you can determine its position and speed. If you wanted to you could apply the formulas of classical mechanics to accurately predict the exact spot where the ball will land. The foundation of this classical physics was first published by Isaac Newton in *The Principia*, three books that are regarded as some of the most important works in the history of science. As long as we limited our observations to large objects, Newtonian physics won.

Have you thought about how you can see a ball in a mechanical sense? Assume it is a night game, and that the source of illumination is light rays from the lights above the field. These light rays (also known as *photons*), are constantly hitting that ball. Some of these photons will bounce off the ball and reflect into your eyes, and the ball appears to move in an uninterrupted and expected direction. The classical world is predictable and behaves as expected, until the outfielder drops the ball . . . but that's another story.

ESSENTIAL

The way large objects interact, as in Newton's classical physics, and the way subatomic particles exists, as in quantum physics, differs to the point that a search has been undertaken for almost a century to try to find a true Unified Theory.

Applying Heisenberg's Uncertainty Principle

Now, what would happen in the subatomic world based on Heisenberg's uncertainty principle? Let's imagine that you are seated in the stands, but instead of a ball we substitute an electron in its place. Well, some of the photons from the light would hit the electron and bounce off it. If these reflected photons entered your eyes, you would then "see" exactly where the electron was located at that instant. However, the photon of light, which is also a subatomic particle, directly affects the properties of the electron and can give it energy. This is because the photon is almost as large as the electron. So, the electron changes momentum when it interacts with the photon, and as a result, it could theoretically reappear anywhere in the field, and this is the uncertainty to which Heisenberg's principle refers. If you really could sit in the stands and observe this, the electron would appear to sparkle in and out of existence, appearing to jump at times between locations. You could only make predictions on where the electron will appear next based on quantum probability and statistics.

In the Heisenberg model, the underlying subatomic fabric of the world behaves in a way that cannot easily be understood. Fixed points of reality do not seem to pre-exist in the subatomic world, only quantum probabilities with inherent uncertainties and inaccuracy. And it is only when you make an observation that these probabilities fall apart into an observed reality.

What these theories propose is that the things that make up a human being, matter and energy, can be interchangeable on a subatomic level. The afterlife could be the reconstructed form of an individual after the physical matter of the body dies.

The Search for the God Particle at the Large Hadron Collider

The Large Hadron Collider (LHC), built near Geneva, Switzerland, is the the world's largest and most powerful particle collider. The circular tunnel is 27 kilometers long (16.8 miles) and is about 600 feet under the ground. This massive machine has been designed to collide opposing proton beams at superhigh energy of 7 TeV. That's 7 trillion electron-volts!

The proton beams were circulated in the collider for the first time in September 2008. However, after shutting down to repair a flaw, it was reopened again in November 2009, and proton beams were successfully circulated through the tunnel once again. In early 2010, the beams were circulated at an energy level of 3.5 TeV, a world record, which is just half of the collider's designed capability, and the collision was recorded in March of that year.

The "God particle," or Higgs boson, and the Large Hadron Collider have been a subject of both discussion and debate in recent times. Not only is the Large Hadron Collider machine and experiment getting the scientific community excited, it is also inspiring awe—and in some cases, fear—among the world's populations.

Higgs boson, better known as the "God particle," is a theoretical subatomic particle that is, according to some, the one missing piece of our present understanding of the laws of nature, known as "the standard model of physics." The particle is thought to be the creator of mass, that is, the creator of elementary particles. This particle is popularly referred to as the "God particle" because the origin of mass in the universe, according to the standard model, was mediated by it. Higgs boson was proposed by British physicist Peter Higgs to explain why some particles have mass, while others, such as photons, do not.

This is especially significant, as at the time of the big bang there was no mass, but only energy. Higgs's theory explains, by means of Higgs bosons and their field, how some particles escaped the Higgs field without mass, while others accumulated mass. The "God particle" is in a way the creator of matter as we know it today and hence holds the key to a number of the universe's mysteries.

To find a Higgs boson, a high-energy environment similar to that after the big bang has to be imitated, which is exactly what the LHC aims to do. The LHC experiment can prove or disprove the existence of this elusive particle, which will be revolutionary for the field of physics.

The LHC particle collision experiments at such high energies that it is expected to shed light on the mysteries of the early and the current universe. Answers to many of the baffling physical questions and issues are expected, and some of the things scientists are looking for are:

- Proof of existence of Higgs boson and validation of the standard model and Higgs mechanism, which explains the origin of mass
- More information about the nature of the dark matter and energy, antiparticles, and other subatomic particles
- Evidence of existence of extra dimensions predicted by string theory

Controversies Surrounding the God Particle Experiment

Even before the Large Hadron Collider was fired, a number of speculations and controversies surrounded the experiment. Most of these were on account of the fact that the high-energy environment being created is getting as close as possible to simulating the birth of the universe. The fear of many is that it may just end up spelling doom for the world.

One of the biggest fears expressed by the critics of the experiment was that smashing protons at 99.9 percent of the speed of light could create small black holes, which can swell to a proportion that they might just swallow up the earth. Physicists, however, claim that no such danger is posed by the experiment, as creation of such black holes is unlikely and even if they were to be formed, they would be too unstable and disintegrate.

There continues to be a host of other similar concerns as the world being created in the LHC is an unexplored arena, one that has never been experienced or seen.

CHAPTER 8

Unraveling String Theory

The question of who we are and where we come from has been asked by every generation for thousands of years. Though the question of our existence was once based on a system of cultural and religious beliefs, now modern-day science is examining the real possibilities of our existence. String theory could explain everything about what man is and combine all modern scientific theories. The principles that make up the universe and the interaction of subatomic particles might indeed prove the existence of an afterlife.

Uniting the Building Blocks of Nature

In the last few decades, our understanding of nature has expanded tremendously. Physicists have relentlessly probed the two extremes: things that are very big, like stars, black holes, galaxies, and even the whole universe; and things that are very small, like molecules, atoms, electrons, and quarks. But so far, even the greatest scientific minds have been unable to reconcile these two extremes. Some of the laws that hold true in one extreme simply don't work in the other extreme. Most physicists believe that this is because an important piece of the jigsaw is still missing. This piece could be string theory, and it can completely transform the way you look at nature.

The Conventional View of Nature

Until recently, it was believed that everything in nature is made of fundamental particles, known as *fermions* and *bosons*. Fermions (like electrons and quarks) were thought to be the building blocks of matter, while bosons (like photons that make up light) were thought to be the building blocks of all forces. But this model has proved inadequate so far in explaining how gravity, one of the most familiar of the fundamental forces, works at a microscopic level.

What Nature Is Really Made Of

String theory is a revolutionary alternative view to this model of nature. According to string theory, the fundamental building blocks of nature are tiny strings (much smaller than observable subatomic particles). These strings manifest as different particles only because of their different vibrations. It means that instead of having multiple fundamental particles, the universe is only built of a single object: strings. All other particles are built using these strings. When you see these strings oscillating in a particular way, you think of them as a particular particle, and when it is some other kind of oscillation, you see them as some other particle.

Another important idea proposed by string theory is that the same strings can manifest both as forces and matter. Forces, such as gravitation and magnetic attraction, are seen as nothing but an interaction of strings. These forces also operate at the subatomic level. They help hold an atom together by creating a strong attraction between subatomic particles. If this force did not exist, the nucleus of the atom would break down and the world as you know it would cease to exist.

QUESTION

How has the study of nature changed?
Within nature there are many different physical laws, some having been discovered centuries ago. These physical laws are still being used today to examine the observable universe. In recent years these physical laws had to be questioned when science began to look at the interaction of subatomic particles.

Understanding Life and Death in a Universe Made of Strings

If string theory is true, your body, your spirit, the air around you, the ground your feet stands on—everything you can see and feel—is made of the same fundamental building blocks. What differentiates you from others is how the strings that you are made of are vibrating.

As these strings are indestructible, death has to be interpreted as a change in the vibration of strings. Some of the strings that a person is made of remain in the dead body and form a different type of matter as the body decomposes. However, some other strings, the ones that make up the force of life, escape from the body and continue to vibrate in the same manner. These strings are referred to as the soul.

Existing in the Afterlife

As the strings that make up the soul continue to exist after death, you can understand why some people receive communication from their dead relatives, especially when they are bothered by some unfinished matter. And as these strings can execute physical forces, they can move objects or occasionally even become visible as apparitions. But as they are not accompanied by the strings that make up the body, you cannot see them in the same way as you see a living person.

The conventional laws of physics are inadequate to explain how strings behave. This could be the reason why so many scientists feel that the afterlife cannot be proven through scientific investigation. Once scientists are able to construct reliable experiments to test string theory, concrete evidence of the afterlife is also likely to emerge. In fact, it could even help develop better means of communicating with dead people. Phenomena that is currently categorized as paranormal could come into the mainstream with new tools and techniques.

There is no doubt that the current understanding of nature is extremely limited. As string theory develops further, it will continue to force you to reconsider some of your most strongly held beliefs.

M-Theory and the Existence of Multiple Dimensions

String theory is a revolutionary new theory in quantum physics. String theory evolved into the M-theory and the existence of multiple dimensions as it gained wider acceptance and momentum among physicists.

M-theory is known as the "theory of everything." It combines all string theories together. The M-theory requires mathematical tools that have not yet been totally accepted in order for it to be fully understood.

Edward Witten, professor of physics at Princeton University, proposed the M-theory in the 1990s. Witten has been described as, "the most brilliant physicist of his generation. One of the world's greatest living physicists, perhaps even Einstein's successor." (Brian Greene, physicist, Columbia University)

In 1995, he suggested the existence of M-theory and used it to explain a number of previously unexplained mysteries of string theory. He sparked a flurry of new research in string theory. Witten said, "All this suggests that string theory is on the right track; otherwise, why would it generate so many unexpected ideas?"

These new ideas run on the premise that there are eleven dimensions of time and space. M-theory suggests that there are many dimensions that are unseen. One of the theories is that the extra dimensions are so tiny that they exist inside atoms.

The Connection to String Theory

String theory was considered the possible answer to a unified theory of physics which Einstein had sought throughout his career. This theory began to branch off with new unexplained questions and needed to be tied together in order to gain the unity that was being sought. With new mathematical calculations the multiple string theories were combined into the unifying M-theory.

The universe is made up of four dimensions:

- Height
- Width
- Length
- Time

Everyone is familiar with height, width, and length. And time gives a total of four measurable dimensions. However, string theory supports the possibility of ten dimensions—the remaining six of which cannot be detected directly. When M-theory was coined, this increased to eleven dimensions.

String theory suggests that electrons and quarks (unseen tiny energy balls) within an atom are moving lines. These lines (the strings) possess only one dimension of length, no height or width.

Every atom is comprised of:

- Electrons
- Protons (quarks)
- Neutrons (quarks)
- Strings (in theory only)

String theory poses that these strings can vibrate, thus giving the electrons and quarks their energy, or charge.

So, according to string theory, of what is the world made? Ordinary matter is made of atoms, which are in turn made of just three basic components: electrons whirling around a nucleus composed of neutrons and protons.

The electron is a fundamental particle, but neutrons and protons are made of smaller particles, known as *quarks*. Quarks, as far as we know, exist, but are so minute that they are not visible even under an atomic microscope.

All matter is comprised of elements from largest to smallest components:

1. All matter
2. Molecular level
3. Atomic level—protons
4. Subatomic level—electrons and neutrons (quarks)
5. Strings (in theory only)

Brian Greene, professor of physics and mathematics at Columbia University, is perhaps the best-known proponent of string theory. He supports the idea that minuscule strands of energy vibrating in eleven dimensions create every particle and force in the universe. He has said, "All we are is a bag of particles acting out the laws of physics. That to me is pretty clear."

ESSENTIAL

With the different variations surrounding string theory, it is an accomplishment to have a consensus generally agreed upon in the all-inclusive M-theory. This is the beginning of more in-depth research into the makeup of this universe and possibly other dimensions as well.

New Possibilities

Could there be other dimensions to time? Could other frequencies exist that we cannot hear? Do other dimensions, also unseen, exist? Some physicists think so, but this leads to deeper questions such as the possibility of the existence of more than one universe.

British physicist and author Stephen Hawking originally believed that M-theory may be the "ultimate" theory, but later suggested that the search for understanding of mathematics and physics will never be complete. He said in his book *Stephen Hawking's Universe: The Cosmos Explained*, "My goal is simple. It is a complete understanding of the universe, why it is as it is and why it exists at all."

It has been claimed that M-theory eliminates the need for God. Actually, it may just provide a possible explanation of the "nature" of God. M-theory hypothesizes that God could be a conscious, intelligent brain permeating the universe.

Some people believe that M-theory will prove or disprove the existence of God. However, most proponents of M-theory insist that it still comes down to personal belief.

M-theory proposed an eleventh dimension. According to the theory, our universe exists on a floating membrane, along with infinite parallel universes. By introducing the eleventh dimension, M-theory successfully united the "competing" theories of string theory. M-theory also provided another crucial aspect of the puzzle in that it explained how the big bang might have occurred, with two universes colliding.

ALERT

Because string theory predicts phenomena we cannot presently measure, such as tiny strings of energy, extra dimensions, and multiple universes, some scientists reject it outright. Others find the mathematical puzzle of the M-theory proof in itself that it must be correct and expect M-theory and the existence of multiple universes and strings to eventually be validated.

Space and Time Here and in the Afterlife

There are two leading theories in physics that help explain most of the phenomena that is observed around humanity. The first is Einstein's theory of general relativity, which explains how gravity works, why planets go around the stars, why black holes and galaxies exist, and a lot of other astronomical phenomena. The second is quantum mechanics, which very accurately explains how particles like electrons and protons behave at subatomic levels, as well as the properties of light and other forms of radiation. However, one of the biggest unsolved problems in physics today is that these theories just don't reconcile. It simply cannot explain how relativity impacts particles at subatomic levels or how quantum mechanics interacts with gravity.

String theory is one of the candidates of a "theory of everything," which has been proposed as a solution to this problem. If proved true, it could be an overarching framework, consistent with both relativity and quantum physics. But its implications could go much beyond and it could even explain the existence of afterlife.

Key Aspects of String Theory

According to string theory, fundamental particles in nature, like photons, electrons, and quarks, are nothing but vibrations of extremely small strings. Just like a guitar string can create different musical notes when plucked, the tiny strings in string theory create different vibrations under different tensions, also known as *excitation modes*. Different kinds of vibrations represent different fundamental particles of nature.

An important difference from the guitar analogy is that in string theory, strings are not attached to anything and they float freely in space and time. An even more interesting characteristic of these strings is that they exist in ten dimensions. The first nine dimensions are in space and the tenth dimension is time. According to string theorists, six dimensions of space are unobservable, as they are either extremely small or they are "curled up" and cannot be detected with conventional experiments. Only the other three dimensions are big enough to be perceived as "real." However, it is the hidden dimensions that define most of the properties of the world.

How String Theory Is Related to the Afterlife

A direct consequence of string theory is that there is a huge number of multiple universes that coexist with this universe, and these universes have their own space and time. Although with the current scientific knowledge it is not possible to communicate between two universes, it is theoretically possible to do it. The idea of multiple universes can be used to explain the concept of afterlife and realms like heaven and hell. It is not only conceivable but also quite probable that these other worlds are universes that exist parallel to the world lived in today.

Physicists believe that other universes would have both similarities and differences when compared to the world of today in terms of space, time, and laws of physics. This is consistent with the description of realms like heaven and hell in almost all religions. Similar physical laws apply in these places as the viewable universe but they have some unique characteristics of their own as well. For example, they can have different physical laws governing time, in which an eternal afterlife existence is possible.

Another possibility is that the afterlife exists in the six dimensions that are hidden. This can explain how dead people are sometimes able to communicate with this side even though they cannot be seen. They can interact with our three dimensions of space but they cannot exist in them the way we do. The six dimensions of afterlife can be right in front of everyone, but are still unobservable. If this is true, psychic ability can be understood as a greater awareness of these dimensions, which are hidden to most people. In the same way that dead people can send messages to this dimension, mediums are able to pick up messages from their dimensions.

ESSENTIAL

Science and religion have at times been at opposite ends when the concept of the afterlife has been evaluated. With modern-day scientific technology it is possible to theorize that other dimensions exist. With all the major religions believing in some type of continuation of the consciences, or soul, after the death of the body, science and religion are beginning to share the same concepts.

The power of this theory is in its beauty and how easily it can explain some of the most complex phenomena, including an afterlife. The history of science shows us that the most important theories are usually the most elegant, but they seem extremely simple once they are understood. String theory also falls into this category.

How String Theory Can Explain Afterlife

If the true nature of matter is as predicted by string theory, you would be forced to rethink concepts like life, death, and the afterlife. You can no longer think about death as an irreversible event that sees the complete destruction of a living being. Death would have to be seen as just a change of state of the strings that a person is made of.

The idea that the same fundamental strings can form both matter and forces can be applied to the distinction between the spirit (force) and the body (matter) of a person. It is possible that at the time of death, strings that form matter stop vibrating or go into some other excitation mode, while those that form the spirit continue to vibrate in the same manner and float in the space-time continuum.

FACT

Classic physics deals with the interaction and makeup of large objects. Quantum physics and string theory deal with the same interaction and makeup but on the smallest subatomic level. With this research, the true makeup of matter is being discovered.

What gives you life is the vibrations of strings that make up matter, and it is perfectly possible that in another realm, a different type of vibration could create a different type of matter. This matter could then be combined with the spirit and would be able to feel sensations in the afterlife, like the pain of hell or the pleasures of heaven.

Another possibility is that after the strings that make up the force of life disappear from one dimension at the time of death, they enter one of the six dimensions predicted by string theory.

Another way in which string theory offers support to the existence of afterlife is that it shows how wrong we can be in our understanding of our world and the nature of matter. There are things that are simply beyond our current understanding. And there is no reason why you should reject them and consider them outrageous until you have complete knowledge of them.

Dark Energy: The Unseen Force

Dark energy is one of the most mysterious subjects of modern-day physics. It was first observed in 1998, and even though more than a decade has passed since then, physicists throughout the world are still clueless about what dark energy is and how it affects everyone. The discovery of the existence of dark energy has fueled speculation that it could be linked to paranormal phenomena. Many theories explaining this relationship have been proposed.

How Was Dark Energy Discovered?

For many years, physicists believed that the universe was expanding, but that it will eventually slow down because of the force of gravity between distant stars and galaxies. However, in 1998, observations made by the Hubble Space Telescope showed that the universe is in fact expanding at an accelerating pace. Not only was this completely unexpected, but scientists were unable to explain the reason behind it. Eventually, physicists came up with the explanation that a "dark energy" permeates the universe and that almost 70 percent of the universe consists of nothing but this energy. Twenty-five percent of the universe is dark matter, which is the invisible matter that does not give off light, x-rays, or any other radiation, but does give off a gravitational force, and only the remaining 5 percent is the observable part of the universe, including the earth, sun, stars, galaxies, and all other forms of matter.

Nature of Dark Energy

Very few facts are known about dark energy. It is believed that it is homogenous, i.e., it has a uniform structure and remains essentially the same throughout the universe. It has an extremely low density, which makes it very hard to make any observations about it through conventional experiments.

The leading theory of dark energy is that it is an inherent property of space. Wherever there is space, there is a uniformly distributed dark energy in it. This theory comes from Einstein's general theory of relativity, which uses a "cosmological constant" to explain how the universe is held together. This cosmological constant is now believed by many scientists to be dark energy.

Another theory that tries to explain dark energy is that it is a dynamic energy fluid, which fills the whole universe. This theory is referred to as *quintessence*. Its name comes from the Greek concept of a pure "fifth element," or the aether that fills up the universe. Proponents of this theory believe that dark energy is not uniform and that it can change in time and space.

Is Dark Energy Related to Paranormal Phenomena?

A lot of people now believe that the existence of dark energy is intricately linked to paranormal phenomena and several theories explaining this relationship have been proposed in the last few years.

There is hardly any doubt now that dark energy is holding the universe together and it is present everywhere. This energy could explain how spirits can move objects and make them float in the air. It can also explain why the conventional laws of physics do not apply to spirits. Dark energy could also act as the channel through which some people are able to communicate with spirits or through which telepathic communication can take place between two people.

ESSENTIAL

Modern science now has the capabilities to measure phenomena that only 100 years ago would not have been possible. The technology available, including computers and space-based experiments, have opened the door to other realms of possibilities that unseen forces are interacting in the universe.

Dark energy can also help explain the concept of a universal consciousness (also known as distributed or nonlocal consciousness), which has been proved by several experiments. It could be the same phenomena that has been referred to in various cultures as *chi, orgone, prana, aether,* or *the Holy Spirit.*

Another theory that relates paranormal phenomenon to dark energy is that this energy carries psychic information and facilitates ghostly activity and psychic abilities. It is also believed that dark energy can pass through objects made of matter as if they did not exist, but this interaction could have a huge paranormal significance and could even be the source of some of our seemingly spontaneous thoughts.

Yet another theory is that the spirit is composed of dark energy that exists in symbiosis with matter of the human body when a person is alive. After a person's death, this energy is decoupled from the body and either exists in the vicinity of where the person died or merges into the aether.

As more is learned about dark energy through new observations, more could also be learned about how paranormal phenomena works. Dark energy could in fact be the key that unlocks the relationship between science and paranormal phenomena, and the next few years could be very exciting for both these fields.

Parallel Universes and Multiple Existences

String theory is one of the most elegant ways of reconciling quantum mechanics, which deals with physics at a subatomic level and relativity, which typically explains the behavior of large objects and the space-time continuum. String theory also indicates the existence of some seemingly weird phenomena that have so far remained in the realm of metaphysics. One such phenomenon is parallel universes.

Everything Is Probable

The idea of parallel universes stems from a key principal of quantum mechanics that everything has a probability associated with it, even reality as you know it. What's more, all possible outcomes are likely to exist at some point. In other words, one form of reality gradually just slips into another form. You can understand this better by considering the example of a die. When you throw the die, you may see it landing on two values, but quantum mechanics says that it lands on all values! This problem had baffled physicists for a long time, until it was proposed that each outcome of throwing a die exists in a different universe, and that a huge number of such parallel universes exist.

Living on a Floating Membrane

String theory further supported the idea of parallel universes. In the initial stages of development of string theory, it got divided into separate theories, all of them predicting the same outcome. This anomaly was fixed with M-theory, which combined different string theories and proposed an overarching framework that has gained considerable approval from physicists.

M-theory postulates that our universe exists in eleven dimensions, one of time and ten of space. In the eleventh dimension, it is possible for a string to gain so much energy that it can expand into a huge floating membrane, on which our universe could exist. Many such membranes can coexist, which means that there could be many parallel universes present along with the one that we live in.

A Copy of You Somewhere Out in Space

In a parallel universe scenario, there are many copies of the same particles existing in multiple universes. By applying a quantum mechanics–based probabilistic framework, scientists argue that in such a scenario, different copies of the same person must also exist in multiple universes. These copies would be more or less identical, but there could be some key differences between them. In fact, different universes could even have different physical laws governing them.

Implications on the Concept of Afterlife

In a parallel universe scenario, the concept of life and afterlife take an entirely different meaning. There is no single "you" living in a single universe. There are many states of "you" living in universes next to each other.

When you take an action or when some other event takes place, there is a chance that, depending on the outcomes of that event, different copies of you branch out into different universes. Death is one such event. When we see someone dying, that reality exists only in the universe that we are in. There is a copy of that person that lives on in a different universe.

FACT

Parallel universes and multiple existences used to be the fantasy of science-fiction writers. Today, with the research in string theory and quantum mechanics, these realms may indeed be possible. Present-day mathematical models are being developed in order to understand these possibilities in greater detail.

Communicating with Someone in a Parallel Universe

It may seem that when a copy of you branches out in a different universe, it will be impossible for it to communicate with this universe. But physicists believe that interaction between different universes does take place. In fact, it has been proposed that this interaction is the cause behind one of the most fundamental forces of nature: gravity.

It is not possible for a copy of a person to come back into the same universe, but there could be ways through which he can send back messages for his loved ones. These messages would seem like paranormal activity to you, as they may not conform to the conventional laws of physics applicable to our universe. They could take the form of apparitions, unexplained voices, forces moving objects, etc. It is possible that psychics are also able to establish such communication through their ability to reach out to different universes.

It should be kept in mind that the concept of parallel universes and multiple existences is no longer metaphysical speculation. These ideas stem from theories that have consistently been proven correct. Quantum mechanics, in particular, has always given predictions that have turned out to be highly accurate in experiments.

CHAPTER 9

Communication with the Afterlife

Throughout history almost all cultures and religions have reported the ability to connect with entities from the non-physical world. Some have called it communicating with the angels or with teachers, and some claim to connect to other humans after their physical deaths. Mediumship has been referred to in many ways, depending on culture and time of practice. From group settings to one's individual connection of prayer, communication with the afterlife has been and continues to be a fascinating and controversial subject.

Mediumship Through the Ages

Mediumship is a way of afterlife communication between a person, medium, and the spirits. The medium is said to possess psychic abilities that help him communicate with spirits, angels, and other immaterial entities. Most mediums attempting to communicate with the spirits of dead people have a direct conversation with them, some go into a trancelike state and relay messages from the netherworld, or permit the spirit to speak through their bodies. During a séance, which is a group event, a medium will attempt to communicate with spirits of the deceased to the group as a whole or directly to individuals involved in the event. Mediumship has deep-rooted beliefs in the concept of an afterlife and is an integral part of the Spiritualist movement that continues to this day. Mediumship has been found throughout most cultures and belief systems around the world.

Mediumship Before the Twentieth Century

The history of mediumship dates back to ancient Greece, where an oracle, a priest, or priestess was said to have the power to prophesize about the future by seeking answers from a particular Greek god/deity by acting as the medium. In the sixteenth century, self-declared English alchemist and medium Edward Kelly claimed to have the ability to contact angels through a crystal gazer. Russian medium Madame Blavatsky (1831–1891), founder of the Theosophical Society, was said to have contacted the spirits of ancient Indian sages for advice and passed them on to devotees.

ALERT

Years later, the Fox sisters would call their "spirit rappings" deliberate hoaxes, but there were subsequent retractions, as it was learned that much pressure was put on the young girls by other established religions to deny the original events. This gave believers and skeptics enough fodder to make their individual contradictory viewpoints.

In 1848, the Fox sisters from New York were the first modern and celebrated mediums who communicated with spirits through "rappings," or short knocking sounds. The Fox sisters gave public séances across Europe and America with attendance from many famous personalities. This began the emergence of Modern American Spiritualism. Trance mediums gained popularity in the 1860s and 1870s. The mediums would go into a deeply altered state and the spirits would convey messages to their minds. The mediums would then speak out what the spirit had communicated, and this was written down by the mediums' assistants. Through the mid-1800s and into the 1900s, many mediums emerged, with séances becoming commonplace across America and parts of Europe. President Abraham Lincoln is also said to have invited mediums (notably Nettie Colburn Maynard) to the White House to relay messages to him from the spirit world.

ESSENTIAL

"My position is that the phenomena of communicating with those who crossed over in their entirety do not require further confirmation. They are proved quite as well as facts are proved in other sciences."
—Dr. Alfred Russel Wallace (1823–1913), co-originator with Charles Darwin of the natural selection theory of evolution

Mediumship in the Twentieth and Twenty-First Centuries

Beginning in the 1930s and through today, a form of mediumship called "channeling" became popular. In this technique, the mediums might go into a trancelike state and "step to the side" of their bodies, which are taken over by teaching spirits who communicate through them. Jane Roberts, Esther Hicks, and Lee Carroll are some of the well-known twentieth-century channeling mediums. Channeling can also be done without entering a full trance state; in this method, information is allowed to flow through the medium to a group or an individual.

William Stanton Moses, another prominent nineteenth-century medium, possessed the ability to levitate, produce lights during séances, and materialize objects. Twentieth-century American psychic and medium Edgar Cayce, believed to be one of the greatest psychics of all time, would perform readings and give advice on health problems in a trancelike state. He is reported to have healed thousands of people where conventional medicine had failed. His thousands of prophecies and psychic readings are still being studied today.

More traditionally, there are also medicine men or shamans who are believed to cure illnesses by obtaining solutions through the spirit world and cleansing the souls of the sick.

Some modern-day mediums, such as James Van Praagh and John Edward, have brought the concept of mediumship out into the open to millions via television shows. Research on mediumship continues by Britain's Society for Psychical Research and those by independent investigators, such as Dr. Gary Schwartz in *The Afterlife Experiments*.

Types of Mediums

Mediumship is a process of communication between a person or persons from the earth plane (medium) and discarnate beings (entities without physical bodies). A medium is said to be sensitive to vibrations from the spirit world, enabling him to communicate with discarnate entities, including angels and guides. Because of this ability, mediums facilitate communication between spirits and people who are not mediums.

Mediumship has been practiced for centuries and is still actively practiced in many parts of the world. Some New Age movements, encompassing astrology, alternative medicine, nature, philosophy, metaphysics, and music, have incorporated mediumship into their belief systems. Mediumship can be broadly divided into two categories: physical mediumship and mental mediumship.

Physical Mediumship

In this form of mediumship, energy systems are said to be manipulated by spirits. The phenomenon can be observed by all those present in the medium's vicinity. It was an important form of mediumship in the eighteenth and nineteenth centuries, where most well known mediums demonstrated physical mediumship during séances. It is still practiced today in controlled environments and under supervision.

In some forms of physical mediumship, a chemical reaction is caused in the medium's body when she comes in contact with the spirit. It is said to be centered in the medium's solar plexus, as opposed to the base of the brain, as in the case of mental mediumship. Here are some of the types of physical mediumship:

- **Raps:** Spirits are said to sometimes communicate through raps and knocks, answering simple "yes" and "no" questions through sounds coming from somewhere in the room.
- **Materialization:** Spirit faces, hands, and complete physical forms are said to have materialized many times during séances. The most famous instance of materialization was that of English medium Florence Cook, during whose sessions a spirit, called "Katie King," would materialize and have conversations with members attending the séance. Materialized entities are different from ghosts or apparitions and occur very rarely.
- **Ectoplasm:** The term *ectoplasm* was coined by French scientist Charles Richet in 1894 to refer to an exteriorized substance emitted from the medium's orifices (ears, mouth, nose) during a séance. It was described as a milky-white, rubbery, clotted substance. Exposure of ectoplasm to light was said to cause injury to the medium, one reason why séances were often conducted in dark rooms.
- **Apports and levitations:** Apports are physical objects like books or flowers, which are said to have been transported by spirits at the scene of a séance. Séances are not necessary to make apports appear; they can be transported by the spirit anywhere or anytime if it so wishes. Mediums have also been known to levitate during séances. The most famous case of this involved the nineteenth-century Scottish medium Daniel Dunglas Home, who was reported to have levitated out of a third story window of a building and then re-entered through a different window.
- **Direct voice:** These are audible voices of a paranormal nature produced during a séance. Trumpets were often used at the scene of the séance to amplify the faint voices of the spirits; however, the voice can also be heard independent of any device. Several investigators recorded voice manifestations in séances conducted by twentieth-century British medium Leslie Flint. There are still mediums that use direct voice as their method of mediumship, but it takes much training and practice to acquire the ability to make the phenomena happen.

Mental Mediumship

In mental mediumship, communication occurs within the medium's consciousness without the involvement of the five physical senses. Due to this, it is also referred to as telepathic mediumship. The following three types are the most popular:

- **Clairvoyance (clear seeing):** In the context of mediumship, clairvoyance refers to seeing images, people, or animals in the head, or mind's eye, that may not be physically present or visible to nonmediums. In some cases, mediums may see a spirit standing before them, as if it were a physical entity. The images seen by mediums may have a symbolic meaning in relation to the spirit's life.
- **Clairsentience (clear feeling):** This is the ability of the medium to sense the presence of a spirit, and it is often experienced. It is common to many people as the feeling that someone is behind you or that someone is staring at you. The medium is just more sensitive and can pick up more details such as feeling the touch of the spirit, a cold breeze blowing, a scent or fragrance, sense the personality of the deceased, or other evidential traits.
- **Clairaudience (clear hearing):** This is the ability of mediums to detect spirit voices in their vicinity. They can be heard within their head. The voices are inaudible to others who may be present in the vicinity. Mediums have also reported hearing spoken thoughts, music, and singing.

Séance: A Group Event

The word *séance* originates from a French word meaning "to sit." A séance is a means of communicating with the deceased. It is believed that during the procedure the spirits are enabled to visit the location where the séance is being held. In some cases the medium leading the communication is used as a vehicle for the spirits to directly communicate with those present. In others, the spirits may make their presence known by smells, sounds, or touch. In rare cases, participants of a séance have also reported spirit sightings during the procedure.

Séance Through the Ages

Man has been attempting to communicate with those who have passed beyond since times immemorial. But in modern times it was the Fox sisters,

Margaret and Kate, who were perhaps the first acknowledged and famed for their ghostly encounters. In the late 1840s, the girls communicated with a spirit in their haunted home using a series of claps and knocks to get answers to their questions. They went on to publicly demonstrate their spiritual powers.

ESSENTIAL

The nineteenth century was also the time for public séances conducted by Paschal Beverly Randolph. Randolph would act as a messenger between his audience and the spirits they wished to talk to. Other famous spiritualists include medium Leafy Anderson, who, in the early 1900s contacted the spirit of Black Hawk, a warrior of the Native American Fox tribe.

When Spiritualism first emerged as a religion and grew into a movement, many self-styled mediums and spirit communicators emerged from various sections of society. They brought news of the dead, how and where they were, and whether or not they were happy. Inevitably, many fraudsters took advantage of the mystic nature of these spiritual activities and made money off gullible believers who were desperate to communicate with deceased loved ones.

Although many mediums and several well-publicized séances came to be exposed as frauds later on, there were still many others that held up to the closest scrutiny. Through the years and even today, séances continue to open the doors between our world and the beyond. Believers come together and combine their spiritual energies to call for spirits to visit them.

Different Kinds of Séances

The movement of Spiritualism encouraged communication with the dead to learn about the world beyond our understanding and the afterlife and to prove the continuity of life itself. In public séances, Spiritualist ministers conveyed messages from the dead to living members of the congregation, which were usually held in Spiritualist churches or camps. At times, a particularly receptive medium would function as the messenger instead of an ordained minister. These public religious services continue today throughout the world and usually contain a healing service as well as a lecture on various spiritual topics.

Group Séances

In this, a group of believers come together at one location to communicate with the spirits. Each one may have a question to ask the otherworld's visitors. The leader of the group séance needs to be a very sensitive medium in order to establish a successful contact with a spirit.

The medium may slip into a trancelike state, allowing the spirits to communicate through him. At other times the information may just be related verbally without any sign of interaction between the medium and the recipients. Sometimes the medium communicates the spirit's message by means of automatic writing. Spirits can also communicate through sounds like knocking or scratching.

Spiritual Circles

Smaller groups of people who are interested in exploring supernatural phenomenon conduct séances in the hope of learning more about the otherworld. These spiritual circle séances are more exploratory in nature, and often the participants do not have any specific questions or wish to contact a particular spirit. They do wish, however, to expand their knowledge of the process and hopefully develop their own mediumistic abilities.

Séances with Manifestations

When Spiritualism was at its peak, many mediums claimed an ability to generate ectoplasmic manifestations of spirits. In these séances, participants could see a translucent shape issue from the medium. It was believed that this ectoplasm was a spirit in physical form. There were other reported manifestations, such as apports of objects or the transfiguration of the medium himself. Transfiguration and physical mediumship are still practiced today.

Séance Tools

Many mediums offer themselves as the vehicle for the spirit to communicate with the living. Others use special tools to comprehend what the spirit is trying to convey. Ouija boards, or spirit boards, are widely used to understand messages from the spirit world. These flat boards with numbers, letters, and symbols come with a planchette, or pointer. In a successful séance, the participants may feel an unseen force moving the planchette to point to different letters and symbols to spell out a message.

Some mediums also use trumpets to hear the spirits talk or slates where the spirits can leave written messages. Sometimes mediums also confine themselves in spirit cabinets from which they would emerge with messages from the netherworld.

Séances—Are They Real?

The existence of paranormal entities like spirits and the possibility of communicating with them through séances has been questioned repeatedly by skeptics and scientists. Famed magician and illusionist Harry Houdini duplicated many of the famous séances conducted during his lifetime and exposed them as illusions. However, Houdini was also a firm believer in the paranormal and often made his beliefs public.

ESSENTIAL

Sir William Crookes (1832–1919) was a physicist, chemist, and one of the most decorated scientists of his time. He discovered the element thallium and was a pioneer in radioactivity. He said, "It is quite true that a connection has been set up between this world and the next."

Several well-known scientists and inventors including Sir William Crookes, Alexander Graham Bell, Guglielmo Marconi, and others firmly believed in the power of séances to reach paranormal entities. Marconi went so far as to attempt a direct communication with spirits using radio signals.

Science has evolved over the years to come up with explanations of many of our ancestors' unsolved mysteries. But there are still many paranormal phenomena, including afterlife communication, that are beyond the reach of science today.

Scientific Studies of the Phenomena

The concept of an afterlife forms a part of the belief system of many religions, including Christianity, Hinduism, Judaism, and Buddhism. The soul of a person is believed to remain intact after death, even as the physical body ceases to exist. The soul is believed to be the identity of the deceased in his afterlife, and it is this identity that sometimes communicates with family members in the living world. This phenomena, referred to as "afterlife communication," has been studied under the purview of spirituality and parapsychology. Communication with deceased loved ones, encompassing geography, religion, and culture, has been recorded for centuries. Modern-day parapsychologists and investigators are trying to provide foolproof evidence of such phenomena through research and experimentation.

Research Before the Twentieth Century

One of the earliest and most influential nineteenth-century compilations of studies on the paranormal, including the phenomena of afterlife communication, was *Phantasms of the Living* (1886) by Edmund Gurney, F. W. H. Myers, and Frank Podmore. An extremely detailed book, it presented 702 scientifically researched and presented case studies of real-life paranormal experiences, some of which were afterlife communication incidents. The incidents related to afterlife communication and were laboriously researched for authenticity by volunteers from the Society of Psychical Research to verify the stories of respondents. The verification consisted of soliciting letters from other parties where these informants had shared their experience, going through diary entries, checking death notices in newspapers, and so on.

ALERT

It should be noted that visual experiences are just one of the types of after-death communication, which also includes hearing voices, feeling a presence, smelling a familiar fragrance, seeing two-dimensional images or visions, dreams, and communication through a medium.

Two such afterlife communication experiences were visual, that is, the deceased appeared in front of their family members, with verbal communication taking place in one case. In the first experience, the dead mother of a woman, visible only down to her waist, appeared before the woman and her fiancé. Another incident recounted in the book involved both visual and verbal communication. A woman, dead for three years, who was the mother of two children, who were also dead, appeared before a woman known to her and thanked her for visiting the grave of her dead children.

F. W. H. Myers (1843–1901), scholar, scientist, and cofounder of the Society for Psychical Research, was one of the first to boldly declare that man had a soul, and that the soul survived death. His book *Human Personality and Its Survival of Bodily Death* was one of the most pioneering studies into the subject of afterlife and after-death communication. He applied scientific methods of observation to a spiritual concept to provide proof of the phenomena.

Research in the Twentieth and Twenty-First Centuries

Regarded parapsychology researcher Karlis Osis (1917–1997) conducted many surveys during the mid-twentieth century to study the phenomenon of deathbed experiences, which have a strong connection to the concept of an afterlife. His experiments studied dying patients who had experienced visions of deceased loved ones in dreams, giving them comfort and removing the fear of dying from their minds.

In 1996, Bill and Judy Guggenheim cowrote a book on the phenomenon of afterlife communication, *Hello from Heaven!* Over a period of seven years, the authors collected a vast number of personal experiences of afterlife communication from several thousand Americans and Canadians. Based on the nature of the experiences, they are categorized into various types (dreams, smells, visions, touch, visual experience, and so on). The book also describes how positive the experiences have been for those individuals, healing them on an emotional and spiritual level. Based on their studies, the authors estimated that one in five Americans have experienced afterlife communication.

Professor of psychology at the University of Arizona Dr. Gary E. Schwartz, who holds a doctorate from Harvard and a professorship at Yale, has tried to provide scientific evidence for the afterlife communication phenomena in his book *The Afterlife Experiments*. The book describes laboratory experiments that Schwartz has conducted with internationally renowned mediums including American John Edward. A lot of care was taken to eliminate possibilities of cheating and fraud. In the experiments, the medium was able to relay information like names and events from the deceased. The experiments were videotaped and the responses of mediums were scored on accuracy. The results showed that the mediums had a 77 to 95 percent accuracy.

Other twenty-first-century researchers of afterlife phenomena include American psychiatric therapist Dianne Arcangel. Her book *Afterlife Encounters* has presented real-life cases of afterlife communication experiences, and the effects of these encounters on the people who went through them. She collected and scientifically researched all the information through rigorous surveys over five years. Her book reveals that 98 percent of those experiencing the phenomena found them comforting.

FACT

Later, Dr. Schwartz, working with his research partner Dr. Linda G. Russek, made the experiment controls even more stringent to the point where mediums weren't allowed to see or hear the sitters. The accuracy even after these controls remained close to 90 percent.

There are many modern-day researchers concentrating much of their efforts on better understanding spiritual experiences such as afterlife phenomena. No one can predict whether the phenomena can ever be proved with substantial scientific evidence in the future, but it is clear that this paranormal and spiritual phenomena will continue to fascinate.

Individual Connections Through Thought and Prayer

Prayer is a means of establishing an emotional and spiritual connection with powers beyond our imagination and direct reach. Different people follow different praying methods and expressions of devotion. The object of this kind of devotion, affection, or faith can be a divinity, a person, a departed relative, an idea, or even a group with influential preachings and principles.

Different schools of belief may have different prescribed methods of prayer. These methods can take the form of hymns, songs, words, or various acts. Some people even believe in simply expressing their faith in their own words extemporaneously.

Why Prayer?—The Significance of Prayer

Most often, people turn to prayer seeking guidance during difficult times. Sickness or trouble of some kind can also prompt fervent prayers for help from the unseen. Deeply religious people believe that their daily prayers reveal to them the right path to life. The reasons for praying are different among different people, but the commitment, faith, and emotions behind the supplication are equally strong.

Praying allows the living to communicate with the universal powers and seek help from them beyond the means of human power. The help desired may be material, spiritual, or emotional. Usually, humans faced with daily challenges of ill health, financial want, and emotional disturbances ask for material or emotional help, like release from a specific worry or anxiety.

The Efficacy of Prayers

Skeptics question the efficacy of prayer in granting the devotee what he desires. But the fact is that devotees through the ages have, without doubt, gained emotional strength and risen above their worldly problems by the power of prayer. A prayer expressed with complete faith in the supreme power gives an immediate sense of calm to the devotee. A deep belief that you have the support and blessing of the power you believe in blossoms in your heart as a result of prayer, helping you face tribulations with confidence. Many medical studies have focused on the power of prayer in recent years, with results showing a significant difference in the healing of ill patients who engaged in prayer.

Faith and Healing

The effectiveness of prayer is perhaps most clearly illustrated by faith healings. The healing of many sick people by Jesus is recorded in the New Testament, establishing the way for many religious leaders to follow suit in later years. There are six incidents described in the four Gospels wherein Jesus restored sight to the blind. Greek mythology also speaks of the centaur Chiron, who could heal with his touch. Every religion has its own share of healing stories.

A study of spiritual healing among those with visual and auditory impairments also concluded that prayers played a critical part in the healing process. These conclusions were recorded in the Study of the Therapeutic Effects of Proximal Intercessory Prayer (STEPP); the results of the research were compiled over a period spanning seven years.

FACT

Many scientists have studied "healing touch," or spiritual healing, which is the ability to cause a healing mechanism to take place by working with the human energy field. Beneficiaries have been examined and the obvious effects of the healing have been recorded in many scientific journals and papers. Two of the more recent papers presented on this subject are by Larry Dossey, MD, and Daniel Benor, MD, both of whom studied spiritual healing at close quarters.

Seeking Help from Beyond the Veil

Prayers can also take the form of a supplication to loved ones who have passed beyond the veil. Often when a family member dies, the grieving survivors are unable to bear the loss. Praying to this departed soul can help bring closure to the grieving person and also help the restless spirit of the dead move on to the higher regions.

Most religions propagate the belief that upon death, the soul moves closer to God. Seeking help from such souls by means of prayer is a way to channel the infinite power of the almighty to fulfill our desires. The need may not always be physical in nature, like money or a job. The supplicant can ask for peace, the ability to pray better, or the well-being of himself or others.

Many religions set aside a special day for communion with the dead. On this day, the dead are remembered by offering special gifts, food, and other items, which they were particularly fond of in their lifetime. The Day of the Dead and the All Saints' Day are examples of such celebrations when the dead are believed to be closest to the living and can actually partake of the offerings made by their living family members. The concept that the living are merely separated by an impenetrable and invisible "curtain" from the departed souls is an integral part of these religious traditions.

Praying is a very effective tool to channel the infinite powers that lie beyond our worldly reach. The old saying that "faith can move mountains" may not be taken literally in today's world, but it is something that should be seriously pondered. It signifies that deep devotion and heartfelt belief in entities beyond imagination and this world can help resolve difficulties that are beyond human capabilities.

CHAPTER 10

Afterlife Evidence
from Mediums

Spirit communication is all about transmitting, receiving, and interpreting information accurately. Giving names might prove spirits' identities. They seldom give us "name, rank, serial number." They impart much more information in a variety of ways, such as by telling secrets, identifying objects, and even exposing causes of death, which may not always agree with the coroner's report. Many statements given by a spirit carry additional information that must be interpreted by the medium. It is the medium's challenge to gather the information and present it in a way that the intended recipient will understand the message.

Personality and Trait Descriptions

Spirits have the burden of proving their identities. It would be nice if they came through and simply stated their names; some do, but not always. If a spirit attempts to give his name, the medium may only hear one or two letters of it, which is usually enough to establish the correct name of the spirit. They send out all the right information; we simply are not tuned to receive it! Spirits communicate telepathically. They are accustomed to sending and receiving mental messages to each other. Comparing their language to ours would be like putting into words what you did on your last vacation compared to what you see in your mind. Spirits vibrate at a higher frequency, which means they transmit more information in a shorter period of time than the living do. The medium receiving these messages must be capable of raising his vibration in order to understand the message.

» CASE: DOMINEERING PERSONALITY

A couple had traveled quite a distance to see me for a "spiritual" reading with the intent of discovering the paths they were on or were meant to take. I informed them that my expertise was in contacting loved ones who had passed. As soon as we began the session, I addressed the husband and stated, "You're here looking for proof that I am able to contact your son, who took his own life." Their deceased son told me that if I didn't give his dad enough evidence of his identity that he would get up and walk out.

He then said to say to his dad, "You need a new inverter for your motor home." The father was surprised, as he had just been told by the RV dealership that the reason the television and refrigerator were not working was because of a bad inverter. I had no clue that they owned an RV.

Typically spirits don't like to be tested. When a sitter challenges the communication or becomes too critical of the delivery of the message, the session can come to a sudden close. The son's personality had to be stronger than the dad's, who was a high-ranking military official. He may have taken control of the reading to compensate for his shortcomings in real life.

Identifying a Spirit

Whatever a spirit was best known for here on earth is most likely what he will project to the medium to validate his identity. There are many ways that a spirit's identity can be conveyed. One technique could be to reference a medical condition. For example, if a person suffered a stroke and lost mobility on one side of his body, the medium may exhibit those same symptoms such as slurred speech and leaning to one side. Once the condition is recognized as being specific to the person when they were here, the symptoms and the condition disappear; the medium returns to normal.

FACT

Mediums don't always remember the messages they give during a reading. The level of concentration is so intense that sometimes information will flow through the medium on a subconscious level. Further scrutiny of information delivered in that manner will accurately reveal the spirit's personality.

›› CASE: HE REALLY IS WITH ME!

A friend of mine wanted to connect with his dad who had passed over when he was only four years old. He had little recall of his dad because he was so young. I attempted to make contact, not convinced that this was going to go very well. At one point I placed both of my hands in front of my face, and as I looked at my palms I rotated them so that I could now see the back of each hand, and stated, "Your dad can't do this." I placed my hands in my lap and wondered why I said that. After a few seconds, I brought my right hand to the same place and said, "He can do this," as I rotated it before my face. I looked down, and it was as if my left arm were missing. I asked my friend if his dad was in fact missing his left arm, and he said that he had lost it in the war.

One of the messages that was given to my friend from his dad was that he was a good father to his children. My friend told me that he had no way to gauge his parenting skills, so this message brought him peace knowing that he had his father's approval. Later during the session his dad did reveal his name.

Relating Shared Experiences

Spirit guides are with us for our lifetime, and they know us all too well. Energy constraints make it difficult to elaborate on the many details that compose a story during a reading. If a spirit wants to convey a long story that would be recognized by the person receiving the reading, the medium's spirit guide will know the history of the medium's life and will create a parallel of something she has done to equal that of the story the spirit wants to tell.

>> CASE: AFRAID OF HEIGHTS

During one reading I was giving to a mother who lost her son to a motorcycle accident, I was reminded by my spirit guide of a helicopter ride that I had taken recently that left me a little nauseous and somewhat frightened. When I saw this reminder I observed a ladder being lowered from the helicopter, and the woman I was giving the reading to was hanging on the ladder frightened and yelling. Her session was ending, and I told her that because of her fear of heights, when it was her time to ascend to heaven, her son would not be part of the process.

I didn't want to end the session on a rather uncomfortable message, so I asked why the metaphor of a helicopter was used. She explained that on her birthday her son took her to lunch, then to the beach where he was a helicopter tour guide. He lifted off, and she screamed so loud that he was forced to land. He told her that he would never take her up again!

>> CASE: EXISTENTIAL HAPPENINGS

I was asked if I could do a reading for a mother whose son had recently passed. Approaching the end of the reading, her son stated that he liked it that his mom had placed her hands under and over his hand, making a "hand sandwich." The mother then relayed that during the reading, she was in the room with her son who had passed two days earlier, and had just cradled his hand as described.

In Pennsylvania, the state where the death occurred, it is allowable to retain the deceased's body at home for up to three days.

When booking the reading, the mother did not want me to know how recently the son had passed, thinking that he might not be able to come through that soon. Most mediums prefer at least a six-month wait period in order to give the person receiving the reading time to further heal. My experience has been that, even within hours of their passing, spirits are able to communicate. Giving a reading that soon must be carefully evaluated in each case.

QUESTION

Do animals communicate from the other side?
Yes, our pets are part of our families and will show themselves, even with other loved ones who have passed to the other side. A pet, particularly a dog, may present itself as a guardian of the person to whom it was most attached. Cats, birds, horses, and other pets may also come through in readings.

>> CASE: SAME PERSONALITY IN LIFE AND AFTERLIFE

Our personalities do not change when we go to the other side. People who are quiet and secretive when they were here are the same when they are contacted during a reading. What happens when a person was bigger than life when he was here? One case I had the pleasure of working on will answer that question.

I was contacted by two women who were interested in having a person-to-person reading. I was warned that they didn't want me to have any prior information about who they wanted to contact. The day of the session, the two ladies sat together on a sofa in my reading area. Before I could start, I saw a woman in spirit sitting across from them on what should have been an empty sofa in my office. I could see her as if she had walked in with the two women. I projected a mental message asking her if she was here to connect with the two ladies sitting across from me. "Yes," she said. "I'm their mother, and I died last month from pneumonia."

When I asked if that was the purpose for the reading, the women were emotional but happy that their mother was present. They had no idea that I could see and talk to her as if she were still in the body.

After several minutes of conversation with their mother, I saw a true American icon appear to her left. I could see and hear him very clearly. "Hey, Chuck, tell them I'm here," he said, and he continued to try to get my attention. I didn't want to reveal his identity because I didn't want the ladies to think that I was hallucinating. Finally I gave in and stated that this famous person was sitting next to their mom wearing sunglasses and boxer shorts. Their excitement said it all. They were the sisters of this star, and the woman next to him was their mother.

Knowing the language of the other side all so well, I asked if there was a reason for their brother to show up in boxer shorts. They told me that years earlier he was visiting their mom and kept his visit a secret so as to avoid unwanted publicity. One evening while walking around in his boxer shorts, police came to the house to warn of vandals in the neighborhood. The officers heard a noise in the closet, opened the door, and saw the celebrity standing there in his boxer shorts. This story was never made public. The sisters brought the family photo album to prove that they were in fact related to the celebrity.

This event was a learning experience for me. The person whom this story is about was able to manifest his spirit so clearly that I could see what he was wearing and hear his voice as well as I could hear the voices of the others in the room. The mother was also able to make herself visible and speak.

High-profile people in real life seem to come through in spirit with more force, even, as in this case, manifesting themselves in body. Even the mother, herself, who was not a celebrity, was sharing the high energy of her son, making her visible to me.

Objects of Significance

Part of the spirit language is the use of objects to convey a message. Necklaces, bracelets, watches, rings, cigarettes, and anything that we use in daily life can be used to put focus on something of significance. Sometimes the object, along with either a feeling or even a scent, will be added to give direction to a statement.

» CASE: HOW WILL YOU KNOW IT'S ME?

During a group reading I gave in a private home, I had just finished giving a reading to one person and was moving on to another when I heard the words "Alcoa aluminum." Next, I felt like I was working in the kitchen of a hot, greasy diner. I could tell that I was connecting with an older male cook who was covering a dish of food with aluminum foil. No one in the group could relate to this description. As I repeated the information to the group, the husband of one of the women present came into the room. He could hear me giving this description and felt that the message was for him.

Many years before his dad had owned a diner, and they had worked in the kitchen together. His dad didn't believe in psychics or mediums. One day, while covering a pan of food with aluminum foil, his dad said to him, "Let's make a deal; whoever passes over first, the other will go to a medium and communicate back a code word that will positively prove his identity." As he looked at the box of aluminum foil he had just used, he said "Alcoa aluminum." There is no way a medium can guess that one! The father and son were reunited during the session with plenty of unique validations; however, his dad never gave his name.

» CASE: RECOGNIZING THE CLUES

I was giving a group reading when I singled out a woman because I connected with her eighteen-year-old daughter who had passed away in a car accident six months earlier. I heard the word "floorboard," and I sensed that her daughter had been with her mother that very morning, as she adjusted the mats on the floor of her car. I didn't understand the relevance of this, but

I passed on the information to the mother. The woman explained that she had gone shopping with her daughter, who had then disappeared into the mall to purchase a gift for her. Since the daughter died the next night, she never had a chance to give it to her mother. The day of the group session the mother went into her daughter's room and found the bag that she had never opened. Inside were two mats for her car. Both had a picture of an angel on them. That morning, she put the mats in her car and asked her daughter to talk about them at the session.

>> CASE: BUNDLES OF JOY

As word traveled around the police department that I was developing my intuitive skills, I found myself doing readings for my coworkers. A female officer approached me, seeking a prediction regarding the possibility of her much-desired pregnancy. I did a session with her, and her father came through. I clearly saw him with a baby in each arm, wrapped in blue, with a look of grandfatherly pride on his face.

A month later, she informed me that she was, indeed, pregnant. Everyone anticipated twin boys. The same month, her sister learned she, too, was pregnant. They each, joyfully, delivered baby boys.

Interpretation of the communiqué should be examined from various angles. Spirits always give the right answer; it is up to us to "plug in" to the most appropriate conclusion.

Presence at Meaningful Events

Spirits have a propensity to gravitate toward emotionally charged events such as birthday parties, weddings, sports events, and other meaningful gatherings. Many have reported feeling the presence of a family member who has passed on at such occasions. Unexplainable colored circles, known as *orbs*, have appeared in family pictures. Many experience this phenomenon on their wedding photographs. Skeptics explain this as lens flair caused by light refracting into the camera lens. Another explanation is dust particles being illuminated by the camera's flash.

Spirit Presence at Group Readings

Large group readings create a much higher energy level, which attracts more spirits into the room. People who do not normally acknowledge spirits around them will report feeling or hearing them for the first time, due to the positive vibes and heightened sense of awareness among the crowd. Competition among the spirits at such events results in them being very creative, so that they will be heard first. They will do things to attract the medium's attention; for example, the medium may see a person, who died while scuba diving, pacing around wearing a tank, mask, and fins.

》 CASE: SHINING STAR

I was helping a friend prepare for her thirty-year-old son's memorial. We were scanning family pictures to her computer, when one of the son, mother, and father appeared on the screen. Out of nowhere, a shower of stars appeared at the bottom of the picture and exited at the top of the computer screen. My friend who was sitting by me, said, "What did you do to create that?" I said, "Nothing, and I've never seen that happen before." Two days later, the brother of the deceased son gave his eulogy. He said that the two competed in their achievements, and he had told his brother that he knew he should "reach for the sky." "No," his deceased brother had said, "reach for the stars."

ESSENTIAL

Vivid dreams, called "visits," many times reveal accurate information from the spirit in an attempt to help solve the unknown cause of death or to give comfort to loved ones. These dreams are brief, colorful, and meaningful to the receiver.

Two days later, the father of the son had a realistic dream that woke him up. He told his wife that he saw the brightest star shining down on him. They both believed that was another sign from their son.

>> CASE: I WILL BE THERE

The first meditation class I attended consisted of eight people sitting in a circle. When the meditation ended, I approached a woman in the group and told her that a twenty-five-year-old female named Gail wanted her to know, "I will be there." The woman told me that her daughter died at the age of twenty-five, and that her daughter's daughter was getting married in a week. The woman came to the session hoping that there would be some proof that Gail would attend her daughter's wedding.

Secrets Exposed

A spirit often wants to "come clean" of unfinished business. He wants to confess, apologize, or explain some actions during his lifetime. The medium does not always understand the message, but must relay the key words as they are thrown down to him, like a deck of cards being scattered on a table-top. Sometimes the messages are to help us, as we are carrying baggage that may be incorrect or misinterpreted. The remaining person may harbor guilt for doing or not doing some particular thing. The spirit wants to set the record straight and help the person resolve misguided issues. The spirit may also receive healing by communicating truth to a loved one, thereby bringing comfort to both.

QUESTION

Do spirits improve upon their communication skills during repeat readings?
Communication may be difficult for spirits initially; they look for the opportunity to contact us, but they have to learn how it is done. They become more accustomed to the process through repetition and listening to other spirits' readings.

We're all here to learn life's lessons. For the most part spirits will communicate that they are okay, and that they are still around us. Warnings of eminent danger may come from the spirit as a suggestion for you to reconsider something that you are doing, to warn you that there may be a negative outcome if you stay on the path that you are on. Placing you in the right job, or selecting a partner for you, is really not their top priority.

ESSENTIAL

Spirits do see the "big picture" when it comes to looking at our lives. Some of what they attempt to impart is censored at a higher level. They know more than they are allowed to tell us. We must learn from our worldly lessons; it's all about choices.

>> CASE: WATCHING OVER YOU

During a phone reading for a woman whose mother had passed over, I felt the tone change from identity validation to concern about the daughter's marriage. Her mother relayed to me that her daughter's marriage was on the rocks. The daughter confirmed this. Mom, in spirit, wanted her daughter to look between the mattresses on her husband's side of the bed while I was talking to her on the phone. Her daughter lifted the mattress and found a scanner. I asked her to turn it on and she said that she could hear my voice coming through the device. Her mom told me that her daughter's husband was having an affair, and that he was monitoring her phone calls on the scanner to find out if she knew about the affair he was having.

Cause of Death Revealed

Police are finding that the crime rate is constantly rising while budget restraints are making case investigations less efficient. They can only spend so many hours on a case, so they try to close them as fast as possible. Murder can be made to look like a suicide. Families that lose a loved one under suspicious circumstances start forming so many "what-ifs." Some cases have been reopened or reclassified as the result of an aggrieved spirit communicating new facts or leads in his case that otherwise would have been ignored.

>> CASE: SUICIDE OR MURDER?

The parents of a girl who had, allegedly, committed suicide asked me to go to the hotel room where she had been found dead. This was a young girl who had spent the holiday weekend there with her fiancé. Neighbors reported that the two had a dispute, and the fiancée packed up and left before daylight. The next day, maids entered the room and found the girl's body hanging from a dog leash, which was tied to the showerhead.

When I entered the hotel room, I was immediately drawn to the shower area and could envision the leash that was used. I could hear her voice say, "I didn't do this." I then went into the bedroom, and although the bed was made, I could see that only the right half had been used by her and a pillow was missing. She had me ask her mother, "What happened to the other pillow?" Her mother stated that the police found that pillow hidden underneath the bed.

I was of the strong opinion that the fiancé had suffocated her with the pillow, then tied her up in the shower to make it look like a suicide. The mother concurred with my opinion. Later, the mother had another reading from a medium, who had no knowledge of the case, and his conclusion was the same as mine.

CHAPTER 11

Solving Crimes with the Help of the Deceased

Many of us would leave no stone unturned if we lost a loved one and the crime appeared to be going unsolved. Evidence can be vague, unpredictable, unreliable, and often inaccurate. A witness may withhold certain information for personal protection, whereas a spirit wants to divulge all of the facts. If the obvious is being overlooked, the spirit tends to be more forceful. A spirit may repeat the same message to many people, hoping that one person will grasp the challenging conundrum.

Naming Suspects

Spirits may come through and actually name the perpetrator. Or they may give one hint at a time, as if on a scavenger hunt, until the person receiving the information puts the pieces together. Spirits are about telling the truth. They will accept the responsibility if they were the cause of their own death.

>> CASE: ALL IN GOOD TIME

Two years after their daughter was murdered, the parents came to me for a session. They did not believe that she had been killed by an unknown intruder at her house during a break-in. I was able to confirm the mechanism of death, which was a baseball bat. The daughter told me that the break-in was staged, and that her husband had committed the crime. While the husband was a person of interest, there was not enough evidence for the authorities to charge him.

The daughter cautioned the parents to back off, and communicated that in twelve months' time, her husband would be charged with the crime and serve time in prison. She did not want her parents to impede the police investigation prematurely. The parents agreed, as they trusted their daughter's message. One year later, I received a call from the family informing me that the husband had been arrested, charged with her murder, and was serving time in prison.

ESSENTIAL

Spirits communicate messages not only about events of the past or present, but also predict future occurrences with precise accuracy.

Providing Evidence

>> CASE: OLEANDER

I went to the scene of the death of a twenty-six-year-old male whose passing was investigated by police, who ruled his death as toxic overload. The mother, who disagreed with the findings, wanted to see if I could pick up any vibrations from her son by going into his apartment. Once inside, I knew that there was a problem with the lighting and the television. She concurred that her son always had the light on 24-7, and the television would be on the moment he arrived home and stayed on until he left. When her son was found, the light and television were off.

He showed me that, in his final moments, something was being poured into his throat. I felt that it was a clear poison. The mother told me that her son came to her in a dream, and was showing her an e-mail on a computer with the word *oleander* written in large letters on the screen. She had no idea what this meant. She did research on the web, and found that oleander is a toxic plant that grows in Florida.

A further key word that was passed down was *monkey*, which the parents identified as their son's nickname. In all, we each felt that the information received was accurate and informative, but it was not enough conclusive proof to convince the authorities to reopen the case. The mother felt the poison may have been overlooked in the autopsy report, and has now employed a private lab to perform extensive tests using blood samples from her son.

The independent laboratory report concluded that death was due to an extreme amount of poison being ingested by the victim. Police have reopened the case and classified it as a homicide.

Locating Bodies

There is an awesome burden placed on any psychic medium when asked to confirm whether a missing person is dead or alive. Simply misinterpreting a message from the spirit could steer an investigation in the wrong direction. The ultimate injudiciousness would be to falsely accuse the wrong person for an offence they didn't commit. The following missing persons case was videotaped and aired before a national audience.

>> CASE: OPEN CASE NOW CLOSED

As a retired police officer and nationally recognized as "the Psychic Cop," I assisted police on a six-year-old missing-person case. I was given absolutely no information or details. At 4:00 A.M. of the day of meeting with the detectives and family, the deceased woke me up in my home and told me that his best friend had murdered him. When he turned around, I observed that he had gray clay, or mud, on the back of his head and down the length of his body. I knew that he had been murdered in a muddy, swampy area.

My first task was to prove that their son was not, in fact, missing, but deceased. I had to prove that I could connect with him on the other side by giving private information to the family that they would recognize as coming from their son. Once this was established, pertinent facts, including location of death, led us to an area that the police had already searched, and believed to be the crime scene. While at the purported crime scene, I felt strongly that this was the location of the actual murder because of the swamp and muddy embankment, but that the body had been removed to another location. Our goal was to find the body.

ESSENTIAL

Time is of the essence when searching for the body of a missing person due to the ravages of deterioration, animal disturbance, and elements of nature. Delays diminish establishing accurate cause of death.

I envisioned a blue pickup truck with something in the back, like a refrigerator, with the door removed. I knew that the body had been placed in the back of this truck, covered over, and removed to another place for disposal. Detectives concurred with this theory, because the owner of the truck, the deceased's best friend, had committed suicide.

QUESTION

Can a person be charged with murder if there is no body found?
Yes, a person can be charged if there is no body found; it is just very difficult to prove.

With this information, I had further images of the suspect dissecting the body and disposing of the remains in a burn barrel in his backyard. Upon visiting the suspect's home, about 100 miles away, we were denied access to the property, but I clearly saw a burn barrel in the backyard of the house in the exact location where I had envisioned it.

Diligent detective work, along with the assistance of the psychic medium, rendered the status of the case changed from a "missing-person case" to "murder-suicide," which officially closed the case.

Locating Missing Persons

High profile cases can present many obstacles for a medium. It is understandable when an investigating officer is reluctant to invest time and energy in information given by a medium. The officer has supervisors, family members, and the media to consider when gathering information that later may be scrutinized by the court system. Mediums walk a fine line when offering information from a spirit that could make them a prime suspect.

›› CASE: FAMILY MEMBER SPIRITS GIVE CLUES

Missing persons may be alive; therefore, it is not possible to connect with their spirit. It is, however, possible to connect with the spirit of a family member who is inclined to assist. The location, and even the health status, of such a person may be specified in order to achieve a safe return.

FACT

Most police departments are reluctant to use physics or mediums to aid in solving a crime. The court system is based upon facts, and cases are difficult to prosecute when information is received from unexplainable sources.

I was called in to work on a highly publicized case involving a missing five-year-old female. I met with her mother and grandmother on day number two of her disappearance. I connected with her great-grandmother, who proved her identity by lifting her chin and plucking an object from that area of her face. "Why is she doing that?" I asked. The mother of the missing child informed me that her grandmother had an accident and that fiberglass was embedded in her chin. She used to pluck out a strand when it would surface. Such an unusual validation served to let me know that the connection was reliable and that I could trust the information that I was receiving.

The great-grandmother went on to tell me that her great-granddaughter was currently alive and being held in a factory-like environment, and that whistles could be heard.

The session was monitored by the many law enforcement agencies present. Unfortunately, no action was taken to search the types of facilities described by the great-grandmother.

Spirits try to help us, and give pertinent information only when the time is right. It is up to us to interpret the data and act upon it. Currently, this young girl is still missing, and the case remains open.

» CASE: GPS COORDINATES FROM ABOVE

A family in California asked if a reading would help to locate their son who had been missing for eight months. There was no evidence to make them believe that he had passed over. Search parties had combed the area to no avail. The police could no longer put man-hours into the case and suggested that they consider seeking a psychic.

The next day, I had a phone session with the family, and their son started the session by showing me a scene of him climbing rocks. His mother confirmed that he was an avid rock climber. There were many more identifiable statements that proved not only that it was their son that I was connecting with, but that he was, in fact, on the other side.

ALERT

Cases can be perilous. There are many elements for a medium to consider before becoming involved in a case, which could be detrimental to his safety.

He showed me a green Chevrolet pickup truck that was quite dilapidated. The mother confirmed that this was an exact description of his truck. I saw myself sitting in the driver's seat of her son's truck. I was looking out of the windshield at large mountainous rocks. Then, like a camera panning down, I could see the speedometer, then the trip meter. The trip meter had 159 miles displayed. Not sure what to do with this information, I waited for the next piece to see if there was anything that I could give to the parents. Next, their son showed me a map of California, and he put an *X* where their house was. Like a video green screen overlay, I saw the numbers *020* floating over the map. I was told to have the parents start at their home and on a map go 020 degrees 159 miles and put an *X* on that spot. I was told that they would find his truck there, with his body next to it.

The next day, the family went, with notes from the reading the day before, to the police in the jurisdiction of where the truck and body should be found. The area was treacherous and required the use of all-terrain vehicles. Investigators found the pickup truck and the remains of their son's body lying next to it.

Substantiating Current Undisclosed Evidence

A common police investigative tool is to withhold information about a crime from sources outside of their jurisdiction. This is usually information that only the perpetrator or victim would know. A medium helping with a case is obligated to give out all information that he receives. There is a thin line between what the medium receives and what he reveals. He does not want to falsely incriminate the wrong person. The medium may set himself up for some type of liability, or even become a potential suspect by knowing too much detail.

ALERT

A medium must use caution when giving out information not known by the public. There could be legal ramifications, or even charges, for revealing information that could impede an investigation.

›› CASE: SELF-FULFILLING PROPHECY

I traveled to a Midwest state to assist the family of a fifteen-year-old female who had been missing for a month. I had been given no other information, nor any facts or details of the case. I met with police detectives and the parents; the first objective was to establish whether or not the missing girl was alive. I was able to connect with her spirit and give many validations. I knew, immediately, that she was on the other side.

The victim gave me the actual name "Roscoe," who was her boyfriend. She also offered information about the location of the boyfriend's family, in another state. Roscoe would spend weekends with his family there. This is where she claimed her body would be found. The police had already interviewed and cleared Roscoe as a suspect after he passed a polygraph test.

The police could only spend limited time with me—less than two days. I took it upon myself to go to the fast-food place where the victim and Roscoe were employed. As I entered the establishment, I was drawn to a particular booth, so I chose to sit there to have a meal. I could see on the side of the booth that part of the laminate was no longer attached to the wood, and a folded piece of paper was drawing my attention. I removed and opened the paper. On one side was a meticulous drawing of a person. Drawn on the flip side was a human brain; just above that was a 45-caliber pistol, and underneath it a casket. My belief was that the victim had made this drawing.

Since I wanted the parents to verify my intuition, I went to their home. Both parents confirmed the drawing was their daughter's; the style and quality matched many of those on her bedroom walls. They allowed me to view her many drawings, and there was no question as to the similarities. In my opinion, she prophesized her own death and wanted to leave a clue behind.

Because the authorities were going in the wrong direction with the case, the victim found it necessary to disclose evidence, which had obviously been overlooked, to me, the medium.

When I left the area, the case had reached a dead end. In the short time I was there, I uncovered many substantive clues that, with more time, would likely have closed the case.

Pulling the Cases Together

Some things are simply meant to be. There is no magic bullet for stopping crime or healing grief. A medium has been given the tools that may help in many ways; knowing how and when to use them requires skill and patience.

Some information given by spirits requires interpretation. This can give false leads to investigators. Not every case a medium works on will be solved. The role of the medium may be to bring hope to the family while giving a positive direction to an investigation and to introduce new leads.

Law enforcement is not ready to give up investigative techniques that have worked for decades. Many departments who use mediums do so secretly. They will ask for assistance from a medium but not offer him recognition or support. The investigators may have worked on a case for months, and they may expect the medium to come up with explanations in a matter of hours, without the help of evidence or witnesses.

FACT

Law enforcement personnel develop a stronger sixth sense out of necessity. Their safety requires that they "read" people being questioned or detained.

Eventually we all end up on the other side. Some spirits are so happy to be there that they do not converse about the event that caused their demise. Spirits enjoy a free will that we do not comprehend. When asked a direct question, they may answer or simply choose to move on to another topic. Investigators expect communication to be like a telephone call: direct and to the point. We are lucky to have this connection with the other side. We have to respect that it is done by their rules, not ours.

CHAPTER 12

Signs from the Other Side

It has been estimated that 20 percent of the population has received some type of after-death communication (ADC). People of all cultures and religions have talked about these special events that have happened to them following the death of a relative or friend. Sometimes these communications come in the form of dreams, other times in the form of physical objects drawing their attention to the deceased. When a sign is requested, it is not unusual to be surprised by what many think is just a coincidence.

Ways Contact Is Made

It has been stated that over 20 percent of the U.S. population has encountered an after-death communication. There seems to be numerous methods for an ADC contact, and they are thought out and well calculated. A majority of people have the ability to recognize signs coming from the other side, but most of the time just brush them off or think of them as wishful thinking. It is not their intention to try to make the connection more difficult than it is, but it is up to the receiver to be able to pick up the sometimes subtle hints that communication is taking place.

Research and Contact

A type of research process is taken on after the death of an individual to find the best way a sign of contact can be made back to the physical plane. Traits, interests, music, and anything that would associate the deceased with the living is processed and of possible use.

However, there are many reasons why no contact will be made at all, as some individuals do not want to interact with the other plane. Sometimes people are not able to accept the possibility of contact, while others may not be emotionally prepared after a passing.

Smells and Sounds

Studies have shown that distinct memories can be associated with a smell or a sound. Childhood memories are filled with the smells of your favorite foods on holidays and special occasions. Perhaps it's the smell of the leather of a baseball glove or the distinct odor of a favorite relative's perfume. Many remember a favorite song or concert that they attended. These are two of the strongest methods that are used to get the attention of a person on the physical plane. Your connection to these methods has been developed over your entire life, and is easily accessed to get a message through.

Nature

Many times people have a close relationship with the natural surroundings of the physical plane. Within these boundaries are methods of contact that can be arranged to show a sign. They can intercede in the action of the animal world, as well as with plants and the weather. If someone would recognize a sign more easily through the action of an animal or perhaps a significant flower or breeze, then this would be implemented in the choice of contact.

ESSENTIAL

> When you ask for a sign from the other side, it is important to then be willing to accept any communication that comes through. Do not be so quick to dismiss coincidences, as these might be the actual signs that you have requested.

Often the sounds of nature are used for some people, as this brings back many fond memories of past love ones, and can be relaxing at the same time. The sound of the wind blowing through the trees, raindrops hitting the ground, or the ocean crashing on a beach are very good natural sounds that can be used to gain your attention about a passed love one.

The Best Time

The best time of contact is when your mind is at ease and your body relaxed. Seeing that the largest obstacle with the method of communication is interference from outside sources, a time is picked when there is the least amount of outside stimulus grabbing your attention. This stimulus can be the overall activity surrounding you, or even things that are on your mind and have kept you occupied throughout the day.

The timing of the communication depends on the individual and the current state the individual is in, how open he is to receiving a message, and how open he is to the possibility of contact from a deceased loved one. These are important issues that have to be addressed before an attempt can be made.

Also, it is found that when you are approaching waking up from a sound sleep or perhaps a daytime nap, this is also a good time for a connection, as many of your burdens and worries and random thoughts are pushed to the side, making it easier for a sign, a contact, to come through.

The process is not limited to these methods, and spirits have vast interacting abilities within the physical plane. All that is needed is an open mind to the possibility and understanding if no sign is to come.

The Dream State

Sigmund Freud believed that dreams were a means of expressing repressed thought. But today, with advancements in science, dreams are thought to be the product of the brain and the still-misunderstood concept of consciousness. Could it be a combination of both of these theories? Could it be a doorway to the other side that is tapped into for cross-communications?

Stages of Sleep

1. **Stage 1:** This lasts for only a few minutes and is very light sleep. The person can be easily woken up by outside disturbances.
2. **Stage 2:** This stage is a much deeper sleep than Stage 1. Dreams begin to start in this stage with unclear images and vague thoughts drifting in the person's mind. However, outside disturbances will break the sleep even at this stage.
3. **Stage 3:** Muscles become relaxed now and blood pressure, heart rate, and breathing become slow and even. Waking a person in this stage is difficult. Only repeated calling of the person's name or a loud noise can awaken him.
4. **REM Stage:** This is the stage when all dreams occur, as it is the deepest state of sleep. The person is difficult to awaken and will take a few seconds to wake up. In this stage, blood pressure and heart rate fluctuate and rapid eye movement takes place. This stage, also known as the REM state, lasts for about ten minutes. Then the person goes back into deep sleep, or NREM stage. The cycle continues between the REM and NREM stages.

Mechanism of Dreaming

As measured by an EEG (electroencephalograph), the electrical impulses generated by the brain during deep dreamless sleep are less than 3 Hz. However, in REM sleep the waves record 60–70 Hz, which is five times more than the waking state! Since there is no physical cause for such high values, the brain activity must be due to some internal activity or external nonphysical activity. The latter view suggests that dreams are a gateway to the supernatural realm, as one's consciousness begins interacting with other dimensions.

Carl Jung, the founder of analytical psychology, has said, "Dreams have a psychic structure which is unlike that of other contents of consciousness." He also described how some dreams seem prophetic in nature, or telepathic.

QUESTION

How can I remember my dreams?
The best way is to keep a pen and piece of paper near your bedside. When you wake up in the middle of the night, first thing in the morning, or whenever you come out of a daydream and you remember something that's significant, write it down.

Contact

The other side is always trying to make contact through the dream state. It is much easier for them to tap into the subconscious state at that level. Not needing to gain attention through outside conflicting stimulus, the dream state is a "communication connector," a highway that is wide open. As soon as you reach your dream state, the road is open and contact can begin.

QUESTION

How do I know if my dream is a visit to the other realm or just my own thoughts?
You may remember that the colors are more vivid, the sounds are more pronounced, and that you recognize the people you see; you know instinctively that it is different from one of your ordinary dreams. These are all clues that you have actually tapped into the other side of existence.

Communication can be visual, as you can see them and they can see you. Many people can remember encountering relatives and friends in their dreams. They can connect with you through speech and sound, as you might relive or enjoy a moment together in a world that is as solid as the one you currently exist in.

The dream state is used to communicate more complex messages that otherwise would be difficult to send during the waking state. While awake, most people are overwhelmed with stimuli from many different sources. Most have pressing responsibilities, and with them as a distraction, complex messages are difficult to receive.

Daydreaming

Daydreaming is a state that is not only healthy, but also an opportunity for the other side to touch in and give insight and instruction you might need at that time. Many times your mind has slipped into a daydream and wandered from thought to thought. This is very similar to being in meditation; thoughts slow down and begin to wander without focusing on any particular thing at any particular point. So this opening allows easy access to insert creative ideas, problem-solving techniques, and other forms of information that may be needed or wanted at that time.

Clairvoyant Dreams

Parapsychologists like Charles Tart believe that dreams are entry points into another realm. The clairvoyant dreams or prophetic dreams are those that seem to foretell the future. Some claim that dreams are gateways to past lives; others say they are ways of gaining knowledge and understanding complex ideas. Many creative expressions such as music and inventions have been formulated in the dream and daydream state.

According to Higgins, you must first understand the possibility and means of communicating with the other side. "Since the beginning of time, dreams have been the most efficient and easiest way for them to communicate with you." So sleep well, keep an open mind, and enjoy the conversation.

The Need for Contact

When a loved one passes away, it leaves a big hole in your life. Not only is the grief immense, but your life also changes in a big way. Some people are completely shattered by such unfortunate incidents in their lives. But if you believe in the existence of the soul after death, it gives some emotional and mental relief that your loved one is not entirely lost.

Some people have even postulated that the dead feel the need to contact with their loved ones in the material world. This may be to offer solace or to make the presence of the afterlife and the alternate world felt. More and more researchers and doctors today agree on the positive effects of after-death contact. It can be stress relieving and may give new meaning to a person's life after a tragedy.

Alleviation from Grief of Loss of Loved One

Many grief and bereavement studies on after-death contact have revealed that the person experiencing such phenomena usually finds it easier to accept the death and cope with the loss of the loved one. Many feel that the unfinished business or suddenness of loss is diluted by being able to contact the deceased. The continuity of the person's existence in another form after death eases the sense of loss and also gives a feeling of accessibility to the departed person.

In 1995, Allan Botkin, a psychology doctor specializing in posttraumatic stress disorder, claimed that he had devised a method of inducing after-death contact in his bereaving and grieving patients. The experience induced by this methodology left the subjects relieved and feeling closer to their deceased loved one.

However, critics of such methods say that such experiences can leave people even more disturbed and affected.

Emotional Solace and Expression of Love/Caring

In many after-death contacts, the deceased are very often observed saying or communicating solace. They deliver messages such as "I'm okay," "I love you," "Don't worry about me," "Go on with your life," and "I'm watching over you." The spirits, by saying such things, seem to be communicating that they want you to move on with your life, and that they still exist around you and love you like before. Such comforting words can be healing for the grieving person. It can give you the strength to gather the pieces of your life and feel at peace with your and your deceased's existence in different worlds.

It is believed that the spirits of the departed try to establish contact with their loved ones through signs to continue the emotional and spiritual bond that they share with them. It is to remind you of the continuing relationship they have with you, though the modes of communication may have changed since death. It is hypothesized that the spirits exist at a higher vibrational frequency than living beings in the material world. In order to establish contact, both the spirit and the receiver have to adjust their frequencies to find a common ground where they can establish communication.

FACT

Many times spirits just want to communicate that they have "made it" to the other side and that they still exist and are not in any pain. The drama in our daily lives does not interest them, as they seem to see the bigger picture of the meaning of life, which is love.

Expanding Your Consciousness to Understand and Feel the World Beyond Sight

Communicating with the dead is said to expand your consciousness to higher levels. When you tune in to the frequencies of the spiritual world, it allows you to experience and feel things beyond the experience of the material world. You channel energies of the otherworld and enter into realms of larger consciousness. Spirits of the deceased loved ones are said to facilitate such experiences.

Believers of the afterlife strongly advocate making such contacts with your departed to feel closer to them and also have a chance to become more educated about the mysterious yet powerful alternate world of spirits.

Death can be devastating for the person who loses a loved one. It can bring grief, hopelessness, and a great sense of loss to the person's life. Observing signs from the deceased can bring acceptance and peace into the life of such a person. It is important to offer support to people experiencing after-death contacts from the deceased. It may just be a lifesaver and a motivation to carry on, with some belief in human existence after death.

Probability and Statistical Evidence

If you were to establish contact with a deceased love one, it would render peace and emotional comfort in your life. This phenomena of ADC by loved ones has been reported widely throughout the world. Most people experiencing such contacts feel exhilarated after the experience. However, there are also a few cases where people feel scared or refuse to acknowledge the phenomena. In any case, the big question is, how do you know if the signs you are observing are truly from your departed loved ones?

Renowned ADC researchers and authors of *Hello From Heaven!* Bill Guggenheim and Judy Guggenheim interviewed 2,000 people of varying backgrounds between 1988 and 1995 across the United States and Canada and recorded more than 3,300 firsthand accounts of ADC with deceased friends or family members. All such recorded incidents were unaided by any medium, hypnotist, or device.

When studied, these experiences revealed patterns of similarities and could be grouped under some high-level classifications. In many cases, the contacts were established repeatedly or multiple times. Many of these signs were unexpected and their odds of natural occurrence were low.

Ways in Which the Deceased Try to Communicate with Us

Deceased loved ones have been observed to contact the living after death in many ways. Some often recorded and narrated ways of contacts are:

- **Physical sensations and fragrances:** Many subjects experiencing ADC report feeling a physical sensation of touch like a toss of hair, pressing of shoulders, a brush against cheek, etc. Some also smell fragrances that they can relate to the deceased.
- **Synchronicity:** "Meaningful coincidences" that relate to the deceased, like spotting the deceased's name in an unexpected place, like a car's nameplate followed by spotting the deceased's favorite restaurant, are common experiences.
- **Telepathy or hearing a voice:** Some people also get messages from the deceased through either telepathy or an external voice. For example, people have reported hearing the deceased's voice on a telephone after the phone rang.
- **Dreams:** These include both one-way and two-way communication between the deceased and the person experiencing ADC.

When what seems like random acts start to occur around an event, there may be an association between the incidences. It does not matter if the subject is a well-known, explained phenomena or something as misunderstood as the afterlife.

How Do You Know If the Signs Are Real?

This is the question often asked by many skeptics and that plagues the minds of people observing the signs from their deceased loved ones. The answer may just lie in the probability of the happening of the event or statistical proof.

When you observe a sign, think about what the probability of the occurrence of the event is. Is it rare enough, and what is the likelihood of it happening? If the event is highly unlikely and it has occurred, it is considered a potentially true case of ADC. Donna Theisen, author of the book *Childlight: How Children Reach Out to Their Parents from the Beyond*, narrates an incident of ADC from her only son, Michael, a month after his death in an accident. While browsing in a gift shop, she saw two tiny cups lying next to each other with messages "love you Mom" and "Michael." She was engulfed with a warm feeling upon seeing the cups. The odds of these two cups lying together were very low considering the dozens of such items being sold at the shop.

Many people also observe signs on a recurring basis, such as a placement of an object in a particular way or at a particular place every day/week/month, or spotting some animals in an uncharacteristic fashion several times. There are also others who observe several signs in quick succession. Such incidents establish a connection that such signs may not be mere coincidences but attempts of contact by the deceased.

Carl Jung has said that such "meaningful coincidences" or "signs" cannot always be traced to a casual relationship. Many of these may be connected to some unexplainable causal principle. He called this "synchronicity." Though many scholars have debated this idea, there are some who stand by it and agree that such events could be triggered by forces beyond our understanding.

Physical Methods Used to Gain Attention

It seems that dreams are a favorite way of communicating between the living and the afterlife. The fact that you are in a relaxed state seems to affect the process of exchanging information. Physical methods are also used, as they give a tangible sense to the contact that a dream state exchange will not provide.

An object used to get your attention can be of solid matter, something that takes up a particular space, but also might be more fluid or something that will stand out—anything to make you take notice and recognize that the departed is trying to connect with you. There have been many ways of how people accept signs, and depending on the individual, the departed will decide the best method of making contact.

Often the objects are ones that trigger fond memories of the loved one who has passed to the other side. These objects could be family heirlooms, a recent gift, or an object that is presented to you that reminds you of the person you were thinking about. At times the object is physically placed where you will notice it, while most often they will direct your attention to the object that you might have over looked. All of these methods and more are utilized with the recognition and sense you gain from a particular object.

If someone is reminded of a family member who drove a big black Cadillac or perhaps had a coin collection then these are the objects that a loved one would use to gain your attention. Other times it could be a ring of significant value, a card one had received, a handwritten letter, or a small token of one's appreciation. There are literally hundreds of different objects that can be presented to you for you to recognize that a sign has been provided by your loved ones.

Different objects will be significant to certain individuals, depending on the relationship to the one that is being contacted. Therefore, the baseball bat to one person might mean nothing, but a baseball bat to someone else whose loved one played baseball throughout his entire life could be the perfect object.

Case Studies

After the loss of a relative or friend, it is not unusual to receive a sign from the other side—millions of people have reported this type of occurrence. It does not seem to make any difference in cultural or religious terms, as the recipients have told of these stories throughout history.

›› CASE: USING SCENT TO MAKE CONTACT

This particular event happened a couple of months after my mother passed to spirit.

That evening, I went out to dinner with a close friend of mine, who had met my mother a few years before she passed. She and my mother got along very well and enjoyed each other's company. This woman was open to the whole idea of contact—or, I should say the possibility of something like that. However, she still had major reservations. When I refer to "reservations" and "open to the whole idea," it means that she, like many of us, is either a little scared by the whole subject or that she might have conflicting thoughts because of her religious upbringing.

After dinner at a local restaurant, we decided to return to the house. It was midspring and all the windows in the house were closed. When we arrived, we entered through the front door and went into the kitchen to put some leftovers into the refrigerator. We had to walk through the dining room in order to access the kitchen.

We might have been in the kitchen for less than three minutes. As we re-entered the dining room, I immediately smelled the most robust scent of freshly brewed coffee that I had smelled since my mother's passing. This was not just the aroma of a cup of coffee that one might have with dinner. Instead, this was the smell you would encounter on a holiday, when a giant urn would be set up to serve a large group. The smell was not there just a few minutes before.

My mother loved her coffee. At the end of her life, she was barely able to consume anything, but she always requested a cup of coffee.

As I continued to walk through the dining room, which had been the scene of many a holiday gathering, I stopped myself from asking my friend, "Do you smell that coffee?" I wanted to get an untainted answer from her without any suggestion from me about what was actually taking place.

Consequently, I just stopped, turned to her and said, "Do you find anything different?" This could have referred to any number of things—from the furniture to the wallpaper to the next room coming up or even the kitchen we had just been in. She stopped, looked at me, and said in the most surprised voice, "Oh my God. It smells like coffee." The whole room was filled with this delicious aroma. She looked at me, and asked where it came from. I told her it must be from my mother, because that would have been a perfect sign to let me know she was around and still with me.

It is important to mention that neither one of us had coffee at dinner. I had not had any in about two years, nor was there even a bean in the house.

We then continued to the living room. As we sat in the living room for a couple of minutes, I mentioned to her that I bet if she went back into the dining room right now, the smell would be gone. She said, "That would be impossible, because the scent of coffee lingers for quite some time. I laughed and said, "Go and see." She immediately got up from her chair, walked back into the dining room, and let out a gasp as she said, "It's gone, totally gone."

To this day, my friend continues to be amazed by what happened that night; and, her witnessing that sign with me brought me great joy, since so many times these signs happen to us while we are alone.

ESSENTIAL

When signs are given it seems that they like to pick objects or some specific thing that is associated with them to gain your attention. Often the connection is made right away and at other times doubt sets in and then a missed opportunity is realized.

» CASE: CHARMING

After my aunt had been dead for about a month, one early Sunday morning, as we often did in the past, my husband and I decided to go to the local flea market. It was a beautiful, warm day and we thought it would be nice to get out and walk around. Right after we arrived, he drifted off to look at tools and I went to browse the aisles. As I strolled in the nice clean air, I remember thinking, "Gee, Aunt Eileen, why haven't you contacted me lately?"

I then thought to myself, "Oh, it is silly to wonder that. I'm sure she's just fine." Just about two minutes later, I found myself rummaging through a table of costume jewelry on which there was a tower, which had necklaces and charms hanging from it. I reached up and turned the tower once to the right, and there before me was a gold necklace with a charm that spelled out "Eileen." My aunt had a wonderful collection of charms she had assembled over the years, and she had been fond of buying charms for me as gifts. This was a gift from her that she didn't have to buy, but it was just as precious to me as any other charm in her collection. (Case studies taken from *Hello . . . Anyone Home? A Guide on How Our Deceased Loved Ones Try to Contact Us through the Use of Signs*, 2009)

CHAPTER 13

Supporting Evidence

For thousands of years there have always been things that go bump in the night. Stories have been handed down through the centuries in writings, paintings, and folklore. The modern-day debate about unexplained phenomena has begun to be looked at with a more scientific view. More people are willing to share their experiences in today's world as a closer look is taken at what has been happening to millions of people throughout history.

Ghosts, Apparitions, and Hauntings

The fear of ghosts and the supernatural is ingrained in every human being right from childhood. Very few people actually accept that there are things that exist beyond our understanding. Some simply choose to believe that paranormal phenomena are just figments of the imagination. Some ghosts and apparitions have been revealed as fakes and illusions, but there are still many instances from different parts of the world that cannot be dismissed with rational explanations.

Observations of entities from the otherworld can broadly be divided into ghosts (or apparitions) and hauntings. Contrary to popular belief, hauntings are most commonly found. A haunting is a "replay" of sorts of a happening that occurred years ago. Certain shocking or horrific incidents affect the location where they take place so significantly that the incident is repeated as if it were a ghostly movie. Specific circumstances trigger this "movie," or it may just happen unexpectedly. Some researchers theorize that it may be some kind of specific point in time, caught in a repeating loop, over and over.

FACT

Many tourists to Gettysburg have reported speaking with a man, bare-foot, dressed in ragged clothes and wearing a floppy hat. The "man" disappears after exchanging a few words. Actors relaxing during the filming of the movie *Gettysburg* encountered a ghost that handed out a few rounds of ammunition. The ammo was later examined and found to be identical to what was used during the real battle. It was more than 100 years old.

The Triangular Field, the scene of the Gettysburg massacre in 1863, still retains an imprint of the incidents that unfolded on the battlefields. Witnesses report seeing Confederate sharpshooters taking aim from the tree cover.

A ghost or apparition is different from a haunting—it is an actual physical form or manifestation of a long-dead living being. Sometimes the ghost can actually interact with the environment and people present there. In some cases, the living may sense distinctive smells, sounds, or even voices, which can be associated with the long-dead person.

Apparitions or ghosts are remnants of the life force of humans. It is generally believed that souls linger in our world as ghosts because they have "unfinished business." But there are many ghosts and apparitions that continue to stay on here because of a strong emotional bond with the living.

Different Types of Ghosts

There are several different types of ghosts you could encounter, and the following lists some of the most common that have been discovered.

Intelligent Ghosts

These are often apparitions that return to communicate something of importance to the living. Many cases have been reported of such apparitions saving living family members from harm or helping them in times of crisis. Farmer James Chaffin appeared before his second son four years after his death in 1921 to reveal the secret location of his last will and testament. Race car driver Dale Earnhardt, Jr., stated on the news show *60 Minutes* that he believed his deceased father, Dale Earnhardt, Sr., a seven-time NASCAR Cup champion, had pulled him to safety after his race car crashed and burned. "I don't have an explanation for it other than when I got into the infield care center, I had my PR man by the collar, screaming at him to find the guy that pulled me out of the car," says Earnhardt, Jr. "He was like, 'Nobody helped you get out.' And I was like, 'That's strange, because I swear somebody had me underneath my arms and was carrying me out of the car. I mean, I swear to God."

Poltergeists

Poltergeists are manifestations of a restless soul in the form of telekinetic activity. The presence of such a ghost may result in moving objects, sounds, equipment malfunction, and other similar activity. Poltergeists are also known to create fires in different parts of the home or make words appear on surfaces.

The most interesting and indeed touching of these is the report of a poltergeist named Danny, aged seven, who wouldn't let anyone sleep in the bed that his mother died in. The case came into the spotlight in the late 1990s when the bed was bought by the Cobb family in Georgia. The poltergeist not only wrote down its name and age but also categorically warned the family with a written message saying, "No one sleep in bed."

Crisis Apparitions

Crisis apparitions often appear when the actual living person is undergoing the occurrence that will lead to his death. The most famous of these is the 1893 sighting of Vice Admiral George Tyron by guests to his wife's tea party back at home. The vice admiral, dressed in official formals, walked through his home at the exact moment his ship sank with him off the coast of Syria.

Other Famous Ghosts/Apparitions and Hauntings

Many hauntings and ghost sightings have been witnessed and experienced over the years by several people. In fact, there are some places in the world that are considered "haunted," or more susceptible to paranormal activity.

FACT

According to a 2005 Gallup poll, 37 percent of Americans said they believe in haunted houses, while 46 percent say they don't, and 16 percent aren't sure. Fifty-six percent of young adults between the ages of eighteen and twenty-nine believe, but belief drops to 39 percent among thirty to forty-nine-year-olds, and 30 percent among fifty- to sixty-four-year-olds.

Among the many well-known haunted places is the Winchester mansion, home of Sarah Winchester, widow of William Wirt Winchester, who was heir to the Winchester Repeating Arms Company. This mansion is considered a place where many spirits reside.

A relic of World War II, the ship the *Queen Mary* is the site of many hauntings by passengers who lost their lives there. Witnesses have seen a little girl, who broke her neck and died when she slid down the ship's banister, wandering about, looking for her mommy. There are many other reports of ghostly phenomena onboard.

The fear associated with any kind of paranormal activity prompts victims to look for ways to get rid of these otherworldly visitors. Most often ghost hunting is an attempt to help the restless spirit move on to the next plane of afterlife. A medium who can communicate with the spirit tries to convey to the ghost that it is time to go. Ghosts that linger in this world to resolve issues or to stay close to loved ones have been persuaded to leave in this way.

ALERT

In some cases, the ghost may be driven by anger or revenge and be unwilling to leave. In such cases, exorcists may be called in to force the spirit to go. However, the success of an exorcism cannot be measured with any accuracy. There have been incidents when hauntings and ghostly visitations have ceased temporarily after an exorcism only to return after a while. Many different religions and cultures have their own way of dealing with unwanted ghosts and hauntings.

Photographic Evidence

Proponents of various theories on life after death may have insufficient factual data to back their beliefs, but may find some support in photographic evidence of ghosts, also known as "spirit photography." Spirit photography, which historically was believed to be the effect of radiation on photosensitive film, first started in the late 1800s when a Boston engraver named William Mumler stumbled upon a puzzling image while doing some experimental self-photographs. In one of his self-pictures, the form of a young woman appeared to be standing next to him. He recognized the figure as one of his late cousins.

Following this, Mumler ventured into spirit photography, which in those times was done using a glass plate coated with a film of collodion (gun cotton dissolved in ether), and containing iodide of potassium. To sensitize this glass plate, it was dipped into a silver nitrate bath immediately before taking a photograph.

Spiritualists and prominent photographers including William Black, a leading photographer in Boston and inventor of photography's acid nitrate bath, investigated Mumler's pictures and his methods, but was unable to find any evidence of fraud at the time.

But while there were fewer believers than skeptics, modern researchers like Alfred Russel Wallace, a co-developer of the theory of evolution, did express belief in the possibility that not all alleged spirit photos were fraudulent.

The *British Journal of Photography* in the 1870s made some references to spirit photography, and one of its editors, J. Traille Taylor, who was a skeptic, studied and experimented with it, using his own camera and assistants, and occasionally produced mysterious results.

Sir William Crookes, a chemist and physicist, studied psychic phenomenon, including spirit photography, and was convinced that it could exist, although his scientific colleagues in the Royal Society remained doubtful.

Famous Spirit Photographs

While William Mumler produced a number of spirit photographs during his time, none of them were as striking as his picture of Mary Lincoln with what appears to be the recognizable image of her late husband, Abraham Lincoln, standing behind her.

FACT

A mysterious photograph taken in 1895 at the Combermere Abbey in Cheshire, England, showed the image of a man seated in one of the chairs in the library of the house. The photograph was taken at a time when no one but the photographer was in the room. While the features of the man in the photo were hazy, many who saw it thought that it resembled Lord Combermere, who was deceased at the time the photo was taken.

In September 1936, Captain Provand, a professional photographer for Britain's *Country Life* magazine, took a series of photos of Raynham Hall in Norfolk, England, one of which showed a female silhouette that Provand did not see at the time the photo was taken, descending a staircase. Experts examined this photograph, and they failed to provide a logical explanation for it. In fact, author and researcher Thurston Hopkins believed in its authenticity and said, "It may well be the most genuine ghost photograph we possess," adding, "and no study of the supernatural is complete without a reference to it."

Due to the nature of the subjects of spirit photography, there is an understandable doubt about its authenticity, although some photos have withstood scrutiny and allegations of fraud.

Modern Spirit Photography

With technological advances in photography equipment and methods, Chris Bailey of Grimstone, Inc., a scientific research organization specializing in investigation of paranormal activities, confirms that it is possible to capture spirits in pictures using digital cameras under certain conditions.

A drawback in using digital cameras for spirit photography, however, is that they do not furnish a negative, making it possible to enhance the photos. However, technology has become more advanced in revealing this type of manipulation. In its defense, digital photography does take away the argument that the ghostly appearances are related to the chemical reactions of the older film.

Electronic Voice Phenomenon

Electronic voice phenomenon (EVP) is a paranormal occurrence in which noises resembling human speech, but not attributable to a living being, are heard in recordings made on electronic devices. The noises are said to be of a supernatural nature and apparently produced by spirits of the dead.

This paranormal phenomenon is claimed to be outside the realm of scientific and normal explanation. The generated voices are usually comprised of words or short phrases uttered quickly. Those experiencing the phenomenon hear background voices of unknown origin on their recordings.

EVP Observations and Research

The early nineteenth century saw a good deal of interest in the subject of spirit communication. Many experiments were attempted to communicate with the spirit world through mediums and Ouija boards. From this interest sprung the idea to try to record voices of those from the other side.

Atilla von Szalay, an American photographer, put together a custom-made recording device to record the voices of spirits in 1956. In the following years, he successfully recorded what were perceived to be spirit voices, and published the results of his experiments in American psychic research journals.

Swedish movie producer and painter Friedrich Jürgenson, considered the pioneer of EVP recordings, was one of the few to dedicate his life to the understanding of the phenomenon. As Jürgenson was listening to his recording of bird sounds, he was amazed to hear human voices on the tape, even when there was no human presence at the scene of recording. After further recording experiments and subsequent studies of the voices, one of which belonged to his deceased mother, he concluded that the recorded voices were those of the dead.

Konstantin Raudive, a Latvian parapsychologist, made several thousand recordings in strict laboratory conditions to investigate this phenomenon. He was successfully able to interpret the recorded messages, spoken in Latvian, German, and French. He would also invite people to listen to the recorded voices and provide their interpretations. Dedicating the latter half of his life to the study of this phenomenon, he published *Breakthrough* in 1971.

QUESTION

How do you make EVP recordings?
Raudive employed several different ways of making EVP recordings. These included recording the microphone voices, where a tape recorder is left running with nobody talking in the vicinity. The other was recording radio voices, where the white noise from a radio, which is not tuned to any station, is recorded.

EVP has now been found using digital recorders that use a device without a physical tape; therefore the phenomenon cannot be associated with the older forms of contact.

Why Does EVP Happen?

The scientific explanations for the phenomenon include radio interference, cross-modulation, static, and ionospheric ducting, which cause disturbances heard as noises on tape. Some sound engineers who have offered to provide their views on EVP claim to have never experienced the phenomenon, even as they spend most of their time listening to hard disk and tape recordings. They attribute the noises to low equipment quality and believe that the noises are misconstrued to be spirit voices.

There are also psychological explanations for the phenomenon; pareidolia is one of them. Pareidolia is a condition where the human brain wrongly interprets random sound patterns to be familiar patterns, thus equating the noise recordings to human speech. However this does not explain how multiple people can hear the same voice and message at different times from the same recoding.

There are still others who believe that EVP does have paranormal roots, suggesting that spirits, ghosts, and discarnate beings are attempting to communicate with the living world through electronic devices. Researchers, even established scientists, across the world continue to explore this explanation through controlled equipment research. Sarah Estep, an EVP researcher, set up the American Association of Electronic Voice Phenomena in 1982, dedicated to ongoing research and spreading of awareness about the phenomenon. The organization currently has more than 200 members.

Apports: The Materialization of Matter

The astonishing and mysterious phenomenon of the materialization of objects out of thin air are called "apports," and at times are associated with spiritual séances and mediumship. Apports can and do happen outside of these events, and might even occur during one's daily life.

ESSENTIAL

The probability of someone misplacing an object and then finding it in the same place is rather high, as multitasking and the responsibilities of daily living cause many to misplace these simple items. But there are occasions when the possibility of an apport could be the answer for that maddening search.

Have you ever lost your keys? Perhaps you have lost a piece of jewelry or a cell phone, only to find them right where they were supposed to be. You swear you looked there twice, even three times, and maybe had a friend look there too, but there was nothing. Then all of a sudden, the missing object appeared.

While much evidence has been collected from séances, some believe the apports to be gifts from demised loved ones, having significant symbolic meanings for those receiving them. Apport appearances during séances, as well as in ordinary daily life, have included jewelry, flowers, keys, pens, coins, and on rare occasions, live animals, which materialized on tables or in laps of those present at the séance. People going about their daily routines have reported feathers floating down upon them, within a closed space or home, when the thought of a loved one entered their minds. This phenomenon has been witness by friends and family members, and has no explanation.

Explaining Apports

The phenomenon of apportation is considered exceptional and one of a kind. While many exhibitions of apports have been proven to be fraudulent, apport mediums have demonstrated the phenomenon to audiences of skeptics, researchers, and medical men under highly supervised conditions. With no signs of fraud evident, researchers have been stumped to explain the phenomenon. For the sake of understanding the phenomenon, one particular theory has been proposed.

Nineteenth-century German professor Johann Zollner put forward the theory of a fourth dimension to explain the phenomenon. The objects are said to be lifted into this four-dimensional space and transported to the desired three-dimension space, similar to lifting an object from an enclosure and keeping it outside. It has been proposed that psychics possess a four-dimensional way of seeing and perceiving things, which is a higher order of experience from the general nonmedium/psychic population.

With regard to séances, the theory put forward to explain apports is that spirits, through their will power, are capable of disintegrating the apport into its basic molecular shape without changing its form. This form is capable of passing through all matter that it encounters on its journey to the scene of the séance. The medium, again through will power, is capable of reintegrating the object. This theory is based on the belief that there is a fourth state of matter associated with higher molecular malleability. In this state, the disintegrated object becomes invisible. Also, as per the laws of science, disintegration is a thermic reaction, one reason why metal and stone apports are searing hot on arrival.

The theories proposed are breathtaking, as they require a whole new perspective and a different, more open-minded view of looking at spiritual or psychic phenomena. Those who have not experienced the phenomenon may find it hard to imagine a fourth dimension or the superior powers of apport mediums, but those from the scientific community who have experienced and researched the phenomenon are convinced of its paranormal nature. With the study of quantum physics and string theory, the idea of multiple dimensions is not as far-fetched as earlier researches had thought.

Animal Reactions to Human Death

Countless people have shared the loss of a dear pet that has become a close companion or member of the family. However, what happens when a pet loses its owner? Are animals capable of not only sensing but mourning their loss as well? If a pet recently faced with the death of its owner acts oddly, is it possible it's sensing or seeing its deceased owner's spirit? This section will examine the possibility that animals' exceptional senses grant them a gateway into the paranormal that humans are oblivious to while detailing pets' grieving processes.

It's common knowledge that animals possess senses that are far superior to humans. Yet, according to Linda Cole in her article "Can Pets See Ghosts?" it seems that their senses are so finely tuned that they can perceive paranormal activity that humans are not able to. She also comments on animals' astounding senses in her inquisitive article, debating whether animals are seeing ghosts or merely behaving oddly:

> *Compared to us, our pets have phenomenal senses we can't come close to. Their hearing is far superior to ours. They can sniff out cancer in people and find hidden explosives. They know, sometimes hours before we do, that a storm is brewing and they need little light to navigate around the furniture in the living room.*

Most find the concept that animals are capable of seeing ghosts utterly ridiculous and dismiss the notion without further consideration. But few would argue against the fact that numerous people have witnessed odd, inexplicable behavior in their pets, like a dog staring intensely at a deceased owner's empty chair, then begin to bark and react in an agitated manner, or a cat reaching out and batting the air.

There are many mysteries to life we can't explain and there's no definitive testing we can use to prove that ghosts share our dimension. Pets, on the other hand, don't try to analyze or examine evidence. They see what they see. If pets really can see ghosts, the only way they can tell us is by their head and eye movements or odd behavior as they follow something through a room or up a staircase.

Clearly, there are processes at work in the universe undetectable to the human eye, ear, nose, and tactile sensitivity. However, animals exhibit outward signs of grief when their owners pass away that are easily observable to their new caretaker.

FACT

Bereavement, grief, mourning, and deep-seated emotions are not foreign to pets that suffer the loss of their owner. Numerous caretakers have observed the acute distress animals are afflicted with in the absence of their friend, companion, and teacher.

Despite the fact it cannot be proven, the notion that animals may be capable of detecting the presence of a paranormal being, such as a spirit or ghost, is made possible by examining their far superior senses and noting inexplicable behaviors. Pets are commonly considered members of the family and like any familial element, they react to the loss of a cherished companion with depression, anxiety, and possibly the sense that their deceased owners' spirit has lingered behind and is still with them.

Case Studies

Ghostly sightings are not restricted to only some places in the world. Every big city and little town has its own share of weird happenings, spooky places, and unexplained visitations. But there are a few places and locations where the intensity of such paranormal activity touches a peak. More than a handful of witnesses have confirmed the presence of otherworldly entities at these locations. Expert psychics and researchers have conducted tests in these locations and come away with certain evidence of a ghostly presence.

The *Queen Mary* Haunting

The imposing hull of the RMS *Queen Mary* has become an inseparable part of the landscape at Long Beach, California. The ship sailed the seas from the years 1936 to 1967 and transported sick and wounded soldiers during wartimes. But it is not the sleek lines or the historic importance of this seventy-year-old ship that draws visitors. The ship is home to many ghostly entities and is the site of many recorded hauntings.

The most poignant of these ghosts is the little girl who broke her neck sliding down the banister. The girl still roams the pool area with her favorite teddy in her arms. Another famous haunting manifests itself as knocks and lights near the engine room 13. Seaman John Henry was crushed to death by the heavy door of this room.

Visitors have also heard frantic knocks and bangs on the sides of the ship. These are said to be caused by the ghostly crew of the cruiser HMS *Curacao*. The *Queen Mary* plowed into this ship and left the 300-odd crew members to die in the freezing waters.

Several paranormal investigators have studied the unexplained occurrences on board this ship and failed to come up with rational explanations.

The Site of the Battle of Gettysburg

Gettysburg, Pennsylvania, was the site of the historic battle that sealed the fate of the Confederate Army during the American Civil War in 1863. By the time the Confederates retreated, they had lost over 28,000 men, whose bodies littered the streets of Gettysburg.

Even before the carnage, soldiers of the Union Army were aided by a silent ghostly soldier who led them to Gettysburg and disappeared. Some believe it was George Washington come to help his men.

There have been innumerable reports of ghostly sightings, and many have heard the screams and groans of the long-dead wounded soldiers at this site. In the Triangular Field, visitors have reported seeing ghostly Confederate soldiers taking careful aim through the foliage.

At Devil's Den, the site of another heavy assault during the battle, electronic equipment fails mysteriously only to start functioning perfectly when it is set up elsewhere.

ALERT

Gettysburg College has its share of ghosts. The haunted sentry atop its Pennsylvania Hall makes his daily rounds even to this day.

The electrical equipment malfunctions and the various smells, sounds, and sights experienced by well-known researchers have served to convince that this site certainly holds more than the living.

The Tower of London

The fact that the walls of the Tower of London stood witness to some of the most brutal and heartless killings ever recorded makes this one of Britain's most famous landmarks and one of the most haunted places on the planet. The first construction at this site dates back to 1066. The towers were later additions to the original castle.

Both Queen Anne Boleyn and Lady Jane Grey, who were beheaded there in the sixteenth century, make frequent appearances in the Tower even today. The gruesome execution of Lady Salisbury has been replayed on many occasions, witnessed by many visitors. In 1541, the executioner chased the unfortunate woman with his ax after she refused to put her neck on the chopping block. The Salt Tower is another area where supernatural beings are said to roam. Dogs are deathly afraid of this place and will refuse to go in.

Guards have reported sightings of two small ghosts that apparently move down the stairs holding hands. These are the two young princes, Richard and Edward, incarcerated in the tower. These princes mysteriously vanished from the tower in 1483. Many believed that the soon-to-be crowned Richard III had them murdered in the tower secretly. The unearthing of a chest in 1674 containing the skeletons of two children has led credence to this theory.

The Tower of London continues to be the site of many such hauntings. Skeptics and believers alike have seen the various specters and experienced the various sensations, sounds, and lights that give evidence of things beyond the ordinary within these hoary walls.

Whether it is a famous haunted house or an entire town, the fact remains that not one but many have experienced the same phenomena and seen the same hauntings or ghostly apparitions in these places. The accuracy of the descriptions and research to date clearly shows that these reports cannot be coincidences or fakes.

CHAPTER 14

Deathbed Visitations

Stories throughout history have explored the concept of something extraordinary happening at the time of physical death. People have explained that they have been in contact with deceased loved ones, angelic beings, and visions of heaven, creating a sense of peace around the time of their transitions. Many cases that seemed to be isolated actually have similar characteristics—even crossing religious and cultural boundaries.

A Long History

Deathbed visitations, or visions, (DBV) is a phenomenon in which people close to death experience visions of deceased family members, loved ones, angels, or a different world. Most people who claim to have experienced this phenomenon were terminally ill patients who died shortly following the incident. The visions usually have a positive effect on people on their death-beds, with most feeling at peace and facing death without fear. Some also feel elated and reassured that they are journeying on to a new world, where they can unite with loved ones they have lost.

Early Historical References of Deathbed Visitations

Historical literature through the ages has several references of death-bed visitations, transcending race, religion, and culture. One of the earliest references dates as far back as 1350 B.C. in Egypt. It is a record on papyrus, now in the British Museum, and attempts interpretations of deathbed visions. Many religious texts including the Bible have also made references to the phenomenon.

In the twelfth century, St. Bogumilus, on his deathbed, saw a vision of Mother Mary and the baby Jesus, surrounded by angels, welcoming him to heaven. In the fourteenth century, St. Alexis Falconieri had a vision of baby Jesus, in which he placed a crown of roses on his head while white doves flew about the room. In a different incident, Anchoress Julian of Norwich in 1373 experienced sixteen visions of "divine love" as she lay dying from a serious illness. She made a miraculous recovery and went on to describe her visions in two books.

Deathbed Visitations in the Twentieth and Twenty-First Centuries

Sir William Barrett, physics professor at Dublin's Royal College, was one of the few from the early twentieth century to investigate the phenomenon. He recorded his scientific research on the subject in his book *Death-Bed Visions*. His interest was triggered by an incident reported by his wife, an obstetrician. She recounted her experience with a woman who lay dying of hemorrhage after she had just delivered a baby. The woman, named Doris, began to speak to someone, who was presumably her deceased father.

What was interesting was that she also began to refer to her deceased sister Vida, who had passed away just three weeks before and whose death had been kept secret from Doris.

FACT

Barrett discovered some surprising aspects of deathbed visitations during his study. He came across instances where the dying persons would see visions of dead friends or family members who they thought were alive. He also found cases where children saw angels without wings, contrary to the normal impressions of angels children hold.

After Barrett, Dr. Karlis Osis of the American Society for Psychical Research conducted extensive research on the phenomenon in the 1960s and 1970s, analyzing several thousand cases and surveying more than 1,000 nurses, doctors, and caregivers. He attempted to study the consistencies and similarities in the experiences between those belonging to Western and Eastern cultures. After conducting extensive research on the subject in India and subsequent comparisons with those from the West, he concluded that the cultural differences have no major impact.

Dr. Carla Wills-Brandon, a researcher on the subject in recent times, has been studying the phenomenon since the late 1990s. Her book *One Last Hug Before I Go* recounts her own as well as many other deathbed visitation experiences.

Various Explanations

Medical professionals argue that these visions occur because the functioning of the brain is affected as a person nears death. The reasons could vary from lack of oxygen, influence of medicines and drugs, to the brain entering into a dreamlike state of REM sleep.

What's so unique about the phenomenon of DBVs, compared to other parapsychological phenomena, is that most of the twentieth- and twenty-first-century visions have been experienced in scientific settings, that is, hospitals. Doctors and nurses who have known patients experiencing DBVs claim that many of these patients had a coherent thought process and did not appear to have had mere hallucinations. Some of them were also not on any kind of medication or drugs that may have resulted in strange experiences. Some patients were even well aware of their existing surroundings and were able to recount the experience vividly. More research into the phenomena is needed to draw conclusions, but researchers are seriously considering the possibility of paranormal activity.

What Is Seen and Heard

During deathbed visitations, it is believed that these beings appear in front of the dying person to help them with the transition from life to death. John W. White, founding member of International Association for Near-Death Studies and author of *A Practical Guide to Death and Dying*, states, "Death challenges us to find the meaning of life, and with it, genuine happiness. It is nature's way of goading us to discover our true condition, our real self—beyond the transience and ephemerally of this material world. And not only this world, but *all* worlds."

There has been a massive increase in the number of reported instances of deathbed visitations, so much so that scientists have stepped in, in order to ascertain the precise cause of this phenomenon. In particular, the scientific world wishes to identify whether these deathbed visitations are anything more than a manifestation of the desires and needs of the person who is dying, or whether there is some supernatural explanation for it all.

Defining Deathbed Visitations

In essence, deathbed visitations are so called because they occur whenever a person is terminally ill and his death is imminent. While the actual content of the visions differ, the basic principle is the same: the dying person sees angels or loved ones who have died appearing before him. Sometimes, this can happen during a person's last moments, when she is literally moments or even seconds from death.

Accounts of deathbed visitations are overwhelmingly positive. Many state that they have been a tremendous source of comfort and peace during the most difficult time in their lives. Terminally ill people have reported that they have been able to accept their fate, and that all doubt and fear have been summarily cast aside with the visitation.

ESSENTIAL

Deathbed visitations temporarily uplift the mood and state of health of the dying person; they feel a sudden sense of elation and peace, and are able to "cross" the line between life and death with ease.

Common Deathbed Experiences

Perhaps one of the most curious aspects of deathbed experiences is that they transcend cultural and social barriers, meaning there is an element of universality associated with them. The following is a breakdown of the most common visions:

- **Crowded rooms:** In this experience, the person is confronted by people from her life, people who she has made a positive impact on, and who have returned to assist the ill person in her hour of need.
- **Angels:** Some people see angels as the stereotypical white light and winged creatures; others simply report a ball of light that emanates a quiet, gentle power. An unusual yet common experience is the appearance of angels without wings, mostly seen by children in their final moments.
- **Stairs/tunnel:** Another common vision is one in which the ill person is confronted with a stairway or tunnel that he needs to climb. The individual is compelled to do so, due to unforeseen forces.
- **Deceased relatives:** Dying people most commonly report seeing familiar people, usually deceased relatives who have come to take them to their world.
- **Sounds/words:** It has also been reported that the comments made by the beings, be they angels or words from God, have provided solace and comfort to the dying person.

To those experiencing the event, it seems there is life after death, and it's a separate world and existence. The angels, deceased relatives, light, and everything else that is seen and heard increases the probability of the existence of an afterlife.

As Dr. Elisabeth Kübler-Ross, a pioneer in near-death studies and author of the revolutionary book *On Death and Dying*, says, "Death is a transition into a higher state of consciousness where you continue to perceive, to understand, to laugh, to be able to grow, and the only thing you lose is something that you don't need any more—and that is your physical body."

Supporting Those Who Experience Deathbed Phenomena

Patients experiencing the phenomena are enthusiastic about sharing it with those close to them, which often includes loved ones and hospital staff attending them. Nurses, caregivers, and loved ones of those who have experienced deathbed phenomenon should have an open mind and empathize with the patients. They don't have to believe it or seek answers; just listening and being there will make a positive difference.

It is reported that the experiences are comforting to not just the patients but also to those around them. Pediatrician Melvin Morse, in his book *Parting Visions*, says that deathbed experiences are empowering and remove fear of death from the patients' minds. They also have a healing effect on family members, who feel at ease, knowing that the dying person did not feel unhappiness or remorse in his last days.

Scientific Studies

In *Encyclopedia of the Unseen World*, Constance Victoria Briggs discusses the form communication takes between the dying and those from the realm beyond death. Reportedly, these communications are often, but not always, telepathic in form. Briggs states, "Research shows that the communication can come in a number of different ways and may occur in the waking state, the meditative state, or the dream state." Communication can be auditory, involving hearing actual voices, or internally, as with thoughts entering one's mind. Deathbed visitation communication can also be visual, seeing a person's spirit with one's eyes open or closed. The spirit-person may be seen fully or in part, and often appears younger than she was at the time of death, and more vibrant, calm, and happy. Briggs explains that the dying individual can also often vividly feel a presence, often accompanied by touch or smell sensations.

Biological Explanations

Many scientists have outlined biologically based reasons that, they say, cause people to experience what only "feels" like out-of-body experiences or visions of loved ones. Melvin Morse, a pediatrician based in Seattle, Washington, has done extensive research in the area of near-death experiences by children, and argues that such limited theories amount to "reductionistic materialism"—basically explaining away anything nonmaterialistic. His research offers what has been dubbed an "interactionist approach," an explanation that encompasses both biology and psychology. Scientists like Morse do not rule out or discredit the notion that one can indeed communicate with deceased loved ones while one approaches death.

In a survey of scientific studies published in *The Near-Death Experience: A Reader*, Dr. Morse found that research not only confirms the reality of deathbed visitations and visions, but also corroborates other reported near-death phenomenon: "Research on near-death experiences validates a host of death-related visions, including premonitions of death, pre-death visions, and post-death visitations. NDEs cannot be understood as an isolated phenomenon, but should be interpreted as being a part of a spectrum of spiritual events which happen to the dying, their families, and caretakers. The salient feature of the NDE is that it is a mystical spiritual experience superimposed over ordinary reality, which is also the hallmark of the death-related vision."

Others Experiencing the Phenomena

Some studies have also looked not only into reports of deathbed visitations between the dying and a loved one, but also by those present who are not dying. The Southwest SIDS Research Institute performed a retrospective case control study focusing on premonitions of sudden infant death syndrome. They found that 21 percent of parents had a premonition of their child's death, sometimes involving hearing or seeing spirits of loved ones or angels, and 7 percent had recorded these premonitions beforehand. Relatives are also reported to have post-death visitations, "typically described in the context of a dream or a waking vision as involving a vividly real hallucination of a dead relative, patient, or friend superimposed over ordinary reality."

FACT

Hallucinations Versus Deathbed Visitations

Peter Fenwick, a doctor of medicine and psychology from the Institute of Psychiatry at King's College in London, who has conducted both retrospective and prospective studies into these and related phenomena, reiterated this sentiment in a lecture for the International Association for Near-Death Studies 2004 Annual Conference, entitled "Science and Spirituality: A Challenge for the 21st Century." He marks the difference between hallucinations and near-death and death-related visions. He notes that while people most often forget hallucinations, near-death experiences and deathbed visions remain crystal clear. Although sick people in intensive-care units, for example, often have hallucinations, "experiences like those do not have the clarity; they do not have the narrative quality; they do not certainly have the positive emotional valence of the typical near-death experience." Fenwick concluded, "So I think, at long last, we are beginning to be able to draw a distinction between hallucinations due to altered brain chemistry and the near-death experience. I think they are different." Healthcare practitioners like Fenwick are routinely witness to deathbed visitations, and in learning to understand what is happening they can be better prepared in their work with terminally ill patients.

Case Studies

Perhaps even more compelling than the scientific research compiled on deathbed visitations are the documented case studies. Accounts of visitations and related phenomenon have trickled throughout all of recorded history, from a vast array of cultures and geographic locations. Here are some contemporary accounts and some of the information and indicators given.

Case studies looking at pre-death visitations can show us information about the time frame in which these visions normally occur, their nature, and even their purpose. In his article "Parting Visions: A New Scientific Paradigm," Dr. Melvin Morse presents a survey of research into deathbed visions and near-death experiences:

Osis and Haraldsson surveyed 5,000 doctors and nurses in the United States and 704 in India. They collected 471 cases of pre-death visions and comment on their similarity to near-death experience, which they also collected. Pre-death visions were typically of brief duration, within twenty-four hours of death, dead and living relatives were often seen, and the purpose of the experience was to take the dying person away and to provide comfort.

But deathbed visits are apparently not confined to the last twenty-four hours of life. Morse also states, "Barrett, Doyle, Madrid et al. report in a prospective case controlled study that dying adults have a marked increase in hallucinations of apparitions in the final week of life."

Visits from departed loved ones to the dying commonly occur not only as a harbinger that the certainty of death is near, but also as a sort of therapeutic "bridge over troubled water," a way to comfort the dying and aid in the transition from life into death. Therapist Sameet Kumar, in his essay "Ascending the Spiral Staircase of Grief" (in Michael Kerman's *Clinical Pearls of Wisdom: 21 Leading Therapists Offer Their Key Insights*), describes this:

One of the most common occurrences on the deathbed is the sense of being visited by deceased loved ones or "emissaries" from the afterlife. People will often feel tremendous relief about being reunited with beloved grandparents, parents, deceased children or pets, and siblings. Again, these visitations, whether believed to be real or imagined, are also indicators that death is near. While these visitations usually comfort the dying, the lucidity of conversations with invisible beings [often] confuses loved ones.

However, it also often comforts loved ones who are not dying, knowing their dying loved ones are passing into a tangible world, have comfort, and are in good hands. Much of the discomfort surrounding these experiences, for those not on their deathbeds, lies in cultural belief systems and taboos surrounding that which is considered unknown. Many therapists assert that whether these experiences are real or imagined, and whether we believe in them or not, they have a very healing and positive effect on the dying.

In his research, outlined in a published lecture entitled "Science and Spirituality: A Challenge for the 21st Century," Peter Fenwick reiterates the theme of the deathbed visitation as serving a purpose of offering comfort to the dying:

> *Common approaching-death experience is of transiting to a new reality. This story was told to me by a woman who was with her thirty-two-year-old daughter as she was dying of breast cancer. In her last two to three days, the daughter described being conscious of a dark roof over her head; then she would go up and go through the roof into a bright light. She moved into a waiting place where beings were talking to her, to help her through the dying process. She conveyed to her mother that everything would be okay, that these were loving beings, and that her grandfather was amongst the beings. She was able to move in and out of this reality, and she was quite clear that it was not a dream. We have been given other accounts by people who describe waiting in a garden, which sounds very similar to the sort of garden that NDErs describe. Light and love are absolutely primary to these experiences.*

In this case study, as with others, light, love, and reassurance are common themes recounted by those experiencing deathbed visitations.

Another account, retold in "Return from the Dead: Investigative Files" in *The Skeptical Inquirer* by Joe Nickell, tells how a Mrs. Haskins of Massachusetts had a near-death experience as a result of a fatal attack of pleuro-pneumonia. For twenty-three minutes her heart stopped as well as apparently her breathing and other vital signs. After her recovery, the woman recounted the story of her experience:

> *She stated she had suffered a fever of 104.5, had a fitful pulse, and experienced shortness of breath, whereupon she declared, "Mother, I'm going to die." Soon she obtained relief: "I felt as if I had been lifted from my bed and was floating up and away on light fleecy clouds. At the*

same time I heard the nurse say: "Well, she's gone." She felt the nurse close her eyes and heard her mother sobbing.

"Then," Mrs. Haskins said, "my little dead baby, Doris, came to me. I held out my arms to her and held her close to my breast. Oh, I was so happy. Baby and I were together again. That was all I thought of or cared for." Little Doris, her first of three children, had died when eight months old, a few years earlier. Now, Mrs. Haskins noted, "she looked happy and healthy," although "she wore the short skirts and white stockings and shoes that she was buried in."

She added: "Her coming back to me was not a shock. It seemed perfectly natural that she should come in that way. So I gathered her up in my arms and together we floated away in perfect happiness." In time though, Mrs. Haskins felt herself gasping for breath, the pain of her illness returned, and she was caught up in her own mother's arms. "Returning to life was the hard part," she insisted. "Dying was peace and happiness."

By reading these recorded case studies of deathbed visitations, we can prepare ourselves and our loved ones for death psychologically and nurture hope in an afterlife. What has been described here is just a sample of the information available on recounted tales of deathbed visitations. In essence, these amazing and moving accounts speak for themselves.

CHAPTER 15

Medical Personnel: Witnesses to the "Crossing Over"

Throughout history, when people died, it usually happened at their home or out in nature, perhaps on a battlefield. With modern medical technology and societal changes, it is more probable that one will pass in some type of medical facility such as a hospital, nursing home, or through the services of a hospice group. It is here that many trained personnel witness the dying process that at one time was experienced only by close family members.

Afterlife Experiments in Medical Settings

Notions of the afterlife have pervaded the annals of human religious, psychological, and metaphysical history. The afterlife is most commonly believed to be an actual spiritual location and embodiment that we venture into after we leave the physical body and earthly plane. Most of us base our ideas about the afterlife on faith and assume it cannot be proven or verified. However, people, ever inquisitive about life after death, have waged research endeavors in various ways throughout time. Contemporary studies have delved into afterlife experiments in medical settings. Beyond forays into mediumship, channeling, and other methods popularly used to investigate the existence of the afterlife, scientists have also looked into its existence using their own methods. Some of this research is based on measured physical observations and case studies, and others on laboratory studies in the context of parapsychology through scientific methods. While many in the scientific community are skeptical about the findings of parapsychology, it is an accepted scientific discipline and provides some compelling information.

NDE

Many researchers consider near-death experiences (NDEs) to be a significant indicator of the presence of an afterlife. As David H. Lund notes in *Persons, Souls and Death: A Philosophical Investigation of an Afterlife*:

> *NDEs became the subject of rather intensive scientific investigation carried over the last three decades, largely by psychologists, cardiologists, and parapsychologists. In some of them, the subject reported information that was objectively verified and yet such that she could not have acquired knowledge of it by normal means. Moreover, some of this information was such that its possession by the NDE subject is apparently most plausibly explained as having its source in the continued existence of deceased persons.*

OBE

In the field of parapsychology, scientists often look into cases of out-of-body experiences (OBEs) as an indicator of life beyond the physical, and thus, the good possibility that the soul continues beyond death. One laboratory-based experiment involved a series of tests performed at UCLA in 1965, as recounted in Robert Pinansky's *After Life, What?* These tests are used as an example of a scientific correlation between reality and the afterlife. In one such test, a psychology professor tested a woman who claimed to have the ability to leave her body:

> *She was placed in a closed room that had only a couch and an observation window. An EKG and cardiograph were attached to her body. On a shelf near the ceiling, way beyond her physical reach, a random five-digit number was placed. After going into a trancelike state, she was able to leave her body and read this number. The odds are 100,000 to one against guessing the correct number. Significant changes took place in the brain wave and cardiogram patterns at this time.*

FACT

Other branches within parapsychology explore apparitions of the dead as heralding the existence of the afterlife. For example, there are many case study accounts of hauntings and deathbed visions that share so many common features that it makes them a compelling study of the potentiality of the afterlife.

Some scientists measure for literal physical changes accompanying alleged afterlife contact, such as with near-death experiences. In a review of *Life After Death: The Evidence* by Dinesh D'Souza, Stephen M. Barr asserts that "D'Souza rightly points out that modern physics has broken the bounds of human imagination with ideas of other dimensions, and even other universes, and has required us to accept features of our own universe (at the subatomic level, for example) that are entirely counter-intuitive." However "counter-intuitive" this evidence may be, it is difficult to ignore. In *Transformed by the Light: The Powerful Effect of Near-Death Experiences On People's Lives* by Dr. Melvin Morse, the author notes:

> *After scientifically studying hundreds of these experiences I am convinced that the NDE itself subtly changes the electromagnetic forces that surround our bodies and each and every cell in it. This change is so*

profound that it affects such things as personality, anxiety response, ability to have psychic experiences, and even the ability in some to wear a watch.

Many scientists argue that when patients flat line or are in critical care, they experience physiological factors that give them the illusion of having had a near-death experience, deathbed vision, or some contact with a realm and with beings signifying the afterlife.

However, as Mark Crislip notes in his review of this research in his article "Near-Death Experiences and the Medical Literature," (*Skeptic* magazine), "If purely physiological factors resulting from cerebral anoxia caused NDE, most of our patients should have had this experience." Yet, good CPR does not lead to cerebral anoxia. Most patients in this study did not have an NDE because they had CPR, so they had blood and oxygen delivered to the brain; thus, they could not have an anoxia-mediated NDE.

In other words, of all the patients studied experiencing the same "cerebral anoxia" under critical care, only a percentage (32 of 282) report NDEs or contact with "the afterlife." This poses issues for the theory that brain chemicals and other physiological factors cause illusions rather than real NDEs, experiences that herald a taste of the afterlife.

Hospice Workers' Stories

The afterlife is a distant, confusing notion to most. However, for workers who specialize in aiding dying patients, known as hospice caretakers, the afterlife is a far more solid place than a religious ideal or comforting dream for the dying. Visions of deceased relatives and angels are frequently debunked as the product of a dying brain. Yet, the sheer volume of reports of otherworldly experiences from the dying and the common ground they all share despite religious, cultural, and geographic differences raises questions and suggests these waking dreams are valid experiences, not mere hallucinations.

As Dr. Carla Wills-Brandon mentions in *One Last Hug Before I Go: The Mystery and Meaning of Deathbed Visions*, hospice workers are extraordinarily accustomed to deathbed visions. These can be experienced as glimpses of the afterlife or otherworldly sightings of angels and passed loved ones. However, how does one know that these visions are more than just chemical reactions that take place in the brain as death approaches or mere side effects of medications? Trudy Harris, author of *Glimpses of Heaven: A Hospice Worker Tells of End of Life Experiences*, an experienced hospice worker, explains how her patients' phenomenal stories caused her doubt to fade:

> *In the beginning when my patients were explaining these experiences to me, I was very skeptical. I began to hear the same stories over and over and over again. . . . After twenty plus years of caring for hundreds and hundreds of patients and hearing the same scene played out over and over and over again, the skepticism went away.*

In *Death-Bed Visions: The Psychical Experiences of the Dying*, William Barrett states: "If these otherworldly visions were simply hallucinations, how could countless patient stories match? In fact, there have been several sightings of angels by dying children who were surprised to find their holy guides arrived without wings." Hospice workers and doctor reports of their dying patients' visions from Europe, Asia, and the United States were found to have eerie similarities. Aside from minor religious differences, the deathbed visions of these patients were consistent.

FACT

Hospice is a set of specialized services emphasizing palliative rather than curative treatment to help patients and families cope with terminal illness. The patient and family are both included in the care plan by being provided a variety of services with quality rather than quantity of life as the main purpose.

›› CASE: KRISTINE

A young nurse new to the hospice field reported the personal, life-altering experience of her first patient's death. Before the patient, an elderly woman suffering from terminal cancer, passed away, her primary nurse, Kristine, committed suicide. The woman was unaware that her nurse had passed away. Yet shortly before her death, she informed hospice workers that Kristine was standing by her bedside. Naturally, the young nurse and hospice workers were astounded and touched (Fawn, "Kristine RN Who Came Back After Death," *www.keen.com*)

Facing Stigma

The stigma surrounding spiritual phenomena keeps numerous people silent about their otherworldly experiences. Elissa Al-Chokhachy defied societal reproach and commented about her personal experience as a hospice nurse of nearly two decades: "Originally, I thought it was really rare that people had these experiences of loved ones after they die. . . . I can now say it's quite common, but very few people talk about it. They don't want people to think they're crazy, and they're not even sure it's real or not." Elissa has found that spiritual visions are so commonplace in hospice care that she wrote a novel detailing these experiences, titled *Miraculous Moments: True Stories Affirming that Life Goes On*.

Clearly this devoted hospice nurse and author has brought the myths surrounding deathbed visions into the light, granting them validity and allowing family members and healthcare workers to openly share their experiences.

"Spiritual Eyes and Ears"

Another hospice nurse, Trudy Harris, was inspired to write about the otherworldly events she witnessed working in palliative care after evidence of an afterlife surmounted her skepticism. Before delving into individual stories, Harris notes the eerie sense declining patients have about their impending fate: "No one has to tell them they are dying. . . . They have developed what I call 'spiritual eyes and ears' and seem to understand things in a way we cannot." With such a vast amount of stories sharing common ground and inexplicable occurrences, many people find their uncertainty melt away.

Despite logical, scientific claims, one thing remains clear: hospice workers are witnesses to otherworldly events. Numerous healthcare workers who have had both the burden and blessing of working in hospice have observed the phenomenal experiences of their patients. What was previously thought to be hallucinations from a dying brain is brought into question as valid, true experiences and evidence of an afterlife.

Hospital and ER Personal Experiences

Quite naturally, hospitals are common areas for the sick and the injured to pass over. Equally natural is the fact that hospital employees who attend to patients bear witness to their crossing over from life into death, and what may lie beyond. Although the training of these hospital personnel makes them traditionally scientifically oriented and skeptical of unexplainable phenomenon, witnessing countless people make their final journey is liable to impress even the most hesitant of minds.

In "Parting Visions: a New Scientific Paradigm," Dr. Melvin Morse details some cases of hospital and emergency staff witnessing the crossing over of patients. He says, "Shared spiritual experiences with dying patients are also reported, which again are strikingly similar to near-death experiences."

One such story involves a nurse:

[She] described a vivid dream in which she accompanied one of her patients through a tunnel into a spiritual light, which occurred at the same time her patient died in the hospital. She stated that during the dream "we burst out into the open-bright light all around us. I felt incredibly peaceful and good. Then I thought, I can't stay, it isn't my time, I have things to do. I looked (at her patient). She had already become part of that glorious white light.

Hospital staff witnessing and even sharing (to some degree) crossing-over experiences of their dying patients may be more common than typically thought. For example, according to Morse, anthropologist D. Lewis "randomly interviewed 100 London nurses and found that 35 percent reported experiences with dead patients, ranging from vague feelings to visual and auditory hallucinations."

In another example, in *The Near-Death Experience: A Reader*, Lee Worth Baily and Jenny L. Yates talk about how one nurse reported witnessing a patient cross over and seeing something "as if the patient were surrounded by a bright glow." She added, "That was a phenomenon she had sometimes observed in the dying."

Some hospital and emergency room staff are witness to their patients' deathbed visions just as they cross over. Wills-Brandon, tells of one doctor describing an interesting case where one of his patients crossed over and seemed to regress to a childhood age just moments before death, as he seemed to see his own passed-on mother.

The doctor said:

While he appeared perfectly rational and sane as any man I have ever seen, the only way I can express it is that he was transported into another world . . . for he said in a stronger voice than he had used since I attended him, "There is Mother! Why, Mother, have you come to see me? No, no, I'm coming to see you. Just wait Mother, I'm almost over. I can jump it. Wait, Mother." On his face there was a look of inexpressible happiness, and the way in which he said the words impressed me as I have never seen before, and I am as firmly convinced that he saw and talked with his mother as I am that I am sitting here.

In another case, Wills-Brandon explains that nurses and doctors at the deathbed of a young boy witnessed not only the boy's dying visions but also a strange change in his physical symptoms, as well as the boy's prediction of his imposing death. These doctors and nurses recount that the boy often talked about his dead mother:

He mentioned her . . . very affectionately. The day he died he had no fever but he said, "My time has come." . . . "My mother is calling. She is standing with her arms open." At that moment his state of mind was clear. He was conscious of his surroundings.

Another hospital worker, Sheila, along with her colleagues' witnessed a remarkable crossing over of a dying patient that forever changed her views about death, dying, and the period of crossing over, causing her to look "upon her dying patients with new eyes and dignity." Wills-Brandon details the story:

One night in 1982 she was working a night shift, attending to a man who was not thought to be in any immediate danger or extremely ill, when at about eight P.M., he began talking very lucidly about a loved one whom he longed to see. Sheila could not tell who this person was, but it was obvious that the man had not seen her in many years and never expected to do so again. The impression is that she must have passed away some years before. . . . At about 9:30 he began talking about this person again, and his vital signs also began to fall. Fearing the worst, more medical staff was brought in. The patient became wonderfully alert, as some people do very near the end. As time went by, it was clear he could see someone there whom no one else could see. Suddenly, his face lit up like a beacon. He was staring and smiling at what was clearly a long-lost friend, his eyes so full of love and serenity that it was hard for those around him to not be overcome by tears.

Sheila follows by saying "There was no mistake. Someone had come for him at last to show him the way." Minutes later the man died, in a state of sublime peace and happiness.

It is not uncommon for personnel of medical settings to witness the events surrounding the dying of a patient. It is also not uncommon for them to witness unexplainable phenomena when such events do transpire.

Nursing-Home Events

Nursing homes are often known to be an arena for the "definitive journey," the human soul's voyage from this life into what lies beyond. With loved ones and caregivers nearby, people often give up their final breaths while resting in nursing homes. Witnesses can attest to the significance and often mysterious and mystical nature of the dying's "crossing over" from life to death, and what awaits after. Many of these testimonies share similar features, and are telling as to what beckons in that twilight period of crossing over.

Case studies and accounts of deathbed experiences witnessed by others in nursing homes sometimes involve the witness having a vision of the dying person leaving her body. Other times, the witness sees unmistakable spiritually charged transformations taking place over the dying individual just before she passes. According to Constance Victoria Briggs in *Encyclopedia of the Unseen World*:

Many individuals have received personal proof of after-death survival by observing their fellow humans at the moment of death. . . . Common characteristics of a deathbed vision include brilliant lights, scenes of great beauty, angels or beings of light, and a sense of calmness and peace. Many deathbed visions involve seeing loved ones that have already crossed over into the spiritual world.

As told in Wills-Brandon's *One Last Hug Before I Go*, a stepdaughter witnesses an encounter with an angelic or spirit-like being, just before her father passes:

I was at the nursing home visiting my stepfather. . . . [He] kept referring to the smiling lady who was sitting on the empty bed in the room. Of course, I couldn't see her. He then wondered out loud why this woman was being so rude. My stepfather thought she should leave the room while he and I had our conversation. He found this most confusing. Then he told me, "She always seems so happy." He said this several times to me. I was concerned about this vision he was having and asked the medical staff about it. They assured me that he was stable for the time being. After that, I decided to go and drove home. As I opened the front door to my house, the phone was ringing. My stepfather had died during my short drive to my residence. I used to be very skeptical of such things, but now I know there is more to life than we know.

ESSENTIAL

Nursing homes are the last place many people will experience before they pass, as children of frail parents can no longer care for them in the way that is needed. Home caregivers and family members often experience the crossing-over process as something special and intimate, compared to the more acute, sudden hospital passing.

As we can see here, those crossing over can have visions heralding the life after life, while being of sound (and even, critical) mind, as this witness testifies.

When it comes to crossing over, communications between a witness and a loved one passing (for example) in a nursing home do not seem to bow to laws of physics, space, or time. As one witness recounts in Wills-Brandon's *One Last Hug Before I Go*, she had a deathbed vision of her mother passing in a nursing home thousands of miles away, while she dreamed:

> *I was asleep at home. My mother had been very ill for some time. I had travelled to the home of my youth to be with her, but had eventually needed to leave her side to care for my young children. When I left my mother's nursing home room, I had known I would never see her again. Flying home, my grief was overwhelming. The night I returned home I was both physically and emotionally exhausted. After dinner with my husband and children, I went to bed. During the middle of the night, I awoke from a very deep sleep. I had dreamed my mother had come to visit me. In this dream, she was with my father who had passed five years ago. Both of them looked happy and healthy. My mother blew me a kiss. Then she and my father turned around and walked off, over a hill. When I awoke, tears filled my eyes, but I also felt a sense of peace. My parents had looked so joyful. I looked at the clock and noted it was 3 A.M., then lay back down and went to sleep. The next morning my brother called to tell me my mother had left us. When I asked him about the time of her death, he replied she had passed at 3 A.M.*

It is not uncommon for those caring for a dying loved one to have their own deathbed visions. As outlined in Carla Wills-Brandon's article "Understanding Departing Visions or Deathbed Visions," "Often times those at the bedside of someone who is terminally ill will experience DBVs." Reports of these deathbed visions are not limited to loved ones, whose testimonies may be criticized as tainted by grief and denial. Hospice and nursing-home staff also report witnessing deathbed visions. Such testimonies can be particularly compelling, given that some nursing-home staff often explain away notions of the spiritual and visions of the soul's passing, or of visages from the afterlife, due to medication or an ailing, dying brain.

Transition Stories from Caregivers

People facing death are usually confronted with spiritual issues and questions as to human origin, life purpose, and the destination after death. The dying also go through intense experiences near their death and during their crossing over, such as having visions, visionary dreams, and other spiritually charged phenomenon. The most likely witnesses historically and practically speaking to a person's crossing over have been, naturally, their caregivers. And as Tad Dunne says in his article "Spiritual Care at the End of Life," "It is important to keep in mind that the work of giving spiritual care occurs originally and essentially within the caregivers."

Hallucinations in Doubt

Some of these experiences near death involve powerful visions, which are too often not taken seriously. However, in "Are They Hallucinations or Are They Real? The Spirituality of Deathbed and Near-Death Visions," L. Betty Stafford focuses on "visions of deceased relatives and friends that persons near death often report." She asks questions about their validity and remarks on how seriously caregivers should perhaps take them: "Are they visions of real people who live in an afterlife environment or are they hallucinations? Most social scientists assume they are hallucinations, but a thorough and careful analysis of the evidence does not point to this conclusion. The argument for the reality of such visions" includes "a theory that makes sense of all aspects of these visions is developed and defended, then tied into our theme: the spirituality of death."

Visionary Dreams

During and before the crossing-over period visionary dreams also occur. In "A Dream Before Dying," Anne Underwood discusses caregivers' observations of dreams of the dying in their care, and the idea that these dreams are indicators of the celestial and the afterlife. Here we see an account given by Reverend Patricia Bulkley and what she witnessed from Charles Rasmussen, retired merchant-marine captain, as he was dying of cancer:

He was consumed by fear until, in a dream one night, he saw himself sailing in uncharted waters. Once again, he felt the thrill of adventure as he pushed through a vast, dark, empty sea, knowing he was on course. "Strangely enough, I'm not afraid to die anymore," he told Bulkley after that dream. Death was no longer an end, but a journey.

As Underwood elaborates, according to Bulkley, "Many people have extraordinary dreams in their final days and weeks. These dreams can help the dying grapple with their fears, find the larger meaning in their lives, even mend fences with relatives. Yet all too often, caregivers dismiss them as delusional or unworthy of attention."

Caregivers' Responsibilities

In a panel discussion about the psychological, emotional, relational, and spiritual experience of the dying and their caregivers, a symposium established to provide "an opportunity to hear and learn from the narratives of older adults who are facing death and their families and caregivers," was summarized by S. Sanders in *The Gerontologist*. This discussion detailed problems that are faced when caregivers do not take seriously the spiritual aspect and phenomenon of dying when a person is crossing over, and the importance of understanding this phenomenon from the perspective of the dying.

NDA

According to Sanders,

Nearing Death Awareness (NDA) is a concept presently recognized primarily by staff and caregivers in some nursing homes, hospitals and hospices. . . . Knowledge of what NDA is, what typical NDA behaviors are and how to respond appropriately can assist people in providing valuable support and comfort, as well as foster preparedness for their own passing when the time comes. Caregivers and loved ones with an open-minded perspective are even more effectively equipped to nurture spiritual growth for the dying in their last days, an immeasurable service deserved by all who pass from this life to the next.

At the same time, it is inherent in a caregiver's role to collect and record these dreams and other crossing-over experiences, making their input invaluable to the understanding of spiritual and psychological deathbed phenomena.

Certainly, there is a commonality among these near-death visionary dreams, worth scientific exploration and deep consideration. For example, in addition to voyage imagery, many see stopped clocks, and are reunited with loved ones.

QUESTION

Is it possible to have a positive experience watching someone die? The living can benefit greatly from observing all the phenomena surrounding the passing and contemplating these experiences as they witness and support the dying throughout their illness and crossing over.

Phenomena Surrounding the Passing

In *One Last Hug Before I Go*, Wills-Brandon highlights more stories about caregivers witnessing dying patients crossing over and some of the strange phenomena surrounding these events. One woman caring for a terminally ill great-aunt reported literally feeling a presence in the room just as and after her great-aunt died:

> *My great-aunt was nearing the end. . . . I had been with her for days, trying to make her as comfortable as possible. . . . She had not had the energy to speak for over a week. One morning, she started weakly calling out for Ted, her brother. . . . Ted had died. . . . My great-aunt called his name softly over and over again for about an hour. Then, as the woman passed, the great-niece says: "Suddenly, I could sense a presence in the room, over her dresser. It wasn't frightening or silly as you would expect a ghost to be."*

In another case, Wills-Brandon tells of a niece caring for her sick aunt, who shared in the crossing-over experience by realizing that her own prayers and intentions were holding her aunt back from making that final journey. She recounts what happened in her situation during the crossing-over period of her aunt:

She looked at me and said, "Joan, I have been over there, over to the beyond and it is beautiful over there. I want to stay, but I can't as long as you keep praying for me to stay with you. Your prayers are holding me over here. Please don't pray anymore." We did all stop and shortly after that she died.

As we can see from these accounts from caregivers, it is not only the dying that can benefit from the information and phenomena they experience in crossing over, but also those who attend, and listen. After all, we will all sooner or later be in their same position.

Unexplained Phenomena in Funeral Homes

History and popular culture are rife with tales of the paranormal. Many of the scenes for these stories include places associated with death and their legacy, sites and homes where people have died, cemeteries, hospitals, and funeral homes. It is fascinating and intriguing, although perhaps unorthodox, to examine accounts of unexplained phenomena occurring in these arenas. One of these areas is the unexplained phenomena as they occur in funeral homes.

According to *Ghost Hunting Handbook* author Marc Tyler Nobleman, funeral homes are one place where spirits often appear, even though proprietors certainly do not advertise this fact:

Though hospitals and funeral homes see death regularly, hauntings are not often reported there. That doesn't mean hauntings don't occur there. More likely it means that the administration doesn't want to publicize something that may make people more anxious than they already are.

Be that as it may, stories of unexplained phenomena related to funeral homes continue to surface and are often published.

Living in a Funeral Home

In an article entitled "Living in a Funeral Home," Victoria Rife recounts some of the experiences her father had as a tenant living in a room rented out to him in a practicing funeral home where he also worked as an assistant funeral director. She says:

> *He had many, many unexplainable experiences while living there. . . . At night the lights would flicker on and off, locked doors would open and then slam shut, unlocked doors would magically lock, things would go and disappear only to reappear later in a weird place, and one night a wall hanging even flew off the wall several feet. My dad had to turn off everything downstairs before retreating upstairs to his home. Some nights he would turn everything off only to get up later and have every light in the house turned on.*

ESSENTIAL

Funeral homes are a special place for people to visit their departed loved ones one last time. The atmosphere is usually peaceful and full of comfort for the visitors. Prayers are often said and fond memories of the deceased are exchanged. This environment can be supportive and help with the beginning of the healing process for many.

The Buildings

Apparently mysterious funeral home activity does not end when these buildings become renovated or transformed somehow. In Buffalo, New York, the building that houses the Iron Island Museum used to be a funeral home. Over the last decade, those working in the building have reported many odd, unexplained occurrences following their discovery of twenty-four containers of unclaimed human remains. Pictures would go missing from tables. Shadows darted about and, occasionally, a voice seemingly came out of nowhere to bid hello. Volunteers dismissed it as "Charlie the Ghost" acting out once again. But now "Charlie" has been reunited with his true identity. He is war veteran Edgar L. Zernicke, whose ashes were in one of the canisters tucked into a basement closet and left behind by Church Funeral Home, which was later sold to Amigone Funeral Home, which donated the building to the museum in August 2000. (Lou Michel, "Staff Links Museum's Ghost to War Veteran's Unburied Remains," September 2010)

Evidently, these now-famous ashes have been moved to Amigone Funeral Home's new location, where they will be buried in September of 2010 at Bath National Cemetery. Whether his ghost will also relocate and continue his haunting at the new funeral home remains to be seen.

Perhaps there is an instructive, as well as healing, aspect to the collusion of funeral homes and supernatural experiences the living bear witness to therein. According to Jeff Belanger in *The Ghost Files: Paranormal Encounters, Discussion, and Research*, "Cemeteries exist more for the living than the dead. When we walk through a place of the dead, such as cemetery, funeral homes, battlefields or even horrific former crime scenes, there's a part of us that consciously or subconsciously tunes in to our own mortality. We think about death, our own inevitable fate.

CHAPTER 16

Miracles

Miracles have fascinated and comforted millions of people throughout history. There have always been conflicting views as to the origin of these events. While many religions believe that miracles are divine interventions, science believes that there is no phenomena that cannot be explained, even if the current technology needed to test the phenomena does not exist at the moment. With the help of modern science, some miracles can now be examined more closely to acquire the origin of the event and to bridge the gap between the religious and cultural views and the scientific community.

Visions by Multiple Witnesses

Phenomena such as visions, healings, and prophecies that fall under the heading of "miraculous" are all events that usually transcend either human powers or defy the laws of nature, as a result of the apparent intervention of divine or supernatural forces. These events are considered by some to be acts of God.

An interesting observation about miraculous visions is that their "greatness" is often comparable to their number of witnesses. Individuals and smaller groups of people witness smaller miracles, and larger, more awe-inspiring miracles are witnessed by crowds of hundreds, even thousands, of people.

Visions in Medjugorje

Since June 24, 1981, six people in the town of Medjugorje in Citluk, Bosnia and Herzegovina, have been seeing visions of Mother Mary, who speaks with them and guides them. The six children, Ivanka Ivankovic, Mirjana Dragicevic, Vicka Ivankovic, Ivan Dragicevic, Ivan Ivankovic, and Milka Pavlovic, saw a beautiful lady with a child in her arms at 6:00 on the Crnica Hill known as Podbrdo. She asked them to come closer but they ran away. The next day at the same time and the same place the lady appeared again, and this time the children embraced her. Ivan Ivankovic and Milka Pavlovic were not there; instead, in their places were Marija Pavlovic and Jakov Colo.

On the third day, when the lady appeared Mirjana asked her name, to which she replied, "I am the Blessed Mother Mary." To this day, these children continue to speak to and see the apparition. The vision tells them to have faith in God.

Our Lady of Lourdes

The shrine of Our Lady of Lourdes in France is one of the most visited shrines in the world because of the healing spring that appeared during the vision of the Blessed Virgin Mary to Bernadette Soubirous, a poor fourteen-year-old girl.

Mother Mary appeared eighteen times to this girl, the first of which was on February 11, 1858. Bernadette saw her in the grotto of Massabielle, where she told her, "I am the Immaculate Conception." On one occasion, she asked

Bernadette to wash her face in the fountain where there was no water. But when Bernadette scratched the ground, a stream of water with miraculous healing powers gushed forth. It is this stream that attracts people from the world over even to this day. Bernadette became a nun and continued to see these visions. She died when she was thirty-five.

ESSENTIAL

When one person is witness to a type of paranormal phenomena they can be open to questions of personal bias, financial gain, or even seeking public attention. However, when multiple witnesses are involved, more critical attention is brought to the event, which then can be investigated without the possibility of one person's own agenda.

The Fatima Visions

During World War I, on May 13, 1916, Mother Mary gave her first vision to three shepherd children, Lucia dos Santos, aged ten, and her cousins Francisco and Jacinta Marto, aged eight and seven, respectively, at Fatima, near Lisbon in Portugal. She asked them to come there for six months on the same date. Various messages were given and people from all of Portugal began to visit the site. In October 1916, to lend credence to the words of these children, as many as 70,000 people saw the "sun dancing in the sky," and then appear to fall to earth before ascending back toward the sky.

Our Lady of the Light, Zeitoun, Egypt

The apparitions of what is called Our Lady of the Light were seen on April 2, 1968, in Zeitoun, Egypt. This apparition was witnessed by tens of thousands of people including Christians, Jews, Muslims, and nonbelievers. At first she appeared surrounded in light in a kneeling position on the roof of a church. Farouk Mohammad Atwa, a Muslim and the first man to see her, was healed from a case of gangrene. Over the next three years, Our Lady appeared repeatedly, usually around two to three times a week. Mostly at night, her apparition would be preceded by orbs of white light, and sometimes white doves would accompany her, at times flying in a cross formation, as she walked around the dome of the church. Everybody could see her and over 100,000 people would gather to view the event.

The Roman Catholic Church finally approved the apparition as a visitation of the Holy Mother. She apparently had a three-dimensional quality with flesh-colored face and hands and she would show up in the thousands of photos that were taken of her, along with the light orbs and rays.

Many people have seen visions of angels telling them what to do, acting as spiritual guides or mentors, helping and guiding or protecting them from harm. Multiple-witness visions add a great deal of weight to the possibilities of the existence of a supernatural world interacting with this physical one.

Healings of Unknown Origin

Almost everyone has heard stories of people miraculously healed after modern medical science has given up hope of a cure. These miracle healings of unknown origin or reason have baffled humankind for centuries. Disappearing tumors, recoveries from deathbeds, and even simple healings of common ailments through prayer, healing touch, distant-healing methods, and many other such paranormal means have been cited, researched, and discussed extensively.

Miracle Healing Through the Ages

Instances of miracle healings have been cited through the history of mankind from the ancient civilizations to the modern world of today. Paracelsus (born 1493), a Swiss physician and alchemist, who is often regarded as the father of modern medicine, is believed to have used not only the physiological but also psychical methods of curing people. He believed that there exists a luminous vital force around us, which could be manipulated to heal people.

Franz Mesmer (1734–1815), a famous psychic healer of the eighteenth century, talked of a universal energy fluid, which could be directed to heal people. He was known for his unconventional methods of healing, which included hypnosis, healing touch, and use of magnets on his patients.

Native Americans have practiced spiritual healing for ages and each tribe has a spiritual leader called a shaman, who is said to have healing powers. Christians strongly believe in the healing power of prayer and many claims of faith healings from across the world are commonly heard.

Various Forms and Types of Miracle Healings

The miraculous healings, which cannot be attributed to natural causes, are associated with paranormal methods or phenomena. There are many ways and methods through which such healings are said to be induced.

In many cases, these are simply said to be the work of God. Most religious healings are said to be achieved through prayers, which in some cultures are performed according to special rituals and practices.

There are also other types of paranormal healings, which are said to be induced through bio-energy or life energy, which flows through all living beings. This universal vital force can be manipulated to relieve patients of their diseases or sufferings. The healing methods, which leverage this paranormal energy and phenomena, include healing through touch, distant healing, and psychic surgery. Alternative healing therapies associated with this school of thought include Pranic healing and Reiki.

Besides these paranormal healing methods, some materials and astronomical bodies are also thought to have miraculous healing powers. Crystal healing is a popular curative therapy adopted by many people worldwide.

FACT

There have been many unexplained cases of healings not associated with medical science. Eastern medicine has utilized various alternative modalities in treatment of the ill, with positive results. Science continues to research the possibilities of healing through touch, prayer, and sound.

Are Paranormal Healings for Real?

Many cases of quackery have been exposed related to miracle healings. Methods like psychic surgery have come under severe criticism after cases of serious fraud were discovered. Noted American psychiatrist Stephen Barrett and medical practitioner W. A. Nolen have extensively studied cases of miracle healings and have found no conclusive evidence that any of the patients were healed by the psychic methods.

However, there are other schools of thought, which believe and try to explain otherwise. There is no doubt that some methods of psychic healings may be fraudulent, but putting all under the same category would be unfair. Doris Kreiger, a New York University researcher, has been studying healing touch and is said to have received positive results from her study of the effect of "therapeutic touch" on hemoglobin. Her sister, Sister Justice Smith, who is a biochemist, has also conducted some successful research on the effect of healing by touch on damaged and whole enzymes.

They believe that the therapeutic touch, even though unexplainable as an exact scientific phenomenon, leverages the power of the dynamic electromagnetic energy field surrounding our body, mind, and soul. These multilayered energy fields connect us with the consciousness of the universe and draw the life force to induce healing in the affected bodies. These alternative therapies of so-called "unexplained" or "miraculous" healings are said to work on the principle of "energy flows where attention goes!"

There are 124 scientific studies reported on in the book *Spiritual Healing* by Dr. Daniel J. Benor that validate the success of various alternative healing methods. Many of the controlled studies were at leading hospitals and research facilities. Therapeutic touch, Reiki, and other hands-on healing techniques are currently being used in hospitals and other treatment facilities across the United States and throughout the world to reduce pain and decrease postoperative recovery times. What at one time may have been seen as miraculous may now be viewed as a new paradigm in healing.

Physical Manifestations

There have been many instances of physical manifestations of God, angels, saints, and departed souls through human history. Such instances have been reported across the world and have strengthened the faith of not only those who witnessed them but also of those who heard or read about them.

Miracles can be defined as physical events that defy the laws of nature. Most miracles show some sort of physical manifestation that is evident not only to the individuals involved, but also to the people around them. According to Father James Wiseman, associate professor of theology at Catholic

University, "There are always going to be some people who see immediately the hand of God in every coincidence, and those who are going to be skeptical of everything. And there is a great in-between."

Physical manifestations surrounding miracles form an integral part of all religions, and an endless number of devotees celebrate these miracles as God's intervention in human lives. Both the Old and New Testaments of the Bible as well as the Koran are filled with accounts of miracles and wonders performed by God, angels, prophets, and saints.

Divine Physical Manifestations

In 1531, Juan Diego, who had recently been converted to Christianity, saw the Virgin Mary five times in Guadalupe, Mexico. The Virgin Mary left her imprint on Juan Diego's cloak. Benoîte Rencurel, a shepherdess from Laus, France, started seeing the Virgin Mary in 1664 and continued to see her throughout her life. In 1830, Catherine Laboure of France saw the Virgin Mary three times and was told to have the medal of the Immaculate Conception made to spread faith in the world. In 1846, in La Salette, France, Maximin Giraud and Melanie Mathieu saw the Virgin Mary. The Blessed Mother appeared in tears and called for penance.

FACT

Stigmata is yet another unexplained physical occurrence. It is regarded as the manifestation of the suffering endured prior to and during Jesus' crucifixion. It involves the spontaneous bleeding of wounds that appear at various parts of the body, such as the hands, feet, forehead, and back.

In the more recent instances, in 1879, the figures of Joseph, Mary, John the Apostle, and a lamb appeared over the gable of a chapel in an Irish village. The figures were surrounded by a bright light and they were seen by fifteen people. In 1932, it is believed that Mary came to five children in a convent in Beauraing, Belgium, calling for the conversion of sinners and identifying herself as the "Immaculate Virgin." In 1933, Mariette Beco of Belgium saw the Virgin Mary eight times in a garden, where she identified herself as the "Virgin of the Poor." In 1981, six girls and one boy saw both Jesus and the

Virgin Mary in Kibeho, Rwanda. The apparitions continued for several years and were last seen in 1989.

Physical Manifestations of Departed Souls

Seeing or interacting with apparitions of the deceased is a very common phenomena. Both natural and induced, after-death communication has been extensively recorded and studied. Children who die young are often reported to be seen as apparitions by loved ones after their death. People on their deathbeds also see apparitions of deceased relatives, symbolizing their getting closer to the otherworld. These miraculous sightings were first studied in detail by the British Society of Psychical Research in the late 1800s. In 1889, a study conducted by the society recorded as many as 32,000 cases of apparition sightings.

Researchers investigating these physical manifestations of the deceased have found most of the subjects to be in perfectly normal, nonhallucinatory states. In addition, some of the sightings have even yielded tangible evidence such as broken things, a signature or words written by the apparition, and recordings on tape. Some apparitions are seen by multiple people (including the apparitions at the Gettysburg battlefield, as previously described). This lends more credibility to the claims. Many of the sightings are unexplainable according to the natural world as we perceive it. These manifestations play an important role in strengthening faith and helping to connect to what is beyond this material world.

According to Jon Butler, Yale University professor of American history, who specializes in American religion, "Most miracles have some physical manifestation that is evident not only to the individuals involved, but may be evident to the people around them. The catch is, how do you explain it?"

Unexplained Evidence

Miracles are events that are beyond explanation of the "natural" state of affairs or science of today. They are events that stir the soul and are often thought to be works of God. There is also another school of thought that connects miracles to metaphysics, and states that miracles are projections of our own soul in an attempt to connect with the mass or self-consciousness. It is probably the reason why many miracles are cited by the observers in times of fear, death, or some other kind of unusual circumstances.

All miracles are associated with unexplained evidence, which the researchers and investigators of modern times are unable to explain scientifically. Science can neither prove nor disprove miracles—if it can, then the event can no longer be called a miracle. People all around the world observe miracles, and their experience results in a strengthening of their belief in the existence of powers beyond the understanding of the human mind and current science.

QUESTION

Is it possible for science to explain every miraculous event?
There are many instances of paranormal miraculous events that have been explained by science. However, there still remains the fact that science might not have the current means to explain all of these occurrences. Until they are completely explained without a doubt, they will remain miracles.

Miracles (depending on the evidence) can be broadly classified into four categories:

- **Miraculous relics:** These are usually relics of religious significance that display unexplained phenomena, like blood tears on a statue of the Virgin Mary and the shroud of Turin.
- **Miraculous images:** These are unexplained images (usually of divine nature), which are spotted at unexpected places, like a religious symbol appearing on some usual object.
- **Divine experiences:** These are experiences that humans go through but are unexplainable by natural laws. This includes experiences such as prophesying, imperviousness to poisons, and speaking in tongues.
- **Faith healing:** The evidence in these miracles is unexplained healing of individuals from incurable conditions or diseases, or healing of the body miraculously, without any intervention of medical science.

Well-Known Cases of Unexplained Evidence and Miracles

Here's a short list of the miracles, which after years of investigation and study, have remained unexplainable.

Weeping and Bleeding Statues of Religious Icons

A number of cases of statues weeping (in many cases blood tears) are heard of from around the world. Famous instances of this include the case of the Weeping Madonna of Toronto, the Jesus painting in the Bethlehem Church of the Nativity, and the statue of Christ weeping olive oil in the Antiochian Orthodox Church, Sydney. Though these incidents are often claimed to be fraudulent, several investigations and tests have only yielded inconclusive evidence.

Crystal Tears of a Lebanese Girl

A Lebanese girl, Hasnah Mohamed Meselmani, produces crystal tears from her eyes. These crystals are as sharp as cut glass, but Hasnah says that she feels no pain when they are produced. These tears are produced as many as seven times a day and have been examined by medical experts, who are unable to find the reason of their occurrence.

Stigmata

Another Christian miracle, which has been reported by people from across the world, is stigmata. Afflicted people receive crucifixion and lashing wounds on their hands, feet, head, and other parts of the body, similar to the way Jesus would have suffered the wounds. These wounds are sometimes visible accompanied with blood, while in other cases these are invisible. They are almost always accompanied with pain and can last for long periods of time.

Francesco Forgione, later known as Padre Pio, was an Italian Roman Catholic priest who became famous for his stigmata. He also manifested various spiritual gifts including the gifts of healing, bilocation, prophecy, miracles, the ability to read hearts, and extraordinary abstinence from both sleep and nourishment. He was granted sainthood after so many miracles were attributed to him.

Ghost Doctor Cures Children in Venezuela Hospital

In May 2008, a strange case of twenty-five children miraculously being healed of life-threatening conditions such as cancer and heart defects in Sacred Heart Hospital in Caracas, Venezuela, came to light. A ghostly spirit of a doctor was claimed to be behind these healings. Many staffers and doctors of the hospital have claimed to have seen the spirit who has brought happiness back into the lives of many ailing children.

These and many more unexplained evidences of miracles have been reported from around the world with scientists and investigators struggling to come up with "reasonable" answers to these happenings. Whether these are divine intervention from God or something supernatural and beyond understanding, they clearly highlight how little is known of the world and its wonders.

Science and the Miracle Phenomena

The term *miracle* comes from the Latin word *miraculum*, meaning "something wonderful." Religious definitions usually refer to a miracle as an unexpected event attributed to divine intervention. Christian Science refers to "a divinely natural phenomenon experienced humanly as the fulfillment of spiritual law." The rise of the New Age movement has shown an increase in paranormal and religious events such as faith healing, divine apparitions, and magical images. However, scientists consider all these as unique natural occurrences, and deny the possibility of any kind of miracle.

Why Science Turns Its Back on Miracles

Miracles are often mistaken to be unexplainable phenomena that are thought by some to have profound meaning. Throughout history, events that were once thought to be miracles have become known simply as rare occurrences with logical, scientific explanations. Examples of these kinds of "miracles" are people being struck by lightning, or the birth of rare animals, such as a white buffalo or red heifer (having obviously genetic causes).

In scientific analysis, phenomena are compared with other similar events so that the mechanisms that made them possible can be understood. Two of the fundamental issues with miracle phenomena are that they are either found to be elaborate hoaxes or they are singular in their occurrence and unable to be compared with for analysis.

Also, because a miracle has to be unexplainable by the laws of nature, a lot of scientists throw out the possibility that a miracle can even exist. The other major issue with miracle claims is in their religious associations, because scientific analysis requires objectivity in a miracle's causality, separating the miracle from its apparent divine creation as well as its supposed support of religiously interpreted "meaning."

Science is an ever-evolving field, thus it may or may not be able to explain all the natural events and occurrences that take place worldwide. But once scientists and researchers find the proper tools to analyze any such event, it ceases to remain a miracle. So for scientists, everything that happens in this world, however incredible it might be, has an explanation, and therefore cannot be referred to as miracles.

ALERT

It is important to keep an open mind when investigating any miracle phenomena and it should not be looked upon with bias or preconceived notions. Following the right scientific protocol in the research of the event is the best way of explaining the phenomena.

How Religions Define Miracles

Because of the past creation of hoaxes to give credibility to religions, sects, or an individual seeking to influence others, the religious definition of a miracle requires that certain criteria be met. Often, so-called miracles have later been revealed to be previously misunderstood scientific phenomena due to either their infrequency or lack of knowledge.

In light of this, some religious authorities, such as the Vatican, restrict the labeling of an event as a miracle to those complex instances that have direct religious association and defy all natural laws as proof of God's omnipotence, adhering to the following rules:

- The event needs to be something that only God can perform and that he's using to point toward himself.
- It has to be certified by a minister.
- It can't be understood in itself but helps to illuminate the understanding of other things.

For any modern-day medical healing to be considered a miracle, the Vatican has access to a pool of sixty-plus doctors covering all the medical branches. Two specialists are assigned to each possible miracle healing to study the event. All scientific causes must be ruled out in order for the event to continue its course of examination toward being designated a miracle.

Lourdes

The Vatican established a medical bureau at Lourdes, France, to establish the authenticity of miracle healings after the apparition of the Virgin Mary in 1858. It is said that a spring was described to Bernadette Soubirous by Our Lady of Lourdes, and it has been associated with over 7,000 miracles. The church takes a very strict scientific approach to the verification of such reports and therefore shares some common ground with the scientific community.

The Search Will Continue

When it comes to supernatural phenomena, there are large gaps in our knowledge, especially when it comes to rare occurrences. Many things that were said to be impossible were later proved to be possible, such as flight, breaking the sound barrier, space travel, relativity, quantum theory, etc.

The intellectual struggle and the resentment it sometimes breeds between people who want to hold true to the belief in miracles and those who want to exercise scientific integrity is unnecessary. In modern-day miracle investigation, both science and religion use the same current knowledge available to try to explain phenomena that baffle the world.

Case Studies

There are many definitions of a miracle that span various cultures and religions. However, the Catholic Church's use of stringent guidelines for determining a miracle and stories of approved miracles will be the focus of this section.

In Catholicism, a miracle is essential for the canonization of a saint and continues to play an essential role within the church. In fact, according to David Van Biema and Greg Burke in "Modern Miracles Have Strict Rules," "of all the faiths that recognize the continuing eruption of the divine in human affairs, Catholicism has gone farthest to systematize that belief."

The Catholic Church recognizes miracles as being works of the divine, either directly or indirectly, through the prayers and intercession of a saint. Saint Augustine of Hippo proposed that the definition of a miracle be subjective by stating that a miracle is "whatever is hard or appears unusual beyond the expectation or comprehension of the observer" ("Miracle," *Oxford Dictionary of Philosophy*, 1996).

The Congregation for the Causes of Saints oversees the mechanisms involved when validating miracles in the Catholic Church. A miracle is usually part of the process to canonize a saint. The chosen supernatural event is deemed authentic or invalid through a complex system of steps divided into two major components.

1. First, the bishop opens the case of an extraordinary event whose servant of God passed away within his jurisdiction. Next, the bishop records the depositions of eyewitnesses before delving into clinical or instrumental documentation. The church has over sixty specialized medical doctors who are used to investigate the clinical portions of the events.
2. In the second portion, the Roman Congregation examines the documents and any subsequent material sent to support the miraculous nature of the chosen event. Eventually, the congregation rules on the matter, effectively closing the case.

ESSENTIAL

Physical manifestations are one of the strongest pieces of evidence when looking at the possibility of a miracle. The evidence presented is more easily examined under scientific protocol than if the event is just observed. This gives all involved the opportunity to truly investigate the origin of the event.

>> CASE: MIRACLE BABY

A great number of modern miracles are medical in nature. In 2001, merely days after his birth, a child was diagnosed with liver failure so severe he required a liver transplant. When the initial donor liver proved incompatible, physicians were certain the baby would pass away. The events that followed astounded doctors and defied medical science:

The child's family prayed to Father George Preca, who was the first Maltese Catholic saint and creator of the Society of Christian Doctrine in Malta. They prayed that he would ask God to spare the life of their child. A glove used during the exhumation of the priest in 2000 also was placed upon the infant's body. Less than a week later, the baby's liver started to function normally, and within another four days the baby no longer required a transplant. Today the child is a perfectly healthy five-year-old. (Caldwell, Simon. "Surgeon Tells of Healed Baby, Crucial Miracle for Malta's First Saint." *Catholic News Service*. May 2007.)

>> CASE: MOTHER MARY MACKILLOP

Even the modern-day marvels are as breathtaking as those from centuries ago. Another story of a modern-day miracle involves the inexplicable recovery of a terminal woman after praying to Mother Mary Mackillop, Australia's first saint:

"The approved miracle involved the healing of a . . . woman with inoperable lung cancer during the mid 1990s. Given just a few months to live, she asked the Sisters of Joseph, which Mother Mary founded, to pray for her, and was given a relic of Mother Mary's to wear. Against all odds she not only recovered but all traces of the cancer disappeared." ("The Miracles That Put Mary Mackillop on the Path to Sainthood." *Herald Sun*. December 2009.)

This was Mother Mary's second miracle and led to her canonization by Pope Benedict XVI.

Although held to strict scrutiny, miracles are still designated by the Catholic Church. The definition and importance of miracles holds steadfast despite the evolving modern era. Surpassing the laws of nature and defying medical science, these phenomenal events continue to touch followers of the church and nonbelievers alike.

CHAPTER 17

Skepticism about the Afterlife

Paranormal phenomena of all types have been subjects of disbelief, controversy, and debate for centuries. In most instances, there are no stated reasons of disbelief. They are debunked at the mere prospect of their existence. Skepticism plays an important and healthy part of any investigation and research. However, when skepticism becomes close-minded thought with preconceived ideas, it starts to take on a definition other than its main purpose, that is, to question new ideas and discoveries with an unbiased, rational thought process.

When Skepticism Is Needed

Whether it is the fear of knowing what exists beyond the sensory world or the unexplained abhorrence of finding out something new and possibly bigger than human existence, the many so-called "skeptics" will debunk these ideas without any due investigation of the available data and information or appropriate critical inquiry. Though there exists some lack of tangible evidence for a lot of these phenomena (including the afterlife), what is even more disappointing is the fact that many researchers are not even willing to investigate these without any biases.

Who Is a Skeptic?

The idea of skepticism came from the Greeks, which meant that nothing should be believed or disbelieved unless proven by what they called the "natural law." The idea in essence means keeping an open mind, asking for evidence, and critically examining it before believing in something. Being a true or "open-minded" skeptic means having no biases or agendas when evaluating the idea in question—essentially being a true guardian of truth, who looks beyond the allegations and unverified opinions. In today's world, being a skeptic has taken on a somewhat different meaning. Any person challenging an idea with or without biases is referred to as a skeptic.

Afterlife and Skepticism

There are many kinds of evidence offered for the existence of the afterlife. In his book *Life After Death: Burden of Proof*, well-known spiritual guru Deepak Chopra discusses six different types of evidence, which include NDE, ESP, quantum consciousness, mediumship, and morphic resonance fields. Skeptics, like modern-day skeptic Michael Shermer, have questioned all these explanations and evidence. Chopra, in reply to Shermer, presented past experimental evidence that reaffirms the existence of the afterlife.

The phenomena most associated with the afterlife, besides mediumship, is the near-death experience. Skeptics argue that there is no empirical evidence of out-of-body experiences, but only narratives from people who claim to have had a near-death experience. They also argue that a NDE is scientifically falsifiable, and that consciousness does not exist outside the body; in fact, self-awareness is merely the notion created by the brain. With the advancement of science, it is argued that the brain can be physically manipulated in behaving and perceiving as desired.

However, the afterlife researchers and believers argue that NDE and the consciousness' existence after death are not scientifically falsifiable as the phenomena are nonphysical and possibly not even measurable currently. There have not been many experiments conducted in the past with the intention of determining the departing of the soul from the body at the time of death that could conclusively prove anything. In addition, prominent afterlife researchers like Dr. Robert Jordan, Dr. P. M. H. Atwater, and Susan Blackmore suggest that it may not be in the capacity of current science to measure the physical forms of energy associated with such phenomena, like many other unexplained and immeasurable forms of universal matter and energy.

ESSENTIAL

"If you are only skeptical, then no new ideas make it through to you. You become a crotchety old person convinced that nonsense is ruling the world. . . . But every now and then, a new idea turns out to be on the mark, valid and wonderful."—Carl Sagan

Similarly, Victor Zammit, an Australian lawyer and a well-known paranormal and afterlife researcher, claims that evidence from EVP has only been debunked by skeptics, but never truly examined for its authenticity. As he puts it, the "inflexibility and the determination of the closed-minded skeptic to block any inconsistent new information" has proved to be a hindrance in progress of the research in afterlife. He also says that Dr. Raudive's (the discoverer of the phenomena) studies have not received the due critical examination so far, which could have lent more insights into the afterlife.

Being a True or Open-Minded Skeptic

True skepticism is about doubting, not believing anything on its face value, and conducting inquiry to find the truth. Mere denial of something does not qualify you as a "true" or "open-minded" skeptic.

From the days of Newton and Darwin when things were perceived to be more deterministic, to today when even science has evolved into believing that the world is full of paradox and ambiguity, we have come a long way. Quantum physics and string theory introduce concepts of a nonlocal universe and the idea that the root to all matter and energy is the cosmic vibrational frequencies, respectively.

Both in their own way suggest that there is a lot in the universe that is still unexplained. Similarly, observations of paranormal and afterlife phenomena may also fall into this realm of "beyond today's science," demanding more investigation with an open mind.

Weighing the Evidence with an Open Mind

The Committee for the Scientific Investigation of Claims of the Paranormal (CSICOP) describes skeptics as those suspending judgment until the evidence is in. From this, it is evident that skeptics support rationalism and scientific theory. When one performs paranormal research and comes up with instances of afterlife phenomena, there are usually two kinds of reactions: some who readily accept the concept, the believers; and others who are wary of believing it unconditionally, the skeptics and debunkers.

An open-minded skeptic is one who does not accept superstitions to explain psychic or physical phenomena. However, if it is proved scientifically, then he will accept the explanation. As Professor Bertrand Russell has said, "We should not go for complete skepticism, but for degrees of probability." This definition best explains the viewpoint of an open-minded skeptic.

A closed-minded skeptic is a person who has already made up his mind about everything. He is so rigid in his nonbelief that even if something can be shown to have a scientific basis, he will still not agree to it. These types are not true skeptics in that they have changed the meaning of skepticism from "those who doubt" to those "who will never accept." This group is also known as pseudo-skeptics.

When skeptics conduct experiments to verify others' findings, their mental makeup will give them different results. For example, a debunker is more likely to reject the results of psychic observations even if they were positive, saying that the experimenter was probably a fraud or unqualified. Closed-minded skeptics see only parts of the jigsaw puzzle because of conscious deletion of segments of knowledge. They are unable to see the whole of it because of their attitude of disbelief.

A scientific approach helps one to refrain from drawing poorly supported conclusions from the evidence, even though one may want the evidence to be proven true.

Many mainstream scientists are skeptics, especially when it comes to paranormal phenomena, because they are wary of anything that cannot be measured or quantified. The very same scientists, who are pretty closed-minded when it comes to accepting paranormal phenomena, talk of black holes and dark matter without batting an eyelid, even though there is no visible proof yet that they exist. They will dismiss without a thought the theories of supernatural and the paranormal while at the same time propounding contradicting theories with extraordinary claims.

QUESTION

What if my religion tells me that something is not possible?
Everyone has to determine his own beliefs when it comes to the possibilities of an afterlife. The fact that science might open a glimpse into that possibility must be accepted, but how you incorporate it into your own faith is your own personal decision.

When analyzing paranormal phenomena, the first step is selection of evidence. There are innumerable instances and incidents to sift through. In the process of selecting the evidence, both believers and skeptics tend to choose that evidence that they are inclined to accept, not that which is relevant or which may make us change our stand.

It is therefore important to focus on the quality of evidence that leads to a conclusion and the method behind it. Keeping an open mind when evaluating a phenomenon makes a person a good skeptic.

Paid Skeptics: The Industry

The world for centuries has had a fascination with life after death, ghosts, and paranormal activities—so much so that an industry of paid skeptics has developed, whereas previously skeptics were motivated by their own beliefs and opinions, not financial incentives.

Research into new consciousness, the existence of ghosts, UFOs, life after death, near-death experiences, quantum physics, and psychic phenomena explores avenues that hint at the existence of other dimensions or levels of reality and consciousness. But some individuals and religious groups find these theories challenging to their own beliefs, sometimes even abhorrent. Without the wherewithal to counter the theories themselves, they employ "paid skeptics."

These days many skeptics are actually paid, by those with a vested interest, to express their opinions publicly on television, radio, online, in newspapers, and magazines. Most recently, it is suggested that many climate change skeptics are paid by oil companies to express their opinions openly.

Types of Skeptics

As previously explained, there are two main types of skeptics. "True skeptics" seek the truth in all matters presented, and "pseudo-skeptics" are fixed in their ideas or their opinions, as are paid skeptics.

TRUE SKEPTICS/OPEN-MINDED SKEPTICS

- Ask questions to try to understand new things and are open to learning about them
- Apply critical examination and inquiry to all sides, including their own
- Are nonjudgmental and do not jump to rash conclusions
- Seek the truth and consider it the highest aim
- Think in terms of possibilities rather than in preserving fixed views
- Fairly and objectively weigh evidence on all sides
- Acknowledge valid, convincing evidence rather than ignoring or denying it
- Possess solid, sharp common sense and reason
- Are able to adapt their paradigms to new evidence and update their hypothesis to fit the data
- When all conventional explanations for a phenomenon are ruled out, are able to accept paranormal ones

ALERT

Professional skeptics have been in business for many years and have been financed by various organizations and corporations to push their agenda to the public. In recent years paid professional skeptics have found that the paranormal arena is ripe for making huge amounts of money in speaking fees, magazine publications, television appearances, and conferences.

PSEUDO-SKEPTICS/CLOSED-MINDED SKEPTICS/PAID SKEPTICS

- Do not ask questions to try to understand new things
- Carry a fixed set of unchanging beliefs that all data must conform to
- Are not interested in truth, evidence, or facts, but only in defending the views of already established conventional beliefs
- Are willing to lie and deceive to preserve their own views, which are their true master
- Are judgmental and quick to draw conclusions about things they know little or nothing about
- Scoff and ridicule what they oppose instead of using unbiased analysis
- Insist that everything unknown and unexplained must have a conventional, "normal" explanation
- Are unable to adapt their existing beliefs to new ideas and deny data that doesn't fit into their beliefs
- When all conventional explanations for a phenomenon are ruled out, are not able to accept paranormal ones

Mostly, the pseudo-skeptics are usually quite fanatical and have little regard for facts, evidence, or truth. They have a preconceived opinion or belief that paranormal phenomena are impossible and therefore set out to debunk, not investigate.

Millions of dollars are being generated and paid to the professional skeptics industry for their opinions and their denial of scientific facts. Magazines, books, websites, television shows, and the speaking circuit are but a few outlets for the professional skeptic to earn a very lucrative living by denying whatever they are paid to deny.

With each new discovery a new denial must be presented in order to keep the money flowing into the industry. One conference in Las Vegas, Nevada, advertised "one of the most spectacular rosters of skeptical speakers ever assembled." The conference offered workshops with titles such as "Skepticism 101," "Skepticism in the Classroom," and "Skepticism and Sexuality."

A skeptic can be sensational and provocative in the media and popular culture. This highlights their motivation for financial gain. Ideally, skepticism should be a tool and method of inquiry to help one learn things and find truth; it should not be used as a cover to defend one's own rigid narrow views or make money.

When Skeptics Become Believers

Afterlife research and communication has generated a lot of interest in recent times, with several scientists and prominent personalities venturing to explore and study the existence of the phenomena. Even several scientifically inclined skeptics over the last couple of centuries opened up to the idea of an afterlife, and after examination and observation turned into believers. Here are a few inspiring stories of some famous personalities who turned from being skeptics to being believers.

Dr. Charles Robert Richet (1850–1935)

Dr. Richet was a Nobel prize–winning physiologist and scientist who began as a materialistic nonbeliever and later became deeply involved in parapsychology and afterlife research. Richet admitted that in the 1870s, he dismissed and even scoffed at parapsychology research being carried out by prominent scientists like Frederic Myers and William Crookes. He later went on to commend both these researchers, saying that he was "equally distinguished by their courage and by their insight."

In the early 1880s, Richet came across the case of an Italian peasant named Eusapia Palladino who was exhibiting phenomena similar to that in the case of D. D. Home (a famous medium) being studied by Crookes. Richet became interested in studying Palladino and Home, and he became involved in several experiments with these mediums. Later on, he went on to join the ranks of famous psychical researchers and also became the president of the Society for Psychical Research in 1905. Richet coined the term *ectoplasm*.

Ian Stevenson (1918–2007)

Ian Stevenson was a highly regarded Canadian professor of psychiatry and a prominent biochemist. Early in his career, after graduating in medicine, he went to work in several hospitals and later became interested and involved in researching psychosomatic illnesses and medicine in the 1940s. It was while studying the cases of psychosomatic illnesses that he realized biochemistry alone was an inadequate explanatory tool, and that psychiatry holds the key in many cases.

During his study of the human psyche, Stevenson found psychoanalysis and behaviorism inadequate to explain personality and human characteristics. His interest in the afterlife phenomena was triggered in the late 1950s when he came across cases of children under the age of ten recalling past lives, suggesting the possibility of reincarnation. He went on to travel the world, studying several cases suggestive of reincarnation, and became more and more convinced of the phenomena's existence. He published a paper on the subject in 1960 and suggested that reincarnation should be a major area of study alongside heredity and environment in understanding human behavior.

ESSENTIAL

The sign of a true open-minded skeptic is his willingness to examine, question, and analyze all the data from at least one paranormal research study before formulating an opinion as to whether the evidence presented is correct or incorrect. Without this ability they must be categorized as a closed-minded skeptic.

Sir Oliver Joseph Lodge (1851–1940)

Sir Oliver Joseph Lodge was a prominent British physicist and mathematician credited with significant contributions in the fields of thermal conductivity, thermo-electricity, and electricity. He was the first to transmit a radio signal, even before Marconi, and was also the developer of the Lodge spark plug. Just like other scientists of his time, Lodge did not believe in the possibility of communicating with an afterlife.

In 1883, he came across stage performer Irving Bishop and was impressed and intrigued by the idea of thought transference and telepathy. He began thinking of the possibilities that can arise from the concept of dislocation between body and mind. He stated, "I began to feel that there was a possibility of the survival of personality." Lodge later went on to study the American medium Leonora Piper in 1889, followed by other investigations and research into methods of different popular mediums of the time. He also wrote a book on communication with the spirit of his son who died in a battle. The book was published in 1916 and was called *Raymond, or Life After Death*.

Sir William Crookes (1832–1919)

Sir William Crookes was a celebrated British scientist of his time. He was a highly regarded physicist and chemist, who is known for his many contributions to the world of science, including discovery of the element thallium and inventions including the spinthariscope, radiometer, and the Crookes tube.

Crookes was an open-minded scientist who was of the opinion that everything deserves an investigation and should not be written off or believed without due study of the subject. He decided to investigate the phenomena of Spirtualism and afterlife communication in the early 1870s. Over a period of three years, Crookes sat through multiple sittings of mediumship with the then-celebrated medium D. D. Home. He became convinced of the psychic powers of the medium and the phenomena of afterlife communication. When he went public with his views, he was faced with widespread criticism, causing him to refrain from publicly speaking on the subject again. However, he remained a firm believer in the afterlife and survival of consciousness after death.

Case Studies: Fraudulent Afterlife Evidence

There is an abundance of cases involving evidence of the afterlife. Personal stories of dying family members and friends are innumerable and heartfelt. However, the otherworldly market permits vague, unverified information, painting a bull's-eye on the backs of grief-stricken customers looking for answers about their deceased loved ones. Fraudulent cases of spiritual mediums and psychics claiming to have a communication line with the deceased are innumerable.

Deceitfully claiming to be in touch with those who have passed on is not a scam limited to modern times. During the late 1800s, a woman and her husband, the Fletchers, falsely claimed they were in contact with the dead in order to con a grieving daughter and gain her inheritance. The exploited woman testified when Mrs. Fletcher was arrested and tried for fraud. According to Montagu Williams in *Later Leaves: Being the Further Reminiscences of Montagu Williams*:

> *I fell on my knees and put the jewels into Mr. Fletcher's lap, thinking I was doing an act of obedience. My mother, through Mr. Fletcher, blessed me for having obeyed her instructions, saying that, if I had not done so, so strong was the magnetism in them, I should have been drawn into spirit life before my time.*

The Society for Psychical Research

Fraud is so widespread in the paranormal field that the Society for Psychical Research was founded in 1882 to "examine allegedly paranormal phenomena in a scientific and unbiased way," and remains a functional nonprofit organization in the present time. The Society for Psychical Research labored intensely to expose deception in spiritual mediums boasting they could communicate with the dead. Not all scam artists fit the public's view of a fraudulent psychic working on the street corner or out of a small shop. In fact, many of these afterlife con artists are professionals with impressive credentials to dissuade suspicion.

Even Harry Houdini, a renowned magician, labored to bring frauds preying on the vulnerable and grief-stricken into the light of truth by writing *A Magician Among the Spirits*. Houdini's text reveals the grim details surrounding several famous psychics and how they fooled customers with hoaxes masquerading as afterlife phenomena. Yet, Houdini was not a skeptic from the start. Spurred by the death of his mother, the awe-inspiring magician sought answers from the spirit realm: "I have never entered a séance room except with an open mind devoutly anxious to learn if intercommunication is within the range of possibilities and with a willingness to accept any demonstration which proves a revelation of truth." His career in magic and his clever wit permitted him to see beyond psychics' and spiritual mediums' veil of deceit.

ALERT

Fraud is generally defined by the law as a deliberate deception or misrepresentation of existing fact made by one person to another while knowing it to be not true in order to secure unfair or unlawful gain.

With the wealth of information, books, and controversy surrounding such a delicate subject for those who have lost a loved one, the opportunity to deceive is immense. Countless people in the throes of mourning have found themselves victims of a scam intended to lighten their wallets instead of providing them genuine glimpses into the afterlife.

As with any occupation, especially in the "get well" field, there are bad apples mixed in with the truly gifted professional. There will always be fraud of some type permeating society, but when it's directed toward the bereaved, it seems so much more harmful.

CHAPTER 18

Do It Yourself: Conducting Afterlife Experiments

It is always fascinating to read about the research and investigations into the afterlife. To try to weigh the evidence of the possibility of such a realm is a daunting task. With modern-day technology it is now possible for anyone to conduct her own look into this often-complex and mysterious subject. The first and most important thing that needs to be achieved is the intent to learn with an open mind.

Using Physical Devices to Investigate

In order to prove the existence of the paranormal, investigators use both conventional and scientific devices to record and track evidences of paranormal activity. Some of the standard equipment an investigator should possess are:

- **A notepad and pencil:** Though it may seem rudimentary, it is important to always keep a paper and pencil handy to note small details that the investigators might need later on, like the immediate reactions of the person experiencing the phenomena.
- **Flashlight and batteries:** Since most of the paranormal activity happens in semi-lighted areas, it is good to keep a flashlight handy. Also, since spirits are supposed to take energy from the sources available, according to paranormal researchers, the flashlight may go off in the middle of an investigation. An extra supply of batteries may be useful.
- **Digital cameras/35mm camera:** Investigators try to capture the scene on digital cameras whenever they sense that a paranormal occurrence is about to happen. High-resolution digital cameras are used to capture light anomalies, shadows, and unexplained shapes.
- **Audio recorder:** This is the most important piece of equipment that a paranormal investigator needs. Investigators try to catch EVP by using tape recorders for recording at the site of activity. During playback, background noises from "disembodied sources" might be heard that were not audible at the time of recording.
- **EMF detector:** Fluctuations in electromagnetic fields are detected with this equipment. Investigators are of the opinion that the presence of a paranormal entity causes these fluctuations. Most of the detectors use a single-axis AC EMF, which is insufficient to detect natural sources. The latest in EMF detectors is the Natural EM TriField Meter, which detects changes in electrical or magnetic fields.
- **Infrared thermal scanner:** This tool measures temperature fluctuations by sending out a thermal beam. Paranormal investigators are able to pick out "hot" and "cold" spots, which might be caused by paranormal activity.

- **Walkie-talkie:** When working in a group it is better to have walkie-talkies to keep in touch with the various members of the group or in case of an emergency.
- **Night vision goggles:** Night vision goggles or even adapters that can be attached to the camcorder are particularly useful to see in the dark, so that one does not mistake a shadow for a spirit.
- **Dowsing tools:** Originally used to divine water, dowsing rods are now used in paranormal study. When the rods cross, it indicates that a source of energy has been found.
- **Video recorder:** It is the most sought-after evidence of afterlife activity. It is used to take a video recording of the event, but such evidence is rare.

ESSENTIAL

Try flattening a piece of Play-Doh and leaving it in an area of possible paranormal phenomena or when trying to contact the other side. Look at it later to see if any physical imprints have been left in it. Make sure to recode your findings, as you may want to try it again under different circumstances.

Newer Ghost Hunting Equipment

Modern equipment is used more for ruling out the possibility of a discarnate being. While it does not indicate the presence of a supernatural being, it helps us to understand the scientific reason for some occurrences, thereby ruling out the possibility of anything surreal.

- **Eight-camera CCTV system:** This ensemble allows the investigator to monitor all areas at the same time continuously for three to four days. It also has a built-in DVD recorder to make instant footage of what needs to be focused on or studied further.
- **Thermal imager:** This device is different from the thermometer in that there is no need for physical contact to measure the temperature changes. It produces images that we can see by measuring the

difference in heat from a distance using the upper portion of the infrared spectrum. Ghosts are believed to emit radiations in this frequency, and the imager is used for capturing that heat variation.

- **Carbon monoxide detector:** High levels of carbon monoxide induce dizziness and other symptoms associated with paranormal experience, even hallucinations. By measuring the amount of carbon monoxide we can rule out that the person was not under its influence when he claimed to have the experience.

Making trials with new equipment and new technology can help establish the presence of the supernatural and explain it in a scientific manner. Look for new methods as they are developed, and network with friends and colleagues to exchange information.

Learning How to Meditate

Meditation is a technique that allows you to train your mind to control emotions and thoughts, and become more aware of self. It helps you elevate to a higher level of consciousness, which in turn relaxes the mind and allows you to look at the worldly things and experiences with enhanced wisdom and objectivity. The positive effects of meditation on emotional, mental, and physical health are well-recognized worldwide.

Basics of Meditation and Key Elements

The Dalai Lama says that the way to gain the most from any doctrine is to incorporate it into your daily life. Meditation, too, is most effective when it is performed in the right way on a regular basis. There are key elements that help make meditation successful:

- **Right time:** The right time for meditation can vary from person to person. Some find meditation easiest to perform just before sleep time, while others like meditating early in the morning. However, it is best to have a consistent schedule for your meditation—both your body and mind will benefit most from meditation if you have a disciplined and fixed schedule.

- **Right physical parameters:** The environment, attire, and posture for meditation is also important and should be in accordance with the comfort of the subject. It is also important that the place of meditation is silent, clean, and uncluttered. Meditation clothes should be comfortable and loose and should allow you to maintain the meditation posture with ease. The Lotus posture is most recommended for meditation.
- **Right frame of mind:** When commencing meditation, the mind should be cleared of all conscious thoughts as much as possible. This does not mean that you stop thinking, which is almost impossible to achieve. The right frame of mind is achieved when thoughts flit across your mind without disturbing your state of calm.
- **Object of focus:** This can be a word, mantra, or a mind picture that you can concentrate on. The object of focus helps bring your mind back on track when thoughts interrupt your meditative mind state.

Meditation is a good way to de-stress every day. A simple meditation involves being consciously aware and relaxing muscles from head to toe. The object of focus helps retain concentration as you continue to meditate. Keeping your eyes closed helps keep distractions at bay, making mental relaxation effective and complete.

QUESTION

How do I stop the random thoughts that flood my mind when I start to meditate?
When learning to meditate it is important to not try to stop these thoughts but to let them just flow. When you try to stop them, you end up focusing on them, and this will stop the meditation process. Try to focus on the gaps between the flowing thoughts.

Establishing a routine for meditation once or twice every day will train your mind to carry out the process with fewer distractions day after day. Begin meditating for a few minutes and gradually extend the time as your control over your mind grows.

Popular Meditation Techniques

There are many techniques of meditation, but some are more popular than others. Transcendental meditation (TM) is one such technique that has been researched and studied extensively. It involves the utterance of a mantra or phrase repetitively throughout the duration of the meditation to help the mind focus. It is simple to learn and is very effective. TM regulates blood pressure, decreases anxiety, and helps resist drug or alcohol cravings.

The complete focus on breathing during yoga is also a form of meditation. Yoga practitioners sense an increase in awareness levels immediately after they complete a session. Taoist meditation techniques, too, focus on the breath. There are two main components here: *jing* (calm) and *ding* (concentration).

Some other popular meditation techniques include walking meditation, loving kindness meditation, vibrational meditation, Vipassana, and movement meditation. The technique that suits one practitioner may not be effective for another. Choosing the technique that you can perform with greatest comfort and ease is important. It is advisable to start meditating under the guidance of an experienced practitioner or teacher.

Resolving Common Problems During Meditation

Meditation cannot be mastered instantly. But with time, you can and will be able to carry out meditation without mental or physical disruptions. Keeping this in mind helps you stay encouraged and positive during the initial stages. In the words of Jon Kabat-Zinn, an acknowledged meditation expert, "If we hope to go anywhere or develop ourselves in any way, we can only step from where we are standing."

Many beginners complain of pain or numbness in the limbs or a prickly feeling in the toes and fingers after they sit in meditation posture for a while. These problems usually pass as the practitioner gets into the habit of maintaining the meditation posture. Those who experience severe discomfort can opt for a more comfortable position, such as sitting on a chair.

Distracting thoughts are another common problem. Avoid making a conscious effort to "not think." As the thoughts come, bring your mind back to your object of focus gently but firmly. With time, the number and frequency of such distracting thoughts will diminish. When you have learned to relax and open your mind, you can achieve advanced learning abilities that can be valuable in your research and understanding of paranormal events.

B. Alan Wallace, practitioner and teacher of Buddhism, explains that mastering meditation is a process and not an event. He says, "Like a good crop, good meditation cannot be forced, and requires cultivation over time." (*Tibetan Buddhism from the Ground Up: A Practical Approach for Modern Life*)

Opening Yourself to Communication

The question of whether life continues in some form after death is still being debated without any widely accepted answer as of yet. Messages from the dead, communication through symbols, visitations by the dead in dreams, and many other occurrences point to some channel of communication existing between our world and that of the spirits. If you desire to make connections to the afterlife, the key is to remain open to all possibilities of communication.

Why Would You Want to Communicate?

The purpose of afterlife communication may differ from person to person. Those left behind often try to reach out to the dead to assuage their grief or any guilt associated with the person's death. Being able to talk to or sense the dead person can bring you a feeling of closure and may ease the pain of the loss. Many turn to their dead relatives for guidance or advice during difficult times. A Ouija board or similar communication tool may be used, or a medium may act as a link to the deceased.

In many other instances, it is the spirit that initiates communication. The spirit may wish to complete unfinished business or help family members during troubled times. A well-publicized occurrence was the appearance of farmer James Chaffin's spirit to disclose the whereabouts of his will to his son. Other spirits simply want their family to know that they are happy. Symbolic or subliminal messages that can readily be associated with the deceased are often experienced in such cases. The deceased may also visit the living in her dreams.

Keep an Open Mind

Everybody loses a loved one at some point of time in her life. But it is only a few who experience a sense of the deceased's continuing presence after the person's death. Mediums are able to sense these "people" owing to their heightened perceptions or extraordinary talents. But many others, who are normal people with no special abilities, have had similar experiences too. Researchers believe that to establish communication with the spirits, you must be prepared to believe when confronted with signs or symbols.

Establishing a Connection Without a Medium

Before you contact a medium, you can try to establish a connection with the spirit yourself. This serves three purposes. One, you can commit to your belief that you can communicate and this helps you keep an open mind about the process. Two, you are just as likely to sense your loved one's presence as the medium, who is a stranger. Three, you can "broadcast" your intent and hope to reach the deceased's spirit; this draws the spirit to communicating with you.

Actively Preparing for Spirit Communication

It is believed that spirits are in a higher state of vibration than the living because they are not burdened by flesh or mired in the denser realm of our world. EVPs, electromagnetic instruments, and other tools have been used to determine the variations in vibrational frequencies between the dead and living. This difference makes it difficult for the living (at lower vibrational frequencies) to communicate easily with them. This is why mediums who can duplicate the vibration are able to reach a loved one's spirit at times when a loved one cannot.

There are many ways to become more receptive to sensing the presence of the dead.

- **State of mind:** Anger, grief, guilt, fear, and other strong emotions are barriers to communication. They close your mind to the subtle signs and subliminal messages that may be conveyed by the spirits. Relax your mind and calm yourself before you try to "reach" your deceased loved ones.

- **Atmosphere:** The atmosphere of the area where you are initiating the communication must be calm and silent. Surround yourself with items associated with the deceased like photographs, personal items, and other things that evoke positive memories of the person. These positive energies call to the spirit and also help keep negative energies at bay.
- **Consciously reach out to the person:** Make a conscious effort in your mind to reach out to the spirit. This, again, "broadcasts" your intent and need to communicate, and this need will draw the spirit to you.
- **Dream state:** Just before you go to sleep, ask your loved one to contact you. They find it the easiest to make contact through the dream state and will often meet you there to communicate. Keep a pad of paper and a pen or an audio recorder next to your bed so when you wake you can record any instances of contact that might have occurred.

ALERT

It is important that when you ask for this communication that you ask for it with the "highest and best intentions" and for it to be "surrounded with the white light of love." This will set the conditions of any contact and will filter out any unwanted residual energy in your field.

Be aware that it may take time; often, several attempts may be required to establish the link. The afterlife is still mostly shrouded in mystery. How the communication happens and what restrictions there are on the spirits are unknown, and every spirit may not be able to communicate in the same manner and at a time of its choosing. Sometimes you may get indirect answers or messages that are not relevant to your questions at all. Still, any such contact demonstrates the possibility of opening a channel of communication, and is a successful attempt.

Creating Studies to Present Evidence

There are a lot of people who believe in the afterlife and don't need any evidence to prove that it exists. But there are others who want to be convinced about the existence of the afterlife and conduct rigorous scientific experiments to look for its evidence. Such people can be used to conduct afterlife experiments and observe the evidence themselves. Here is an overview of different methods to collect afterlife evidence.

EVP

Electronic voice phenomena, or EVP, is also a widely used technique to look for evidence of the afterlife. EVP recordings are usually made by increasing the sensitivity of the equipment being used to record the voices in the background. The most important part of conducting a reliable EVP experiment is to use an isolated area or a quiet room so that the possibility of stray noises is minimized. As far as the equipment is concerned, you can go for a portable digital voice recorder, but make sure that it is good quality. You should also keep in mind that it is not easy for everyone to understand the voices recorded in EVP. You have to listen carefully and patiently. With some practice, you'll be able to detect words and phrases in the recordings. There is computer software on the market that can help you cut out the background "white noise" and increase the quality of your recordings.

Using Mediums

Gifted mediums can help you communicate with your dead relatives. There are different kinds of mediums, and one type that can create reliable evidence is direct-voice mediums. These mediums can relay communication from a dead person in the deceased's own voice. It may not be easy to find such a medium to conduct the experiment, but if you are fortunate, you may be able to arrange such an experiment. The voice can then be analyzed to show that it came from a source other than the medium's voice box. Other mediums that can bring through personalities, physical traits, and specific evidence are great to utilize and may be easier to find and work with.

Out-of-Body Experiences

Out-of-body experiences, or OBEs, have been observed for centuries, and highly consistent experiences have been reported throughout the world. Although many of these experiences have been spontaneous or involuntary, it is possible to induce and consciously control an OBE. There are several teachers who train people to induce an OBE. It is usually achieved by learning to fall asleep without losing mental wakefulness, practicing lucid dreaming, and learning to get into a deep trance. Successfully achieving an OBE shows that the human body is separate from the entity that contains consciousness. When the body dies, there is no reason for this separate entity to also cease to exist. After death, it can enter into the afterlife where it can exist without the body.

ALERT

It is important to be able to furnish all the necessary records of your study. This means you must look at each study with an open mind and record all of the basic data surrounding the event or subject. Without this your studies might not be taken seriously.

Studying Experiences of Others

Besides these firsthand experiments, you can also carry out studies of phenomena experienced by others. Prominent phenomena that directly act as evidence of existence of afterlife include:

- Xenoglossy, where a person is able to speak or write a particular language without ever having learned it or having been exposed to it
- Viewings of apparitions and other signs of the presence of a dead person
- Near-death experiences, where a person comes back from the dead and has a vivid memory of that experience
- Spontaneous recall of past life, where a person starts narrating accurate facts, including places and names, about her past life

When carrying out studies of secondhand experiences, make sure that you record all the facts correctly. Carefully interview those who witnessed the phenomenon and the person who experienced it. Be rigorous in your research so that it can stand up to the scrutiny of a skeptic. Always remember that just as there are many believers in the afterlife, there are also many critics, and to be able to convince them, you need evidence that can withstand a scientific trial.

Recording Your Findings

Paranormal occurrences such as seeing a ghost or a vision are some of the evidences of an afterlife. Paranormal phenomena that have been recorded scientifically are said to be more valid than unsubstantiated claims. Proper documentation of these events is therefore necessary, not only to ensure credibility but also to aid in subsequent investigations. With the use of certain techniques, it is possible to record your findings so that these phenomena can be explained.

ESSENTIAL

The basic equipment needed for recording sightings or findings need not be expensive. You should have a camera (either film or digital), a tape or digital audio recorder, pen and paper, and, optionally, an electromagnetic detector and a laptop computer.

Steps to Record Personal Findings

The recording must be done as soon as possible after the experience. It is important to do this when the experience is still fresh in your memory. Write down the following details:

- **Location:** Write down the exact location of where you were when you had the experience. Was it in your home? If so, in which room? Was it outside? Where exactly? Be very specific.
- **State:** What state were you in? Were you sitting, standing, lying down, facing something or someone? Had you taken any kind of drugs or stimulants, or had you been drinking? Were there other people with you? Were you tired, sleepy, or wide-awake? Were you excited? Had you just read a book on this topic or been with someone who had narrated a similar experience? Anything at all that might have induced this state must be noted.
- **Environmental conditions:** Record whether it was night or day, bright or gloomy. If it was night, was the lighting adequate, or were there dark shadows? Was it a full moon or no moon?

- **Description of the phenomena:** If it was something you saw, describe it objectively. Write down its shape, color, the clothes it was wearing, its weight, etc. If it was something you felt, then describe the feeling in detail.
- **Proximity:** How close were you to the phenomenon? Try to give as accurate an estimation as possible.
- **Action:** If it was something you saw, record what it did. Were its arms raised? Did it move? Did it make any noises? Try to remember and record as much detail as possible.
- **Timing:** Be sure to record the duration of the experience. (Write down the starting and ending time.)
- **Submit report:** Hand over your report to a legitimate paranormal research group in your area or a nationally recognized organization. Ask other witnesses to sign the report to provide authenticity.

ALERT

To add weight to your recordings, write down your details such as name, address, age, gender, and any other relevant information. Make a drawing of the area and of what you saw. In some cases, these drawing are very helpful. Take a picture of the phenomenon. Many times people forget to capture the phenomenon even though they have a camera. Photos lend greater authenticity to your statement.

Steps to Record Other People's Findings

According to Richard Southall, author of *How to be a Ghost Hunter*, a four-step approach is to be followed.

1. **Interviewing the eyewitness(es):** When a sighting is reported, the person(s) who saw or felt the phenomenon must be interviewed. His body language must be noted while recounting the experience.
2. **The area history:** Independent of the witness, the area's history regarding such occurrences must be tabulated.

3. **Investigating the area:** This includes photographing the area, determining the right time to investigate, and following up on every lead to the phenomenon.
4. **Conclusions drawn:** From the recorded data, decide and conclude the investigation by citing what the experience is likely to be.

It is believed that ghosts (being electromagnetic in origin) create disruptions in these types of fields. Use an EMF detector to record the baseline readings of an area and the readings when a phenomenon is said to have occurred.

Ghosts are supposed to interfere with certain frequencies. EVP can be captured using tape or digital recorders and replaying the recording. If there is an unexplainable sound in the recording, it could be credited to the presence of a paranormal being. There is software available for your computer to help you record your EVP events and to help with clarifying the quality of the recoding.

Documenting your investigations will go a long way in explaining these phenomena and proving the theories regarding paranormal entities and events.

Participating in Established Current Research

When Galileo first invented the telescope, he presented it to the pope. Rather than accepting the invention as an advancement of scientific thought, the church shunned it as an "instrument of the devil." Today, a telescope is a basic tool in astronomy.

The study of the afterlife and communication with the dead often gets similar treatment from nonbelievers. However, with more and more research and detailed study being undertaken by scientists and researchers in recent times, the concept of life after death is slowly gaining acceptance. Many more people are coming forward to share their paranormal experiences and participate in established research programs.

Ongoing Afterlife Research

Independent researchers have recorded voice imprints of the deceased through EVP recordings under supervised conditions. All of these findings and ongoing research only serve to prove that there are many things that are beyond our understanding. In fact, many of these phenomena are of such a complex nature that they are difficult to describe.

Experiencing These Phenomena

It does not always require a medium or someone with special capabilities to communicate or sense the presence of a spirit. There have been many cases of family members seeing, hearing, or experiencing a dead relative's presence.

Many paranormal and psychical scientific research organizations welcome such individuals to come and share their experiences with them. These accounts help the researchers get more information about the paranormal occurrences and help them study the nature of the afterlife.

Participating in Afterlife Research

There are many ways in which you can participate in afterlife research. One of the easiest ways is to send your "out-of-the-ordinary" experiences to paranormal research organizations for further study. For instance, the Society for Psychical Research studies paranormal experiences sent in by people from across the world. You need to furnish some specific details of what the experience was.

QUESTION

How can I participate if I have never done any research?
If you volunteer to work with established organizations, they will walk you through the steps of what you need to do to become associated with the group. They will provide the needed training and any resources you can access to learn more about that particular investigation.

Active Participation

Participation in a specific research project is also possible with many research centers. In this case, you may be asked some specific questions that help gather data pertaining to an ongoing research project. Profiles of various interested volunteers are collected by such organizations, and participants may be called depending on their experiences cited in their application. The University of Arizona (conducting the SOPHIA project), the American Society for Physical Research (ASPR), and the Rhine Research Center are some reputed research centers where such active participation is possible.

Volunteering with a Paranormal Study Group

You can also volunteer with informal paranormal research groups in your locality to get some direct exposure to such phenomena. There are many such groups, such as the International Paranormal Research Association. Most are nonprofit research organizations that welcome interested volunteers who are willing to participate in studies and help with their research work. The American Ghost Society even offers a certificate course in ghost study, and the organization accepts members who are willing to actively research paranormal events.

Most researchers request detailed information about you and any previous paranormal experiences you may have had. This information helps them judge your level of sensitivity to the paranormal, your attitude toward the paranormal phenomenon, and the intensity of your past experiences.

Preparing Yourself for Participation

While it is evident that paranormal experiences are not restricted to mediums alone, it is also true that not everyone senses such phenomena. Before participating in a research of paranormal activity, it is necessary for you to keep an open mind. This helps you accept the phenomenon just as you would accept normal occurrences, provided you have compelling evidence. Your acceptance or rejection of these phenomena must be based on an objective and open-minded assessment of what you experience.

If you have already experienced some events or sensations that are out of the ordinary, then maintaining a detailed written journal will organize your feelings and thoughts, and will ensure that you remember exactly what happened sequentially. This journal will also provide the information that you may be required to give when you participate in a project.

The study of afterlife and other paranormal phenomena is not restricted to "specially" empowered mediums or believers alone. If you are interested in exploring what happens beyond this world and have the right mindset to accept clear evidence, then you should participate in paranormal research. And as Stephen Hawking says, "Real science can be far stranger than science fiction and much more satisfying."

APPENDIX A

Glossary of Terms

afterlife: The continuation of one's existence after the death of the physical body.

angel: One of a class of spiritual beings; a celestial attendant of God.

apparition: Supernatural appearance of a person or thing; a ghost or phantom.

apport: The production of objects by apparently supernatural means at a séance.

Buddhism: A religion that originated in India, based on the life and teachings of the Buddha (Siddhartha Gautama). Buddhists believe that people will undergo multiple reincarnations based on how morally and justly they lived their previous lives.

Christianity: A monotheistic religion based on the life and teachings of Jesus. It has several different denominations. Catholicism, Protestantism, and Eastern Orthodoxy are the largest, which have similarities and differences in their theories of the afterlife.

clairaudience: Clear hearing; the ability to hear sounds beyond ordinary capacity, as the voices of the dead.

clairsentience: Clear feeling; a form of extrasensory perception, the ability to sense energy around one's self.

clairvoyance: Clear seeing; the ability to see objects or actions beyond the range of natural vision.

consciousness: The awareness of one's own existence, sensations, thoughts, and surroundings.

dark energy: A unseen force that affects the behavior of photons and other particles throughout the universe; makes up most of the universe.

dark matter: A form of unknown matter invisible to electromagnetic radiation; makes up the majority of the matter in the universe.

death: The cessation of all the vital functions of an organism, including brain waves.

deathbed visitations: The viewing of deceased relatives or angels when one is close to death.

dimension: A property of space, a direction or possible measurement of space or time.

direct voice: The ability of a medium to speak in the exact voice of a discarnate being.

ectoplasm: The mysterious visible substance that is exuded by a medium or sitter in a group séance.

electronic voice phenomenon: The audio recording of what is thought to be a disembodied spirit.

ghost: A disembodied spirit; the sighting of a deceased being whose image is possibly caught in a time loop.

Gnosticism: A religion of nonhierarchical interpretation of the Christian message; a system of religious doctrines, possessing knowledge of spiritual matters.

Hades: The underworld, commonly referred to as hell.

Heisenberg uncertainty principle: Named for Werner Heisenberg, the principle of quantum mechanics. The principle puts limits on how much an observer can ever know about the position and velocity of an object at one particular time.

Hinduism: The common religion of India, based upon the religion of the original Aryan settlers as expounded and evolved in the Vedas, the Upanishads, the Bhagavad-Gita. Buddhism and Jainism are outside the Hindu tradition but are regarded as related religions.

Islam: The religious faith of Muslims, based on the words and religious system founded by the prophet Muhammad and taught by the Koran.

Judaism: The monotheistic religion of the Jews, having its ethical, ceremonial, and legal foundation in the precepts of the Old Testament and in the teachings and commentaries of the rabbis as found chiefly in the Talmud.

Large Hadron Collider (LHC): A particle accelerator at the European Laboratory for Particle Physics near Geneva, Switzerland, containing a circular underground tunnel 27km (16.8 miles) in circumference, around which two streams of particles are sent in opposite directions before being brought together in a high-energy collision.

life review: One segment of a near-death experience, reported by participants as viewing their entire life in a very brief moment with all the emotions and consequents being understood.

meditation: The act of meditating; self-thought; reflection; contemplation of one's self.

medium: A person through whom the spirits of the dead are able to contact the living.

mental mediumship: The relaying of information, via the varied aspects of thought transference, or mental telepathy, without using any of the five physical senses.

miracle: An extraordinary event in the physical world that surpasses all known human or natural powers and is ascribed to a supernatural cause.

M-theory: A theory that involves an eleven-dimensional universe in which the weak and strong forces and gravity are unified and to which all the string theories belong; thought to be a unifying theory.

mysticism: The beliefs, ideas, or mode of thought of mystics; a belief of a spiritual intuition of truths that transcends ordinary understanding.

near-death experience (NDE): A sensation or vision, as of the afterlife, reported by a person who has come close to death.

out-of-body experiences (OBE): A vivid feeling of being detached from one's body, usually involving observing it and its environment from nearby.

phenomenon: An amazing or incredible fact, occurrence, or circumstance observed or that is observable.

physical mediumship: The process whereby someone in spirit form works or operates through the mental and physical energies of a medium and causes something physical to happen on the earth plane. When the phenomena occurs, everyone is able to see and/or hear it.

quantum physics: The branch of physics based on quantum theory.

quantum theory: A branch of theoretical physics; a body of scientific principles describing the behavior of particles and their interactions on the atomic and subatomic levels.

reincarnation: The belief that the soul, upon death of the body, comes back to earth in another body or form.

Scole experiment: A five-year investigation into life after death that took place in the English village of Scole in 1993 involving a group of mediums.

séance: A group meeting in which a medium attempts to communicate with the spirits of the dead.

skeptic: A person who questions the validity or authenticity of something purporting to be factual.

skepticism: A skeptical attitude; doubt.

spirit: The principle of conscious life; the soul, the essence of a human; a conscious, incorporeal being.

Spiritualism: The religion, philosophy, and science that believes in the proof of the continuity of life through the communication with spirits of the dead. This is accomplished through a medium who is particularly susceptible to their influence.

string theory: A mathematical entity used to represent elementary particles, in terms of a small but finite string-like object existing in the four dimensions of space-time and in additional space-like dimensions. The theory of such objects (string theory) avoids the many mathematical difficulties that arise from treating particles as points.

telekinesis: The movement of a body caused by thought without the application of a physical force.

Universalism: A system of religious beliefs maintaining that all men are predestined for salvation.

Wicca: Witchcraft; benevolent nature-oriented practices derived from pre-Christian religions.

Additional Resources

Books and Articles

D'Souza, Dinesh. *Life After Death: The Evidence* (Washington, DC: Regnery, 2009).

Filkin, David. *Stephen Hawking's Universe: The Cosmos Explained* (New York: Basic Books: 1998).

Green, Michael B., John H. Schwarz, and Edward Witten. *Superstring Theory. Vol. 1, Introduction* (Cambridge: Cambridge University Press, 1998).

Harris, Trudy. *Glimpses of Heaven: True Stories of Hope and Peace at the End of Life's Journey* (Grand Rapids, MI: Revell, 2009).

Higgins, Joseph M. *Hello . . . Anyone Home? A Guide on How Our Deceased Loved Ones Try to Contact Us through the Use of Signs* (Fall River, MA: Joseph M. Higgins, 2009).

Lund, David H. *Persons, Souls and Death: A Philosophical Investigation of an Afterlife* (Jefferson, NC: MacFarland, 2009).

Martin Ellis, Melissa. *The Everything® Ghosthunting Book* (Avon, MA: F+W Media, 2009).

Morse, Dr. Melvin, with Perry Paul. *Transformed by the Light: The Powerful Effect of Near-Death Experiences on People's Lives* (New York: Villard Books, 1992).

Pinansky, Robert. *After Life, What?* (San Diego: The Book Tree, 1995).

Raymond, Moody A. *Life After Life* (New York: HarperCollins, 2001).

Ring, Kenneth, PhD. *Mindsight: Near-Death and Out-of-Body Experiences in the Blind* (Palo Alto: Williams James Center for Consciousness Studies at the Institute Morris of Transpersonal Psychology, 1999).

Schwartz, Gary, PhD, with William L. Simon. *The Afterlife Experiments* (New York: Atria Books, 2002).

Solomon, Grant, and Jane Grant, in association with the Scole Experimental Group. *The Scole Experiment, Scientific Evidence for Life After Death* (London: Judy Piatkus Publishers, 2000).

Turner, Dr. John L. *Medicine, Miracles, and Manifestations: A Doctor's Journey Through the Worlds of Divine Intervention, Near-Death Experiences, and Universal Energy* (Franklin, NJ: Career Press, 2009).

Wills-Brandon, Carla, PhD. *One Last Hug Before I Go: The Mystery and Meaning of Deathbed Visions* (Deerfield Beach, FL: Health Communications, 2000).

Websites

Authors' Websites
www.josephmhiggins.com
www.chuckbergman.com

Deathbed Visions
Dr. Carla Wills-Brandon's research
www.near-death.com/deathbed.html

The Human Consciousness Project
www.nourfoundation.com

A Lawyer Presents the Case for the Afterlife
"Irrefutable objective evidence" presented by Victor Zammit
www.victorzammit.com/book

National Spiritualist Association of Churches
www.nsac.org

On-I-Set Wigwam Spiritualist Camp
www.onisetwigwam.com

Index

After-death communication
(ADC), 177–90, 182–84
best time for contact, 179
case studies, 187–90
dreams and dream state, 185
emotional solace and love and
caring, 183–84
evaluating, 186
evidence, 184–85
expansion of consciousness,
184
fragrances, 185
grief, alleviation of, 183
methods, 185
physical methods to gain
attention, 187
physical sensations, 185
synchronicity, 185
telepathy, 185
types of contact, 178–79
Ahmad, Mirza Tahir, 27–28
Al-Chokhachy, Elissa, 224
Alighieri, Dante, 44, *see also*
Dante's hell
Alzheimer patients. *See* Coma
and nonresponsive Alzheimer
patients, communications with
Anderson, Walter Truett, 85
Angels, 40–42
and Buddhism, 40–41

case studies, 52–56
and children, 55–56
and deathbed visitations, 211
interventions by, 41–42
and Islam, 41
and major religions, 40
and near-death experiences, 55
Animal reactions to death, 201–2
Apparitions, 192–93, 194
Apports, 143, 199–201
Arcangel, Dianne, 150
Atoms, 127
Atwater, P.M. H., 102, 255
Augustine, Saint, of Hippo, 250

Bailey, Alice, 110–11
Bailey, Chris, 197
Baily, Lee Worth, 225
Baldwin, Terry, 54
Barr, Stephen M, 221
Barrett, William, 208–9, 223
Bartlett-Gustina, Joanna, 37
Baynes, Cary, 7
Becco, Mariette, 243
Belanger, Jeff, 235
Bell, Alexander Graham, 147
Bennett, Alan, 66
Bennett, Diane, 66
Benor, Daniel, 53, 54, 242
Benson, Herbert, 89

Bishop, Irving, 262
Black, William, 195
Blackmore, Susan, 88, 255
Blavatsky, Madame, 140
Boleyn, Anne, 204
Borysenko, Joan, 78
Botkin, Allan, 183
Brain and consciousness, 74–76
Brennan, Barbara, 111
Briggs, Constance Victoria, 212, 227
Brinkley, Dannion, 101
Buddhism, 6, 7, 30–32
and angels, 41–42
and esotericism, 33–34
heaven and hell, 49
Bulkley, Patricia, 230–31
Burial, 9–10, 13–14
Burke, Greg, 250
Butler, Jon, 244

Cameras, 266
Campbell, Laurie, 60
Cantrell, Gary, 36
Carbon monoxide detector, 268
Carpenter, James, 72
Carrington, Hereward, 88
Carroll, Lee, 141
Cayce, Edgar, 141
CCTV system, 267
Celtic beliefs, ancient, 12–14

Chaffin, James, 193, 271

Chakras, 110–11

Channeling, 141

Chinese beliefs, ancient, 6–8

Chips, Godfrey, 17

Chopra, Deepak, 254

Christ, 35, 151

Christianity, 22–24

  Catholicism, 22–23

  Eastern Orthodox, 24

  heaven and hell, 48–49

  and mysticism, 35

  Protestantism, 23

Clairaudience, 144

Clairsentience, 144

Clairvoyance, 144

  vs. telepathy, 81

Cole, Linda, 201

Coma and nonresponsive
  Alzheimer patients,
  communications with, 82–84

Communication with afterlife

  atmosphere, 273

  consciously reaching out, 273

  dream state, 273

  electronic voice phenomena
    (EVP), 274

  mediums, 274

  opening yourself to, 271–73

  out-of-body experiences
    (OBEs), 274–75

  preparing for, 272–73

  reasons for, 271

  recording findings, 276–78

  scientific study of, 147–50

  secondhand experiences, 275

  state of mind, 272

  studies, creating, 273–74

  without a medium, 272

Confucius, 8

Consciousness, 74–76

  and meditation, 76–80

  telepathy, 80–82

Cook, Florence, 143

Cooper, Sharon, 68–70

Coover, John E., 81

Cornwell, J., 75

Crick, Francis, 75

Crime-solving with help of
  deceased, 168–75

  body location, 169–70

  evidence, 168–69, 173–74

  missing persons' location,
    171–73

  suspects, naming, 168

Crislip, Mark, 222

Cromie, William, 89

Crookes, William, 196, 260, 262

Dalai Lama, 268

Dante's hell, 44–47

Dark energy, 132–34

Daydreaming, 182

Death

  clinical vs. conscious, 96–97

  legal definition of, 96

Deathbed visitations, 208–17

  angels, 211

  biological explanations, 213

  case studies, 214–17

  common experiences, 211–12

  crowded rooms, 211

  deceased relatives, 211

  defined, 210

  described, 210

  explanations, 209–10

  history of, 208–10

  scientific studies, 212–14

  sounds/words, 211

  stairs/tunnels, 211

  supporting those who
    experience, 212

  visitations to others present, 213

  vs. hallucinations, 214

De Broglie, Louis Victor, 117

Deceased loved ones

  and deathbed visitations, 211

  and near-death experiences
    (NDEs), 99–100

Demiurge, 32

DeRose, Keith, 36

Diego, Juan, 243

Dimensions, 127, 128–29

Direct voice, 143

Dowsing tools, 267

Dreams, 180–82, 185

  daydreaming, 182

  dream state, 273

  stages of sleep, 180

Druidism. See Celtic beliefs,
  ancient

D'Souza, Dinesh, 221

Dunne, Tad, 230

Earnhardt, Dale, Jr., 193

Earnhardt, Dale, Sr., 193

Eastern religious influences, 18–19

  vs. western beliefs, 19–20

Ectoplasm, 143

Edward, John, 60, 142, 149

Egyptian beliefs, 3–6

  Book of the Dead, 4, 5

  Field of Rushes, 5, 6

Einstein, Albert, 109, 117

Electronic voice phenomenon
  (EVP), 197–99, 274

Ellison, Arthur, 66

EMF detector, 266
Engel, Gregory S., 114
Enlightenment. *See* Transformation consciousness, wisdom, and enlightenment
Esotericism, 33–34
    and Buddhism, 33–34
Estep, Sarah, 199
Experiments, 58–60
    do-it-yourself, 266–80

Faith healings, 151–52, 245
Fatima, 239
Fenwick, Peter, 64, 214, 216
Field of Rushes, 5, 6
Flint, Leslie, 143
Fontana, David, 66, 67
Forgione, Francesco, 246
Fox sisters, 140–41, 144–45
Foy, Robin, 66, 67
Foy, Sandra, 66
Fresnel, Augustin-Jean, 115
Freud, Sigmund, 180
Funeral feast, Celtic, 13
Funeral homes, phenomena in, 233–35

Gettysburg, 192, 203–4
Ghosts, 192–205
    types of, 193–95
Gnosticism, 32–33
God particle, 119–21
Gray, Jane, 204
Greek beliefs, ancient, 8–10
Green, Celia, 88
Greene, Brian, 126, 128
Guggenheim, Bill, 149, 185
Guggenheim, Judy, 149, 185
Gurney, Edmund, 148

Haraldsson, Erlendur, 51, 215
Harris, Trudy, 223, 224
Hauntings, 192
Hawking, Stephen, 128, 280
Heaven, 42–44
    Chinese beliefs, ancient, 8
    Christian, 22–24
    comparisons, 48–50
    Hinduism, 49
    individual existence of, 43
    Islam, 49
    justice and judgment, 43–44
    permanence theory of, 43
    and religions, 43
    reward theory of, 42
Heisenberg, Werner, 117
Heisenberg uncertainty principle, 117–19
Hell. *See also* Dante's hell
    Chinese beliefs, ancient, 8
    Christian, 22–24
    comparisons, 48–50
    Dante's version of, 44–47
    Hinduism, 49
    Islam, 49
Hermeticism, 34
Hertz, Heinrich, 116
Hicks, Esther, 141
Higgs, Peter, 120
Higgs boson. *See* God particle
Hinduism, 28–30
    heaven and hell, 49
Holgate, Stephen, 64
Horne, Daniel Dunglas, 143, 260, 262
Houdini, Harry, 147, 263
Human consciousness and spirit continuance after death, 70–72

Human consciousness project, 63–66
Human energy field, 110–12
    seven-layer model, 111–12

Infrared thermal scanner, 266
Islam, 26–28
    and angels, 41
    heaven and hell, 49

John Paul II, 22
Jordan, Robert, 255
Joseph, Rhawn, 3
Judaism, 24–26
    Kabbalistic, and mysticism, 35
Jung, Carl, 76, 181, 186
Jürgenson, Friedrich, 198

Karma, 29–30
Keen, Montague, 66, 67
Kelly, Edward, 140
Kreiger, Doris, 242
Krishna, 29
Kübler-Ross, Elizabeth, 212
Kuck, Mark, 54
Kumar, Sameet, 215

Laboure, Catherine, 243
Large Hadron Collider, 119–20
Levitations, 143
Lewis, D., 225
Lincoln, Abraham, 141, 196
Lincoln, Mary, 196
Lodge, Oliver Joseph, 261–62
Lonbardo, Tom, 85
Lourdes healings, 249
Lundahl, Craig R., 55

Marconi, Guglielmo, 147

Materialization, 143

Mathieu, Giraud, 243

Mathieu, Melanie, 243

Maxwell, James Clark, 116

Maynard, Nettie Colburn, 141

McCreery, Charles, 88

Medical personnel as witnesses to
  crossing over, 218–35
    afterlife experiments in medical
      setting, 220–22
    caregivers, 230–33
    hospice workers, 222–24
    hospital and ER staff, 225–27
    near-death experiences, 220
    nursing homes, 227–29
    out-of-body experiences
      (OBEs), 220–22

Meditation, 76–80
  benefits of, 79–80
  and consciousness, 77–78
  how it works, 79
  how to, 268–71
  resolving common problems,
    270–71
  techniques, 270
  types of, 78–79

Mediums
  history, 140–42
  mental mediumship, 143–44
  physical mediumship, 142–43
  types, 142–44
  using, 274

Mediums, and afterlife evidence,
  156–65. See also Crime-solving
  with help of deceased
    cause of death revealed, 165
    group readings, spirits at, 162–63
    identifying a spirit, 156–57
    meaningful events, presence at,

162–63
    objects of significance, 160–62
    personality and trait
      descriptions of spirits, 156–57
    secrets of a spirit, 163–65
    shared experiences, relating,
      157–60

Medujugorje, 238

Mesmer, Franz, 240

Messelmani, Hasnah Mohammed,
  246

Metzger, Wolfgang, 81

Michel, Lou, 234

Min, B. K., 75

Miracles, 238–51
  case studies, 249–51
  Catholic Church's guidelines,
    249–50
  definition by religions, 248–49
  divine experiences, 245
  divine physical manifestations,
    243–44
  faith healing, 245
  healings, 240–42
  images, 245
  physical manifestations, 242–44
  relics, 245
  and science, 247–48
  and unexplained evidence,
    244–45
  visions by multiple witnesses,
    238–40

Mohammed, 26

Mohler, R. A., Jr., 23

Monroe, Robert, 87, 88

Moody, Raymond, 61–63, 94

Morse, Melvin, 104, 212, 213, 215,
  221, 225

Moses, William Stanton, 141

M-theory, 126–29
  and parallel universes, 135
  and string theory, 127–28

Multiple universes, 130–31

Mumler, William, 195, 196

Myers, F. W. H., 80, 148, 149, 260

Mysticism, 34–35
  and Christianity, 35
  and Kabbalistic Judaism, 35
  Sufism, 35

Native American beliefs, 14–17

Near-death experiences (NDEs),
  93–106, 254–55
    being of light, 62–63, 99
    of the blind, 68–70
    bright-light experience, 62
    case studies, 104–6
    characteristics of, 97–100
    children's study, 102–3
    and choice, 100
    clinical death vs. conscious
      death, 96–97
    and deceased loved ones, 99–
      100, 100–1
    defined, 94
    in different cultures, 94–95
    Dutch study, 103–4
    investigations, 61–63
    and knowledge, 98–99
    and life review, 99, 101–2
    medical personnel as witnesses,
      220
    and out-of-body experiences, 97
    and science, 95
    scientific studies, 102–4
    Seattle Children's Hospital study,
      104
    and silver cord, 98

Near-death experiences—*continued*
 and telepathic communication,
  100
 and time, concept of, 98
 and tunnel and light, 98
Nearing death awareness (NDA),
 231–32
Neurological explanations, 3
Newton, Isaac, 115, 118
Nickell, Joe, 216
Nobleman, Marc Tyler, 233
Nolen, W. A., 241
Northrop, Suzanne, 60

Orbs, 162
Osgood, Charles, 20
Osis, Karlis, 149, 209, 215
Ouija boards, 146–47, 271
Our Lady of Lourdes, 238–39
Our Lady of the Light, 239–40
Out-of-body experiences (OBEs),
 86–91, 274–75
 case studies, 89–91
 explanations for, 88
 induction of, 87–88
 medical personnel as witnesses,
  220–22
 and near-death experiences
  (NDEs), 97
 types of, 87

Palladino, Eusapia, 260
Palmo, Tsering, 90
Paracelsus, 240
Parallel universes, 135–37
Paranormal phenomena, and dark
 energy, 133–34
Pareidolia, 199
Parnia, Sam, 64

Past lives. *See* Reincarnation and
 past lives
Peat, F. David, 76
Peveler, Robert, 64
Photographic evidence of afterlife,
 195–97
Photosynthesis, 113–14
Pinansky, Robert, 221
Pink, D. H., 74, 76
Piper, Leonora, 262
Planck, Max, 116, 117
Podmore, Frank, 148
Poltergeists, 193
Prayer, 150–53
 and afterlife, 152–53
 efficacy of, 151
 faith healings, 151–52
Provand, Captain, 196
Purgatory, 22

Quantum physics, 108–21
 and biology, 113–14
 entanglement, 109
 God particle, 119–20
 Heisenberg uncertainty
  principle, 117–19
 human energy field, 110–12
 and photosynthesis, 113–14
 quantum tunneling, 114
 subatomic particles, 108
 substances that make up
  physical beings, 109–10
 wave-particle duality, 115–17
Quantum tunneling, 114
Queen Mary, 194, 203

Raps, 143
Rasmussen. Charles, 230
Raudive, Konstantin, 198, 255

Raynham Hall, 196
Reilly, Carmel, 55
Reincarnation and past lives,
 50–52
 and children, 50–51
 past life therapies, 51–52
Religious icons, weeping and
 bleeding statues of, 246
Rencurel, Benoîte, 243
Research, participating in,
 278–80
Resurrection
 Islam, 27–28
 Judaism, 26
Rhine, J. B., 70–72, 81
Rhine, Louisa, 71, 72
Rhine Research Center, 70–72
Richet, Charles, 143, 260–61
Rife, Victoria, 233
Ring, Kenneth, 68–70
Roberts, Jane, 141
Roman beliefs, ancient, 10–12
Rosicrucianism, 34

Sacred Heart Hospital in
 Venezuela, 247
Sainthood, 250
Salisbury, Lady, 204
Sanders, S., 231
Schneider, Susan, 89
Schrödinger, Erwin, 113
Schwartz, Gary, 58–60, 142, 149
Scole experiment, 66–68
Séances, 144–47
 group, 146
 history of, 144–45
 and manifestations, 146
 reality of, 147
 spiritual circles, 146

tools of, 146–47
types of, 145
Shermer, Michael, 254
Skepticism, 254–64
    fraudulent afterlife evidence,
      262–64
    paid skeptics, 257–60
    pseudo/closed-minded skeptics,
      259–60
    skeptics becoming believers,
      260–62
    true/open-minded skeptics,
      256–57, 258
Sleep, stages of, 180
Society for Psychical Research,
    263–64, 279
Socrates, 9
Soubirous, Bernadette, 249
Spiritualism, 37
Spong, John Shelby, 43–44
Stafford, Betty, 230
Steiger, Brad, 55–56
Stevenson, Ian, 261
Stigmata, 246
String theory, 124–37
    and afterlife, 125–26, 130–32
    key aspects, 130
    and life and death, 125
    and M-theory, 127–28
    nature components, 124–25
    and parallel universes,
      135–37
Sufism, 35
Synchronicity, 185

Taoism, 7
Tart, Charles, 182
Taylor, E., 89
Taylor, J. Traille, 196

Telepathy, 80–82, 185
    and near-death experiences
      (NDEs), 100
    studies and evidence, 81–82
    and technology, 82
    vs. clairvoyance, 81
Theisen, Donna, 186
Thermal imager, 267–68
Thompson, R., 74
Tower of London, 204–5
Transformation consciousness,
    wisdom, and enlightenment,
    84–86
Tyrrell, G. N. M., 86

Umipeg, Vicky, 69–70
Underwood, Anne, 230, 231
Universal consciousness, 134
Universalism, 36

Van Biema, David, 250
Van Lommel, Pim, 87, 90, 95,
    103–4
Van Praagh, James, 142
Velmans, Max, 89
Video recorder, 267
Virtue, Doreen, 42
Von Szalay, Atilla, 197

Wake, Celtic, 13
Wallace, Alfred Russel, 195
Wave-particle duality, 115–17
    black body radiation, 116
    de Broglie's hypothesis, 117
    Huygen's wave theory, 115–16
    Newton's theory, 115
    photoelectric effect, 116–17
Webster, James, 68
Weor, Samael Aun, 33

Western religious influences, 17–18
    vs. eastern beliefs, 19–20
White, John W., 210
Wicca, 36–37
Wilber, Ken, 85
Williams, Montagu, 263
Wills-Brandon, Carla, 209, 222,
    225–26, 228, 229, 232
Winchester, Sarah, 194
Winchester, William Wirt, 194
Winchester mansion, 194
Wiseman, James, 242
Witten, Edward, 126

Xenoglossy, 275

Yates, Jenny L., 225
Yin and yang, 7
Yoga, 29–30
Young, J. D. E., 89
Young, Thomas, 115

Zammit, Victor, 67, 255
Zernickes, Edgar L., 234
Zollner, Johann, 200
Zoroastrianism, 43
Zukeran, Patrick, 51

We Have

EVERYTHING®

on Anything!

The Everything® list spans a wide range of subjects, with more than 500 titles covering 25 different categories:

Business	History	Reference
Careers	Home Improvement	Religion
Children's Storybooks	Everything Kids	Self-Help
Computers	Languages	Sports & Fitness
Cooking	Music	Travel
Crafts and Hobbies	New Age	Wedding
Education/Schools	Parenting	Writing
Games and Puzzles	Personal Finance	
Health	Pets	